ARCHITECTURAL DETAILS

AND MEASURED DRAWINGS
OF HOUSES OF THE TWENTIES

William A. Radford

DOVER PUBLICATIONS, INC.
Mineola, New York

Published in the United Kingdom by David & Charles, Brunel House, Forde Close, Newton Abbot, Devon TQ12 4PU.

Bibliographical Note

This Dover edition, first published in 2002, is an unabridged republication of the volume published as *Architectural Details for Every Type of Building: A Practical Drafting Room Guide for Contractors, Builders, Lumber Dealers, Millmen, Draftsmen, and Architects* by the Radford Architectural Company, Chicago, in 1921.

Library of Congress Cataloging-in-Publication Data

Radford, William A., 1865–
    [Architectural details for every type of building]
    Architectural details and measured drawings of houses of the twenties
/ William A. Radford.
        p. cm.
    Originally published: Architectural details for every type of building.
Chicago, Ill. : Radford Architectural Co., 1921.
    Includes index.
    ISBN 0-486-42156-2 (pbk.)
      1. Building—Details—Drawings. I. Title.
TH2031 .R32 2002
692'.2—dc21

                                                                    2002019235

Manufactured in the United States of America
Dover Publications, Inc., 31 East 2nd Street, Mineola, N.Y. 11501

Logical Methods in Architectural Drafting

A KNOWLEDGE of architectural drafting is vitally essential to the carpenter, builder or contractor, who would develop both himself and his business to the greatest possible extent.

The builder who is able to work out a neat and accurate set of drawings or "plans" fully dimensioned and detailed, leaving nothing to chance, has a very decided advantage over his brother, who, without fully conceived ideas and plans, starts building, and trusts to luck and good fortune that everything will work out all right. Even rough sketch drawings with approximate dimensions are better than none, but only full and detailed sets of plans are advisable.

In evolving a set of working plans the first logical step is the sketch. The purpose of the sketch is to fix the various ideas of either the builder or his client or of both and to give some definite basis for a start.

The medium for the sketch may be either pencil, pen and ink, water color or wash, the first named being the most common and the simplest to use.

The value of the sketch to the "builder architect" can hardly be over-estimated, because if well and attractively done, it may bring valuable contracts, which might not be obtained if this means of expression were not used.

Preliminary or "thumb nail" sketches, as they are sometimes called, should not be over 3 or 4 inches in size. They are not drawn to any definite scale and their chief purpose is to show arrangement. They should, however, be kept in proportion as much as possible.

The type of plan for such a sketch must of course be determined upon before the first drawing is made and the deciding factors are, first, the character of the site, and, second, the style of the exterior.

If we analyze any number of house plans we will find that they may be broadly classified into two general types, namely, the central entrance or central hall type, and the side entrance or side hall type. In the first named, as illustrated (Fig. 1), we have a symmetrical arrangement of rooms opening from a central hallway. This is the typical "Colonial" plan and calls, as a rule, for that style of elevation. In Fig. 2 we have the second type shown; note that in this type we have a plan that is unsymmetrical and is adapted especially to the narrow city lot.

We will take as an illustration of the logical steps to follow in making a sketch the first type, or central hall plan. First determine the approximate proportion of the floor plan, says two as to three. 1. Sketch center line. 2. Draw front and rear outside wall lines representing the width of the wall by a single line. 3. Side wall lines. 4. Locate main partition lines. 5. Minor partition lines. 6. Rough in approximate position of openings, doors and windows.

Study carefully at this time the relation of rooms and the circulation.

In like manner sketch second floor plan. It will be found that the basement, as a rule, logically takes its arrangement from the first floor plan, so we need not consider it in the first sketch.

After line sketches of the plans are made, the front elevation and then principal side elevation should be drawn.

The style of the exterior having been decided, determine first the proportion of the front wall—that is, the height from the ground to the under side of the cornice compared with the width. This height in the ordinary two-story house varies from 20 to 24 feet.

1. Block in this rectangle with center line.
2. Block in height lines for windows and doors.
3. Draw vertical outside lines for windows and doors, determining their positions approximately from plans.
4. Draw roof, taking height as ¼, ⅓ or ½ depth of plan, depending on judgment of designer.
5. Draw in porch or porches according to style of exterior.
6. Darken or shade window openings and show shadow under cornice.
7. Sketch in background.

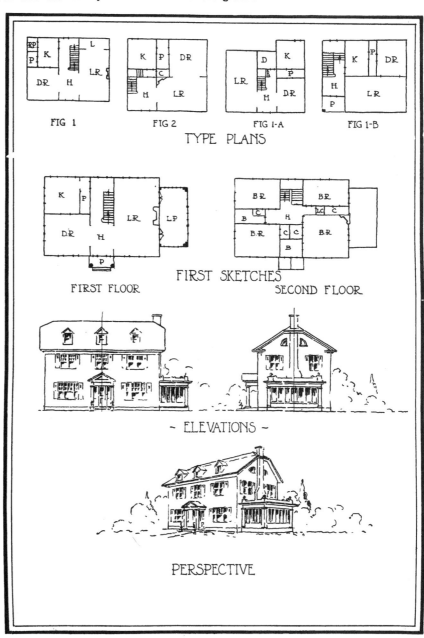

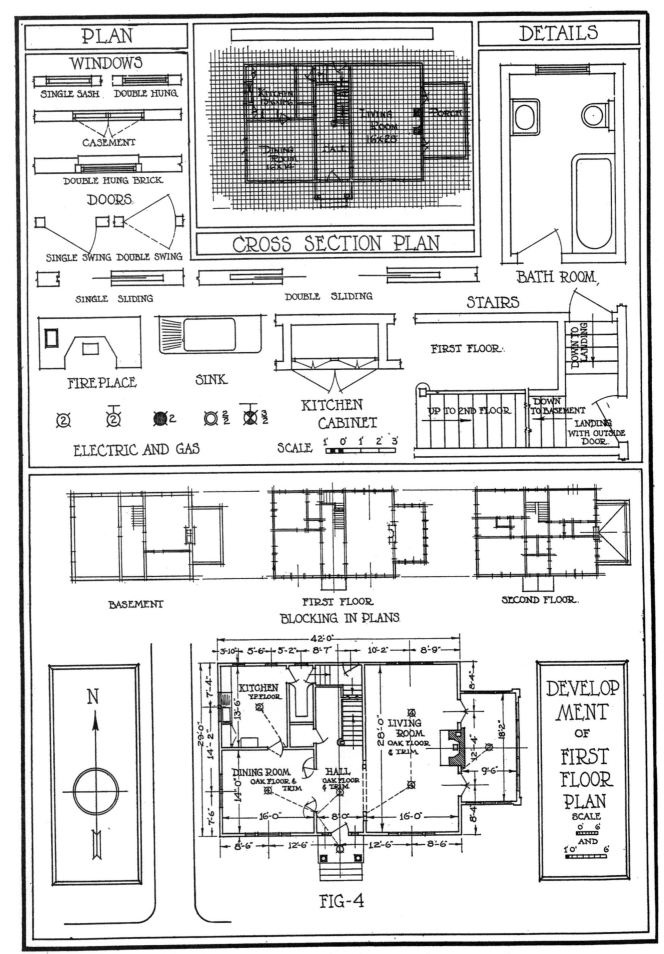

FIG-4

Illustrating Logical Method of Developing the Floor Plans of a Residence.

TYPICAL ELEVATION DETAILS

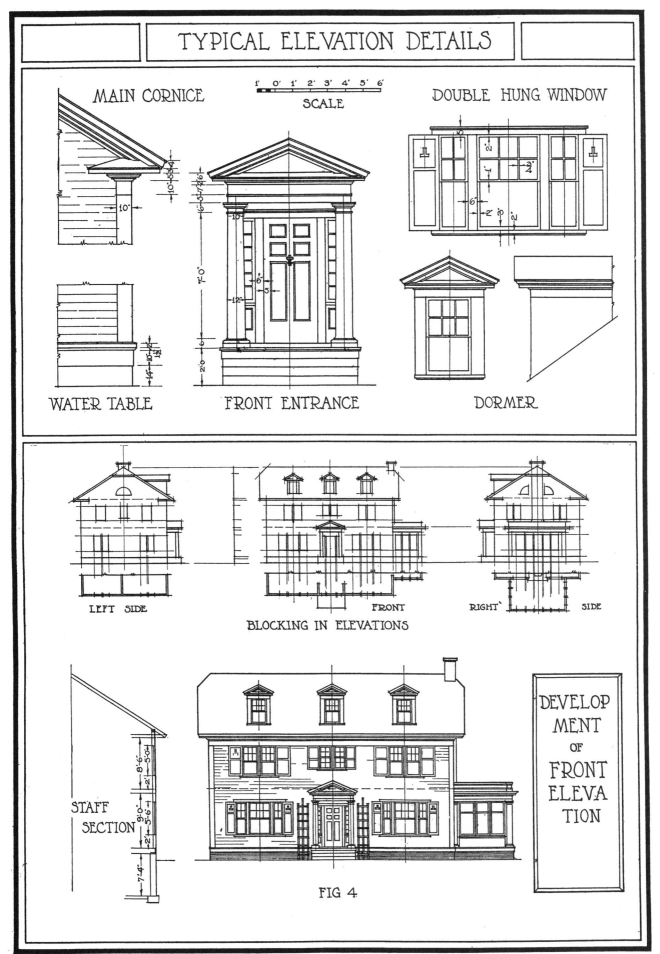

MAIN CORNICE

SCALE

DOUBLE HUNG WINDOW

WATER TABLE

FRONT ENTRANCE

DORMER

LEFT SIDE

FRONT

RIGHT SIDE

BLOCKING IN ELEVATIONS

STAFF SECTION

FIG 4

DEVELOPMENT OF FRONT ELEVATION

Illustrating Logical Method of Developing the Elevations of a Residence.

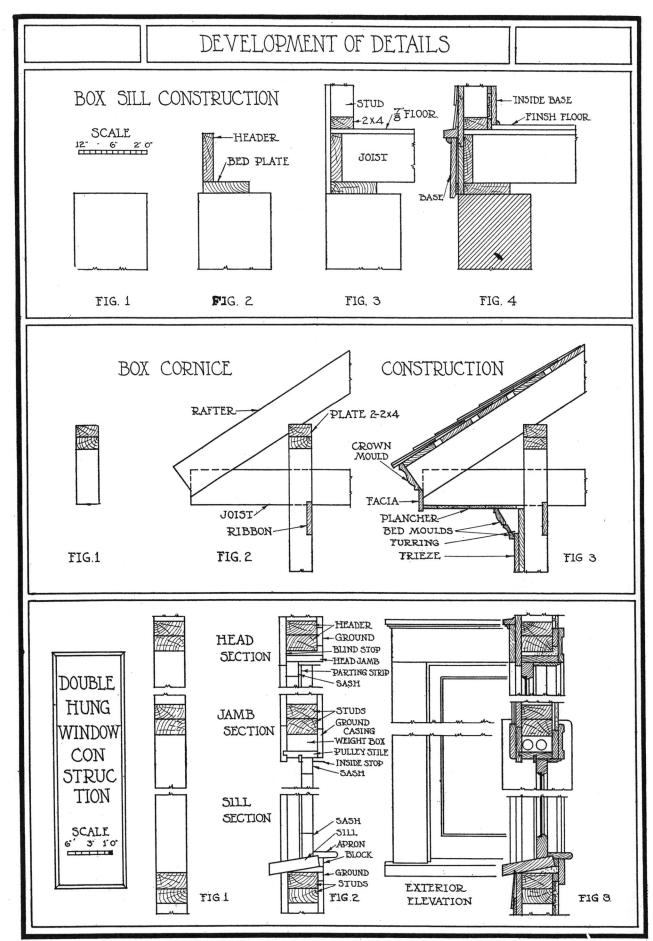

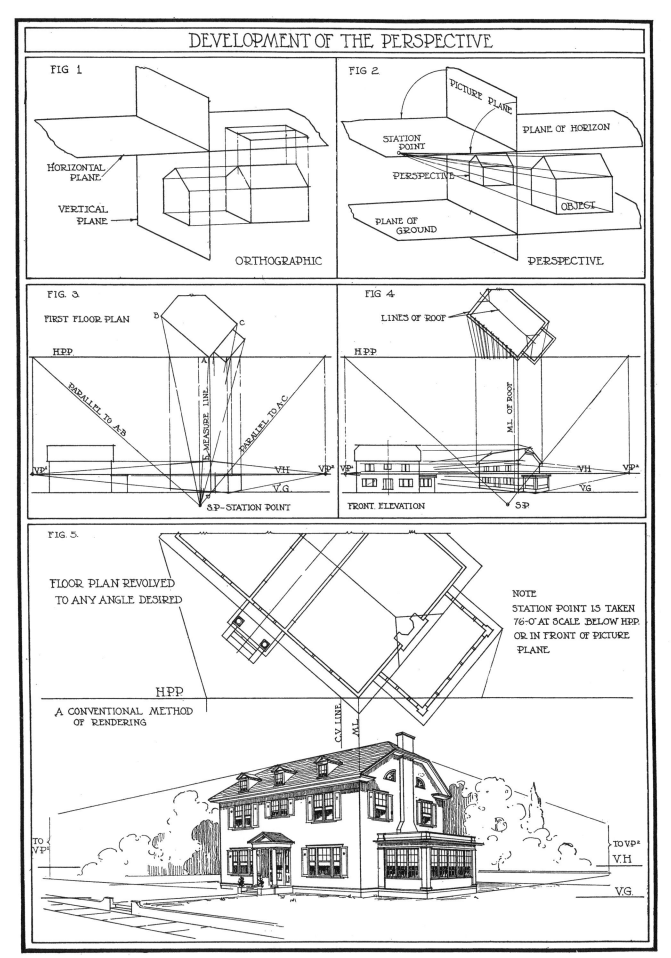

DEVELOPMENT OF THE PERSPECTIVE

FIG 1

HORIZONTAL PLANE

VERTICAL PLANE

ORTHOGRAPHIC

FIG 2

PICTURE PLANE

PLANE OF HORIZON

STATION POINT

PERSPECTIVE

OBJECT

PLANE OF GROUND

PERSPECTIVE

FIG. 3

FIRST FLOOR PLAN

H.P.P.

PARALLEL TO A-B

PARALLEL TO A-C

MEASURE LINE

B

A

C

VP¹ V.H VP²

V.G.

S.P—STATION POINT

FIG 4

LINES OF ROOF

H.P.P.

M.L OF ROOF

VP¹ V.H VP²

V.G.

FRONT ELEVATION

S.P.

FIG. 5.

FLOOR PLAN REVOLVED TO ANY ANGLE DESIRED

NOTE
STATION POINT IS TAKEN 76-0" AT SCALE BELOW H.P.P. OR IN FRONT OF PICTURE PLANE

H.P.P.

A CONVENTIONAL METHOD OF RENDERING

C.V. LINE

M.L

TO VP¹

TO VP²

V.H

V.G.

The Fundamentals of Architectural Perspective Drawing.

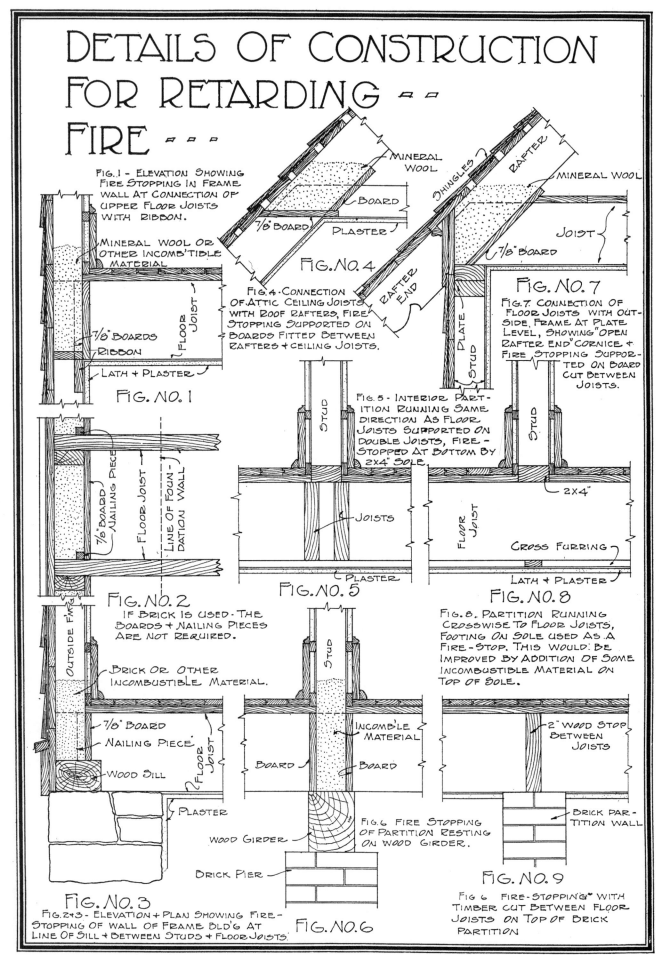

DETAILS OF CONSTRUCTION FOR RETARDING -- FIRE ---

FIG.1 - ELEVATION SHOWING FIRE STOPPING IN FRAME WALL AT CONNECTION OF UPPER FLOOR JOISTS WITH RIBBON.

MINERAL WOOL OR OTHER INCOMB'TIBLE MATERIAL

7/8" BOARDS
RIBBON
LATH + PLASTER
FLOOR JOIST

FIG. NO. 1

MINERAL WOOL
BOARD
7/8" BOARD
PLASTER

FIG. NO. 4

FIG.4 - CONNECTION OF ATTIC CEILING JOISTS WITH ROOF RAFTERS, FIRE STOPPING SUPPORTED ON BOARDS FITTED BETWEEN RAFTERS + CEILING JOISTS.

SHINGLES RAFTER MINERAL WOOL
RAFTER END 7/8" BOARD JOIST

FIG. NO. 7

FIG.7. CONNECTION OF FLOOR JOISTS WITH OUTSIDE FRAME AT PLATE LEVEL, SHOWING "OPEN RAFTER END" CORNICE + FIRE STOPPING SUPPORTED ON BOARD CUT BETWEEN JOISTS.

PLATE STUD

7/8" BOARD NAILING PIECE
FLOOR JOIST
LINE OF FOUNDATION WALL

FIG. NO. 2

IF BRICK IS USED - THE BOARDS + NAILING PIECES ARE NOT REQUIRED.

FIG.5 - INTERIOR PARTITION RUNNING SAME DIRECTION AS FLOOR JOISTS SUPPORTED ON DOUBLE JOISTS, FIRE-STOPPED AT BOTTOM BY 2x4" SOLE.

STUD JOISTS PLASTER

FIG. NO. 5

STUD 2x4" FLOOR JOIST CROSS FURRING LATH + PLASTER

FIG. NO. 8

FIG.8. PARTITION RUNNING CROSSWISE TO FLOOR JOISTS, FOOTING ON SOLE USED AS A FIRE-STOP. THIS WOULD BE IMPROVED BY ADDITION OF SOME INCOMBUSTIBLE MATERIAL ON TOP OF SOLE.

OUTSIDE F'M'G
BRICK OR OTHER INCOMBUSTIBLE MATERIAL.
7/8" BOARD
NAILING PIECE.
WOOD SILL
PLASTER
FLOOR JOIST

FIG. NO. 3

FIG.2+3 - ELEVATION + PLAN SHOWING FIRE-STOPPING OF WALL OF FRAME BLD'G AT LINE OF SILL + BETWEEN STUDS + FLOOR JOISTS.

STUD INCOMB'LE MATERIAL BOARD BOARD WOOD GIRDER BRICK PIER

FIG. NO. 6

FIG.6 FIRE STOPPING OF PARTITION RESTING ON WOOD GIRDER.

2" WOOD STOP BETWEEN JOISTS
BRICK PARTITION WALL

FIG. NO. 9

FIG 6 FIRE-STOPPING" WITH TIMBER CUT BETWEEN FLOOR JOISTS ON TOP OF BRICK PARTITION

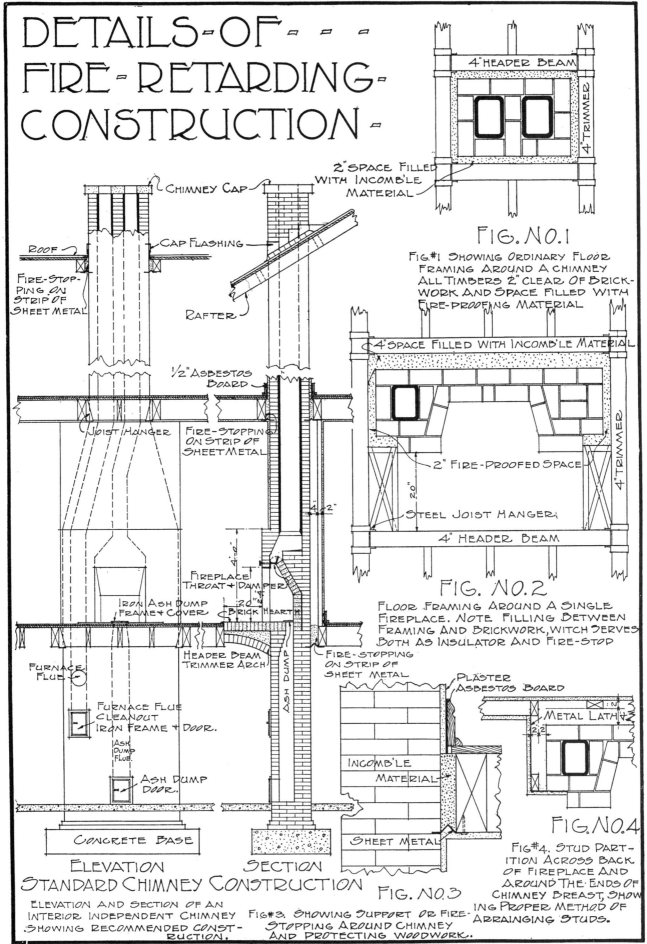

DETAILS·OF·
FIRE·RETARDING·
CONSTRUCTION·

4" HEADER BEAM
4" TRIMMER
2" SPACE FILLED WITH INCOMB'LE MATERIAL

FIG. NO.1
FIG#1 SHOWING ORDINARY FLOOR FRAMING AROUND A CHIMNEY ALL TIMBERS 2" CLEAR OF BRICK-WORK AND SPACE FILLED WITH FIRE-PROOFING MATERIAL

CHIMNEY CAP
CAP FLASHING
ROOF
FIRE-STOP-PING ON STRIP OF SHEET METAL
RAFTER
½" ASBESTOS BOARD
JOIST HANGER
FIRE-STOPPING ON STRIP OF SHEET METAL

4" SPACE FILLED WITH INCOMB'LE MATERIAL
2" FIRE-PROOFED SPACE
20"
STEEL JOIST HANGER
4" HEADER BEAM
4" TRIMMER

FIG. NO.2
FLOOR FRAMING AROUND A SINGLE FIREPLACE. NOTE FILLING BETWEEN FRAMING AND BRICKWORK, WITCH SERVES BOTH AS INSULATOR AND FIRE-STOP

FIREPLACE THROAT + DAMPER
IRON ASH DUMP FRAME + COVER
20"
BRICK HEARTH
HEADER BEAM TRIMMER ARCH
ASH DUMP
FIRE-STOPPING ON STRIP OF SHEET METAL

FURNACE FLUE
FURNACE FLUE CLEANOUT IRON FRAME + DOOR.
ASH DUMP FLUE.
ASH DUMP DOOR.

PLASTER ASBESTOS BOARD
METAL LATH
INCOMB'LE MATERIAL
SHEET METAL

FIG.NO.4
FIG#4. STUD PART-ITION ACROSS BACK OF FIREPLACE AND AROUND THE ENDS OF CHIMNEY BREAST, SHOW ING PROPER METHOD OF ARRAINGING STUDS.

CONCRETE BASE
ELEVATION
SECTION
STANDARD CHIMNEY CONSTRUCTION
FIG. NO.3

ELEVATION AND SECTION OF AN INTERIOR INDEPENDENT CHIMNEY SHOWING RECOMMENDED CONST-RUCTION.

FIG#3. SHOWING SUPPORT OR FIRE-STOPPING AROUND CHIMNEY AND PROTECTING WOODWORK.

How to Lay Up Chimneys and Arrange the Floor and Roof Framing in Relation to Them to Make a Fire-Safe Structure.

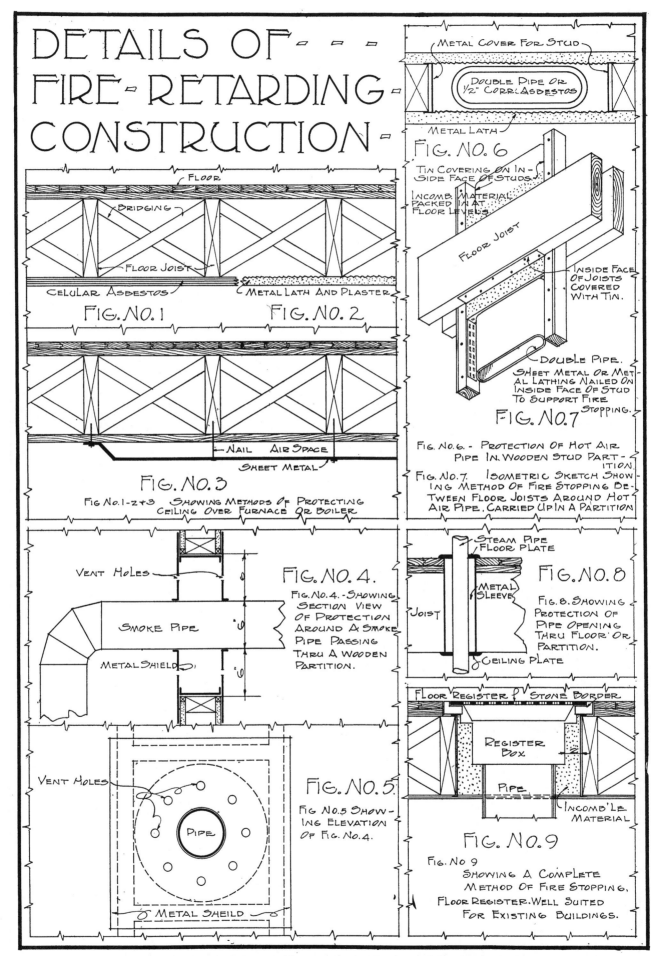

DETAILS OF FIRE-RETARDING CONSTRUCTION

METAL COVER FOR STUD

DOUBLE PIPE OR 1/2" CORR. ASBESTOS

METAL LATH

FIG. NO. 6

FLOOR

BRIDGING

FLOOR JOIST

CELULAR ASBESTOS

METAL LATH AND PLASTER

FIG. NO. 1   FIG. NO. 2

TIN COVERING ON INSIDE FACE OF STUDS

INCOMB. MATERIAL PACKED IN AT FLOOR LEVELS

FLOOR JOIST

INSIDE FACE OF JOISTS COVERED WITH TIN.

DOUBLE PIPE.

SHEET METAL OR METAL LATHING NAILED ON INSIDE FACE OF STUD TO SUPPORT FIRE STOPPING.

FIG. NO. 7

NAIL   AIR SPACE

SHEET METAL

FIG. NO. 3

FIG. NO. 1-2+3 SHOWING METHODS OF PROTECTING CEILING OVER FURNACE OR BOILER

FIG. NO. 6. - PROTECTION OF HOT AIR PIPE IN WOODEN STUD PARTITION

FIG. NO. 7. ISOMETRIC SKETCH SHOWING METHOD OF FIRE STOPPING BETWEEN FLOOR JOISTS AROUND HOT AIR PIPE. CARRIED UP IN A PARTITION

VENT HOLES

SMOKE PIPE

METAL SHIELD

FIG. NO. 4.

FIG. NO. 4. - SHOWING SECTION VIEW OF PROTECTION AROUND A SMOKE PIPE PASSING THRU A WOODEN PARTITION.

STEAM PIPE
FLOOR PLATE

METAL SLEEVE

JOIST

CEILING PLATE

FIG. NO. 8

FIG. 8. SHOWING PROTECTION OF PIPE OPENING THRU FLOOR OR PARTITION.

FLOOR REGISTER   STONE BORDER

REGISTER BOX

PIPE

INCOMB'LE MATERIAL

VENT HOLES

PIPE

FIG. NO. 5

FIG. NO. 5 SHOWING ELEVATION OF FIG. NO. 4.

METAL SHIELD

FIG. NO. 9

FIG. NO 9 SHOWING A COMPLETE METHOD OF FIRE STOPPING, FLOOR REGISTER. WELL SUITED FOR EXISTING BUILDINGS.

Details of Fire Guards to Build in Around Heating Plant Pipes for Protection

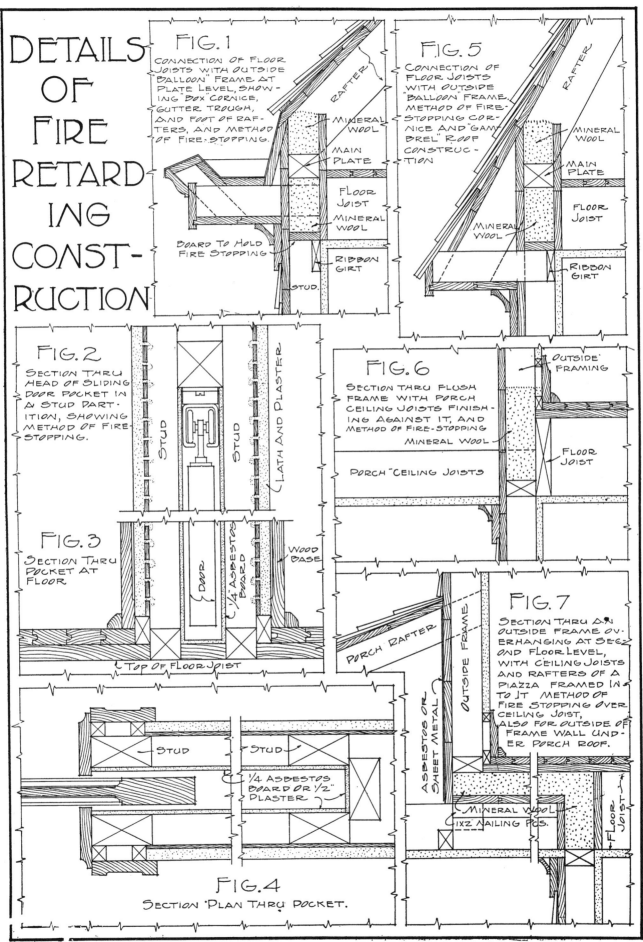

DETAILS OF FIRE RETARDING CONSTRUCTION

FIG. 1

Connection of Floor Joists with Outside "Balloon" Frame at Plate Level, Showing "Box" Cornice, Gutter Trough, and Foot of Rafters, and Method of Fire-Stopping.

Rafter
Mineral Wool
Main Plate
Floor Joist
Mineral Wool
Board to Hold Fire Stopping
Ribbon Girt
Stud.

FIG. 5

Connection of Floor Joists with Outside "Balloon" Frame, Method of Fire-Stopping Cornice and "Gambrel" Roof Construction.

Rafter
Mineral Wool
Main Plate
Floor Joist
Mineral Wool
Ribbon Girt

FIG. 2

Section Thru Head of Sliding Door Pocket in a Stud Partition, Showing Method of Fire-Stopping.

Stud
Stud
Lath and Plaster

FIG. 3

Section Thru Pocket at Floor

Door
¼ Asbestos Board
Wood Base
Top of Floor Joist

FIG. 6

Section Thru Flush Frame with Porch Ceiling Joists Finishing Against It, and Method of Fire-Stopping

Outside Framing
Mineral Wool
Porch Ceiling Joists
Floor Joist

FIG. 7

Section Thru an Outside Frame Overhanging at Second Floor Level, with Ceiling Joists and Rafters of a Piazza Framed Into It, Method of Fire Stopping Over Ceiling Joist, Also for Outside of Frame Wall Under Porch Roof.

Porch Rafter
Outside Frame
Asbestos or Sheet Metal
Mineral Wool
1x2 Nailing Pcs.
Floor Joist

FIG. 4

Section Plan Thru Pocket.

Stud
Stud
¼ Asbestos Board or ½" Plaster

Details of Fire Retarding Timber Construction, Showing How to Do It the Better Way.

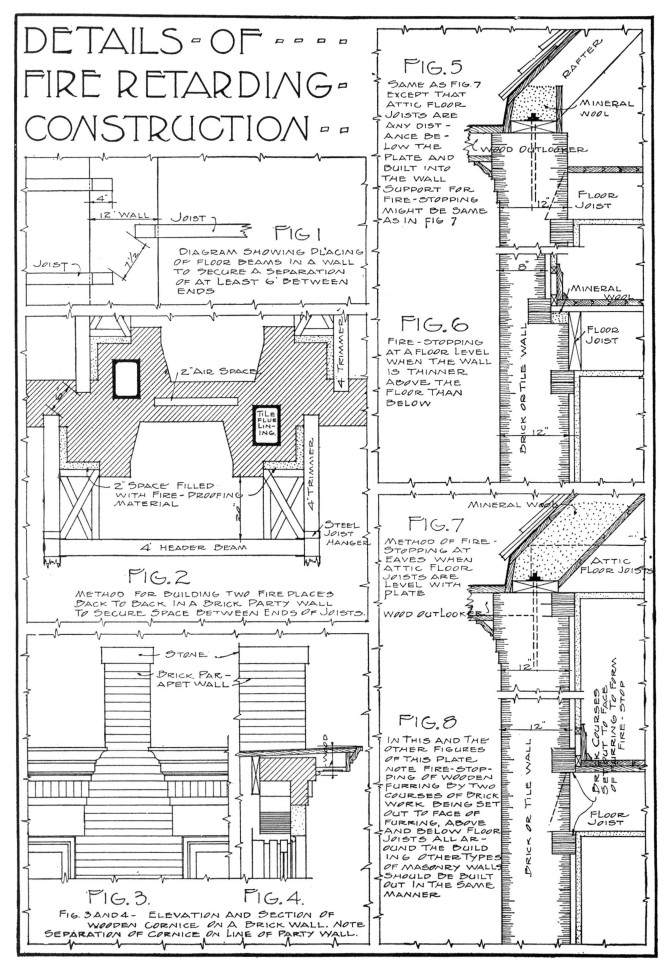

DETAILS·OF···
FIRE RETARDING·
CONSTRUCTION··

FIG 1
DIAGRAM SHOWING PLACING OF FLOOR BEAMS IN A WALL TO SECURE A SEPARATION OF AT LEAST 6' BETWEEN ENDS

4"
12' WALL
JOIST
JOIST
7 1/2"

2" AIR SPACE
TILE FLUE LINING
2" SPACE FILLED WITH FIRE-PROOFING MATERIAL
4' HEADER BEAM
4" TRIMMER
STEEL JOIST HANGER

FIG.2
METHOD FOR BUILDING TWO FIRE PLACES BACK TO BACK IN A BRICK PARTY WALL TO SECURE SPACE BETWEEN ENDS OF JOISTS.

STONE
BRICK PARAPET WALL
WOOD

FIG.3.   **FIG.4.**
FIG. 3 AND 4 - ELEVATION AND SECTION OF WOODEN CORNICE ON A BRICK WALL. NOTE SEPARATION OF CORNICE ON LINE OF PARTY WALL.

FIG.5
SAME AS FIG.7 EXCEPT THAT ATTIC FLOOR JOISTS ARE ANY DISTANCE BELOW THE PLATE AND BUILT INTO THE WALL SUPPORT FOR FIRE-STOPPING MIGHT BE SAME AS IN FIG 7

RAFTER
MINERAL WOOL
WOOD OUTLOOKER
12"
FLOOR JOIST

FIG.6
FIRE-STOPPING AT A FLOOR LEVEL WHEN THE WALL IS THINNER ABOVE THE FLOOR THAN BELOW

8"
MINERAL WOOL
FLOOR JOIST
BRICK OR TILE WALL
12"

FIG.7
METHOD OF FIRE-STOPPING AT EAVES WHEN ATTIC FLOOR JOISTS ARE LEVEL WITH PLATE
WOOD OUTLOOKER

MINERAL WOOL
ATTIC FLOOR JOISTS
12"

FIG.8
IN THIS AND THE OTHER FIGURES OF THIS PLATE NOTE FIRE-STOPPING OF WOODEN FURRING BY TWO COURSES OF BRICK WORK BEING SET OUT TO FACE OF FURRING, ABOVE AND BELOW FLOOR JOISTS ALL AROUND THE BUILDING OTHER TYPES OF MASONRY WALLS SHOULD BE BUILT OUT IN THE SAME MANNER

12"
BRICK COURSES SET OUT TO FACE OF FURRING TO FORM FIRE-STOP
BRICK OR TILE WALL
FLOOR JOIST

Details of Brick Walls with Mineral Wool Filler at Eaves and Floors; Also Double Fireplace Detail.

Framing to Prevent Unequal Shrinkage-Settlement

SKETCH No. 1 shows a cross-section of a "balloon" frame taken from an actual example. It is a glaring violation of all the principles of good construction, fire-resistance and sanitation. It's a fire trap, a vermin harbor, and is subject to a disastrous amount of *unequal settlement*. At "A" is shown the original condition of the framework just after being built. At "B" is indicated, graphically, the dilapidated and deplorable condition of affairs, a year later, after the inevitable shrinkage-settlement has taken place. And it is to be especially noted that the faults shown are not the result of settlement itself, but rather the result of the *difference* in settlement of corresponding and adjacent parts. If an engineer were to design a foundation in such a manner as to be productive of the faults shown, he would, most assuredly, be considered an exceedingly poor engineer. And rightly so. Why, then, in the name of common justice, is not the builder who, day after day, continues to design and frame the timber superstructure in the manner shown, deserving of the same amount of condemnation as the discreditable engineer? Wherein is the difference between an incompetent designer of foundations and an incompetent

designer of timber framing? As a matter of fact, the latter, in this particular case, is more to be censured than the former, for, in residence construction, seven cases out of ten the evils resulting from unequal settlement can be traced to the timber framework rather than to the foundation.

In the "balloon" framing, shown in Sketch No. 1, the exterior studding extends in one length from sill to rafter plate. Hence, the amount of shrinkable timber contributing to the total vertical settlement of the exterior wall is made up of the 4-inch sill and the 4-inch rafter-plate, equaling 8 inches in all. In like manner, the shrinkable bearing-timber in the interior partition is made up of the 10-inch girder, the two sets of 10-inch floor-joists, the two layers of 1-inch sub-flooring, the two 2-inch partition-soles, and the two 2-inch partitioning caps, totaling 40 inches. Hence, assuming an ultimate shrinkage of ½ inch to the foot, the exterior wall will settle 1/24th of 8 inches, or only ⅓ inch, while the interior partition will settle 1/24th of 40 inches, or 1⅔ inches. And the *difference* of 1⅓ inches is bound to cause trouble—floors sag, door frames are thrown out of square, plastering cracks, and the upper partition sometimes

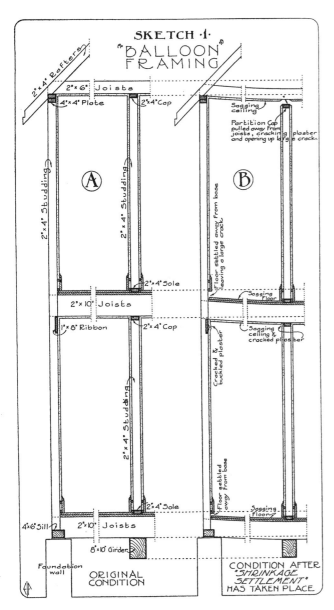

Showing Settlement Which Is Customary with Balloon Framing.

Showing Shrinkage Settlement with Drop-Girt Framing.

parts company with the ceiling overhead or, perhaps, pulls away from the floor and hangs suspended from the ceiling-joists. Trouble enough, surely! But that is not all. Damaging local settlement also takes place at the outer ends of the floor joists, often leaving a wide gap between the finish floor and baseboard, as shown exaggerated in the sketch. At the second floor line the total shrinkage of the 1-inch sub-floor, the 10-inch joists, and the 8-inch ribbon, will measure the magnitude of the gap equaling, in this case, about ¾ inch, for this shrinkage will always be *downward,* in the direction of the load, while no compensating relative settlement will take place in the vertical studding which extends thru this "zone" of horizontal bearing-timber. The base does not move in relation to the studding. But the floor *does.* Hence, the gap. At the interior partitions, however, the vertical studding does not extend thru the floor-construction. Therefore the base and the studding *both* move downward in response to the settling floor. In other words, the settlement is here *general* rather than *local.* Hence, no gap occurs between the finish floor and base. On the other hand, if the settlement continues, the base might buckle, or become split, because of the relative upward thrust of the excessively sagging floor. Moreover, this general settlement, not being equalized, is bound to open up a crack in the plastering at the junction of the ceiling and wall underneath. And, finally, the wide ribbon supporting the outer ends of the second floor joists, is liable to more relative shrinkage than the plastering that covers it. This is the cause of numerous

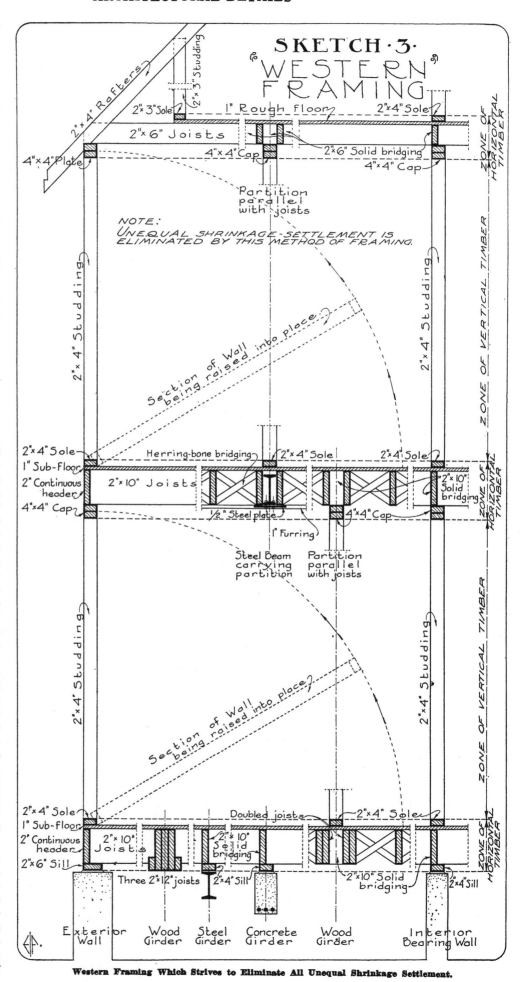

Western Framing Which Strives to Eliminate All Unequal Shrinkage Settlement.

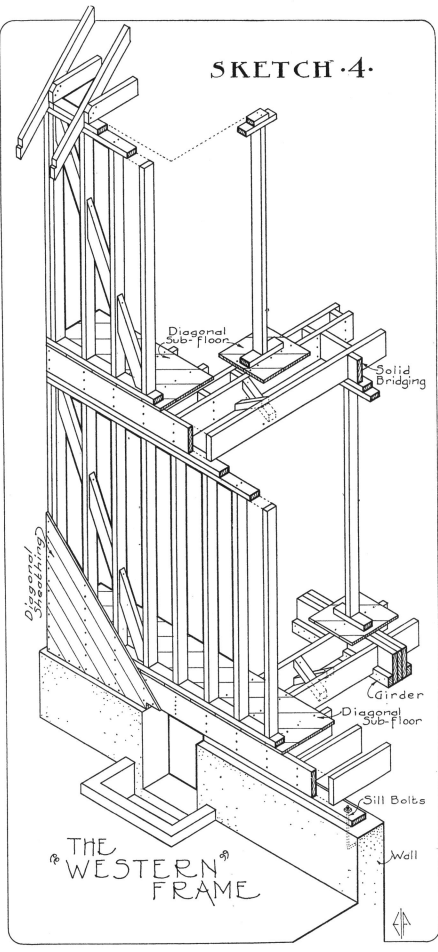

SKETCH ·4·

Diagonal
Sub-floor

Solid
Bridging

Diagonal
Sheathing

Girder

Diagonal
Sub-floor

Sill Bolts

Wall

THE
"WESTERN"
FRAME

Perspective of All Wood Western Frame. Designed to Prevent Unequal Shrinkage Settlement.

plaster cracks in this vicinity and, if this shrinkage is excessive, the plaster will buckle and, perhaps, fall from this portion of the wall.

Sketch No. 2 shows a cross-section of a "drop-girt" frame as called for by the most approved practice. At "A" is shown the original condition of the frame upon completion, while at "B" is shown the same construction after the usual shrinkage-settlement has taken place. While this frame is far superior, in every way, to the "balloon" frame, yet it is, nevertheless, subject to the same resultant evils, even tho these evils be of lesser extent. In the "drop-girt" frame, the second-story exterior studding and the outer ends of the second floor joists are supported upon the 4-inch by 8-inch girt, while the upper interior partition studding rests upon the 2-inch partition cap of the story below, as clearly indicated in the sketch. Moreover, the 6-inch by 14-inch first-floor girder is framed with the top of the joists. Consequently the *general* settlement has been almost, but not entirely, equalized. There will still be a slight sag in the floors and ceilings, but probably not enough to crack the plastering. The sag in the first floor, in this instance, is equal to the difference in settlement between the 14-inch girder and the 10-inch joists, amounting to but 1/24th of 4 inches, or a little more than an eighth of an inch, while the sag in the second floor will be not quite one-quarter of an inch, and the sag in the second-story ceiling will equal the difference in the total general settlement of the exterior and interior walls, amounting to exactly an eighth of an inch. But, as before said, this slight sagging will probably cause no serious damage. However, the *local* settlement occurring at the outer ends of the first floor joists, and at *both* ends of the second floor joists, cannot be so easily overlooked. At all of these points, as shown in the sketch, the vertical studding extends into the "zone" of the floor-construction. Hence, the floor settles *in relation to the studding* and therefore opens up a gap between the floor and base, being more pronounced at the second floor-level because of the greater depth of shrinkable material existing there between the top of the sub-floor and the bearing-surface of the joists. A gap of ½ inch or more is not an uncommon occurrence. An attempt to remedy this fault is sometimes made by placing a base-shoe at the junction of base and floor, and nailing same to the floor only, thus keeping the gap "covered."

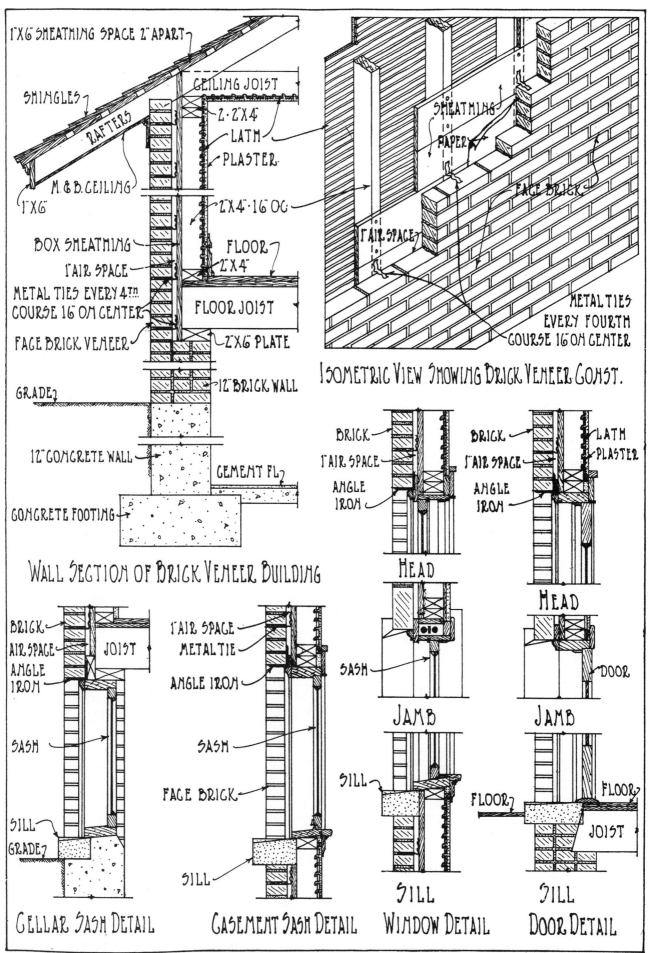

1"X6" SHEATHING SPACE 2" APART

SHINGLES

RAFTERS

M.& B. CEILING

1"X6"

BOX SHEATHING

1" AIR SPACE

METAL TIES EVERY 4TH COURSE 16" ON CENTER

FACE BRICK VENEER

GRADE

12" CONCRETE WALL

CONCRETE FOOTING

CEILING JOIST

2-2"X4"

LATH

PLASTER

2"X4"-16" O.C.

FLOOR 2"X4"

FLOOR JOIST

2"X6" PLATE

12" BRICK WALL

CEMENT FL.

Wall Section of Brick Veneer Building

SHEATHING

PAPER

1" AIR SPACE

FACE BRICK

METAL TIES EVERY FOURTH COURSE 16" ON CENTER

Isometric View Showing Brick Veneer Const.

BRICK

1" AIR SPACE

ANGLE IRON

Head

SASH

Jamb

SILL

Sill Window Detail

BRICK

1" AIR SPACE

LATH PLASTER

ANGLE IRON

Head

DOOR

Jamb

FLOOR

FLOOR

JOIST

Sill Door Detail

BRICK

AIR SPACE

ANGLE IRON

JOIST

SASH

SILL

GRADE

Cellar Sash Detail

1" AIR SPACE

METAL TIE

ANGLE IRON

SASH

FACE BRICK

SILL

Casement Sash Detail

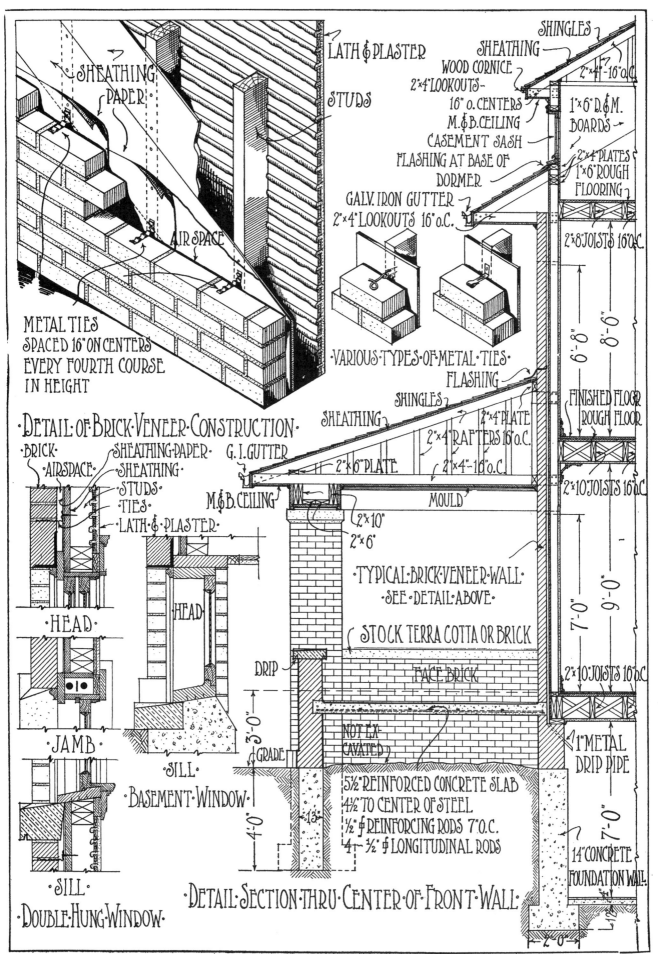

SHINGLES

SHEATHING
WOOD CORNICE
2"×4" LOOKOUTS-
16" o. CENTERS
M.&B. CEILING
CASEMENT SASH
FLASHING AT BASE OF
DORMER
GALV. IRON GUTTER
2"×4" LOOKOUTS 16" o.C.

2"×4"-16" o.C.

1"×6" D.&M.
BOARDS

2"×4" PLATES
1"×6" ROUGH
FLOORING

2"×8" JOISTS 16" o.C.

SHEATHING
PAPER

LATH & PLASTER

STUDS

AIR SPACE

·VARIOUS·TYPES·OF·METAL·TIES·
FLASHING

METAL TIES
SPACED 16" ON CENTERS
EVERY FOURTH COURSE
IN HEIGHT

·DETAIL·OF·BRICK·VENEER·CONSTRUCTION·

·BRICK·
·AIRSPACE·
SHEATHING·PAPER·
·SHEATHING·
·STUDS·
·TIES·
·LATH·&·PLASTER·

·HEAD·

·JAMB·

·SILL·
·DOUBLE·HUNG·WINDOW·

G. I. GUTTER

M.&B. CEILING

HEAD

DRIP

GRADE

·SILL·
·BASEMENT·WINDOW·

SHINGLES
SHEATHING

2"×6" PLATE

2"×4" PLATE
2"×4" RAFTERS 16" o.C.
2"×4"-16" o.C.

MOULD

2"×10"
2"×6"

·TYPICAL·BRICK·VENEER·WALL·
·SEE·DETAIL·ABOVE·

STOCK TERRA COTTA OR BRICK

FACE BRICK

NOT EX-
CAVATED

3'-0"

4'-0"

13"

2"×10" JOISTS 16" o.C.

6'-8"

8'-6"

FINISHED FLOOR
ROUGH FLOOR

9'-0"

7'-0"

2"×10" JOISTS 16" o.C.

1" METAL
DRIP PIPE

7'-0"

14" CONCRETE
FOUNDATION WALL

5½" REINFORCED CONCRETE SLAB
4½" TO CENTER OF STEEL
½" ⌀ REINFORCING RODS 7' O.C.
4 - ½" ⌀ LONGITUDINAL RODS

·DETAIL·SECTION·THRU·CENTER·OF·FRONT·WALL·

2'-0"

Details of Brick Veneer Construction—Four-Inch Face Brick Bonded to Wood Sheathing at Every Joist by Means of Metal Ties in Each Fourth Mortar Joint.

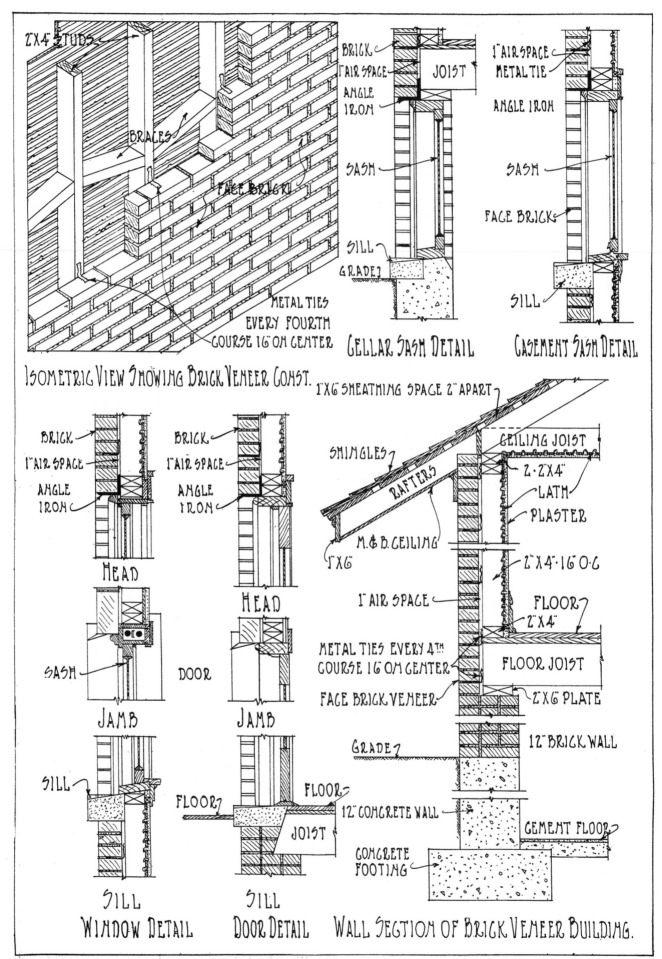

2"X4" STUDS

BRACES

FACE BRICK

METAL TIES EVERY FOURTH COURSE 16" ON CENTER

ISOMETRIC VIEW SHOWING BRICK VENEER CONST.

BRICK
1" AIR SPACE
ANGLE IRON
JOIST
SASH
SILL
GRADE

CELLAR SASH DETAIL

1" AIR SPACE
METAL TIE
ANGLE IRON
SASH
FACE BRICK
SILL

CASEMENT SASH DETAIL

BRICK
1" AIR SPACE
ANGLE IRON
HEAD
SASH
JAMB
SILL

WINDOW DETAIL

BRICK
1" AIR SPACE
ANGLE IRON
HEAD
DOOR
JAMB
FLOOR
JOIST
SILL

DOOR DETAIL

1"X6" SHEATHING SPACE 2" APART
SHINGLES
RAFTERS
M.& B. CEILING
1"X6"
1" AIR SPACE
METAL TIES EVERY 4TH COURSE 16" ON CENTER
FACE BRICK VENEER
CEILING JOIST
2-2"X4"
LATH
PLASTER
2"X4"-16 O.C.
FLOOR
2"X4"
FLOOR JOIST
2"X6" PLATE
GRADE
12" BRICK WALL
12" CONCRETE WALL
CEMENT FLOOR
CONCRETE FOOTING

WALL SECTION OF BRICK VENEER BUILDING.

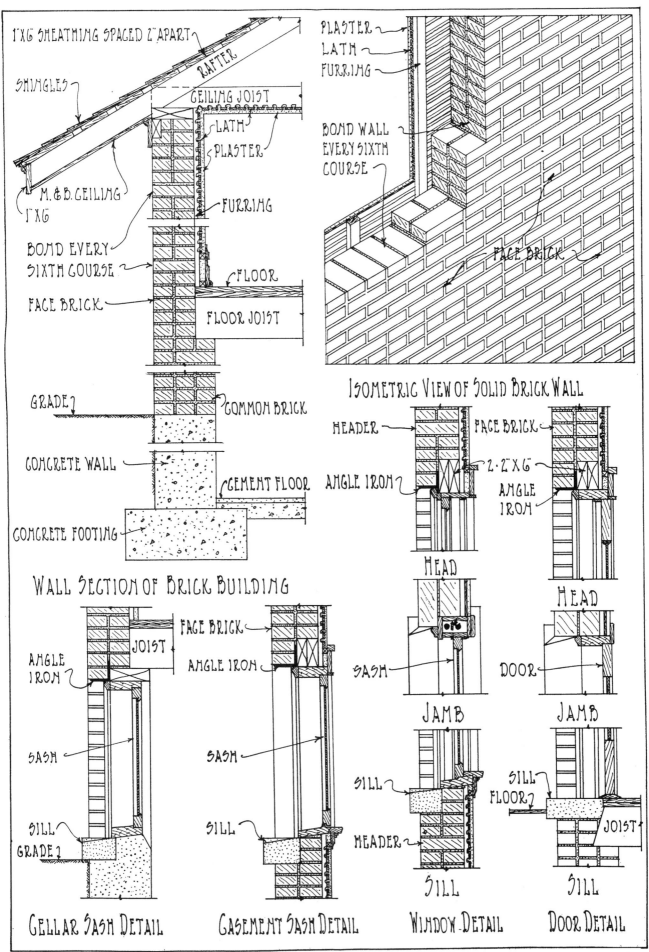

1"X6 SHEATHING SPACED 2" APART

RAFTER

SHINGLES

CEILING JOIST

LATH

PLASTER

M.&B. CEILING
1"X6

FURRING

BOND EVERY
SIXTH COURSE

FLOOR

FACE BRICK

FLOOR JOIST

GRADE

COMMON BRICK

CONCRETE WALL

CEMENT FLOOR

CONCRETE FOOTING

PLASTER
LATH
FURRING

BOND WALL
EVERY SIXTH
COURSE

FACE BRICK

ISOMETRIC VIEW OF SOLID BRICK WALL

WALL SECTION OF BRICK BUILDING

HEADER

ANGLE IRON

FACE BRICK

2-2"X6"

ANGLE IRON

HEAD

HEAD

SASH

DOOR

JAMB

JAMB

JOIST

FACE BRICK

ANGLE IRON

ANGLE IRON

SASH

SASH

SILL

SILL

SILL

FLOOR

SILL
GRADE

SILL

HEADER

JOIST

CELLAR SASH DETAIL

CASEMENT SASH DETAIL

WINDOW DETAIL

DOOR DETAIL

Structural Details of the All-Brick Wall Type of Construction in Which a Masonry Bond Is Used Between the Face Brick Outer Courses and the Common Brick Backing.

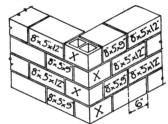

"X" = 8"x5"x5" CORNER TILE

Corner Bonding Detail for 8-Inch Walls of 8 by 5 by 12-Inch Hollow Tile.

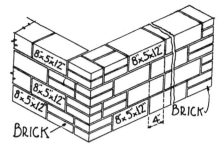

Detail for Bonding Corners and Finishing Around Openings of 8-Inch Hollow Tile Walls with Common Brick.

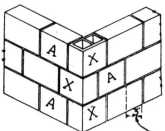

THIS BREAKING OF JOINTS THROUGHOUT MAY BE MADE 6" BY HAVING THE TILE MARKED "A" CUT TO 9" LENGTHS. X = 8"x5"x8" CORNER TILE

Corner Bonding Detail for 5-Inch Walls by 8 by 5 by 12-Inch Hollow Tile.

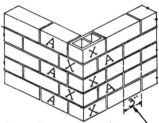

THIS BREAKING OF JOINTS THROUGHOUT MAY BE MADE 6" BY HAVING THE TILE MARKED "A" CUT TO 9" LENGTHS "X" = 8"x5"x4" CORNER TILE

Corner Bonding Detail for 5-Inch Walls of 4 by 5 by 12-Inch Hollow Tile Laid on the 5-Inch Bed. When Laid on the 4-Inch Face for 4-Inch Walls, the Corner Tile Would Be of 4 by 8-Inch Sections Cut to 4-Inch Length (4 by 8 by 4-Inch), Giving a 4-Inch Breaking of Joint.

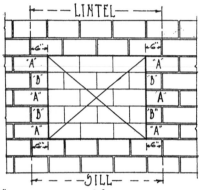

"A"-FULL SIZE TILE "B"-HALF SIZE TILE

Diagram Showing Placing of Opening in Hollow Tile Wall Having a 6-Inch Bond Between Courses.

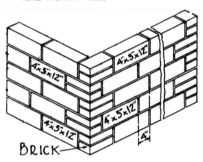

Detail for Bonding Corners and Finishing Around Openings of 4-Inch Hollow Tile Walls with Common Brick.

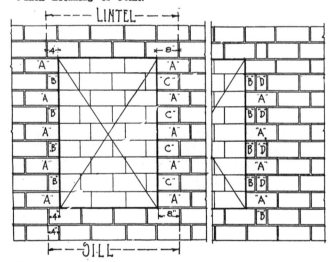

Diagram Showing Placing of Opening in Hollow Tile Wall Having a 4-Inch Running Bond Between Courses.

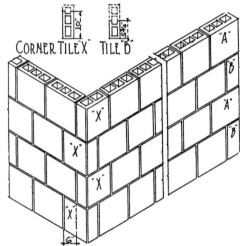

CORNER TILE "X"   TILE "B"

Corner and Jamb Detail for 4-Inch Walls of 4 by 12 by 12-Inch Hollow Tile. Detail for Wall 3 by 12 by 12-Inch Hollow Tile Would Be Similar, Excepting That Corner Tile "X" Would Be Cut as Close to 9 Inches as Possible.

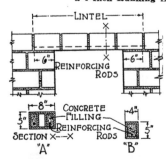

Section "A" for 8-Inch Walls of 8 by 5 by 12-Inch Tile; Section "B" for 4-Inch Walls of 4 by 5 by 12-Inch Tile and for Combining with Section "A" to Form Lintel for 12-Inch Wall Built of These Two Shapes. Similarly for 16-Inch Thick Wall Two Lintels of Section "A" Would Be Used.

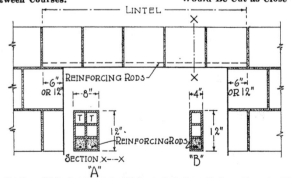

Section "A" for 8-Inch Walls of 8 by 12 by 12-Inch Tile; Section "B" for 4-Inch Walls of 4 by 12 by 12-Inch Tile and for Combining with Section "A" to Form Lintel for 12-Inch Wall. Lintels Made of Single Blocks Similar to Section "A," but 10 and 12 Inches in Thickness, Are Used for 10 and 12-Inch Walls, Respectively. All Lintels for Section "A" Type for Fairly Wide Openings, Particularly for 10 and 12-Inch Walls, Should Have One or Both of the Cells "T" Filled with Concrete, Reinforced with a Light Rod or Heavy Wire to Prevent Breakage in Handling.

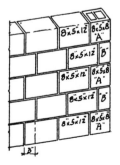

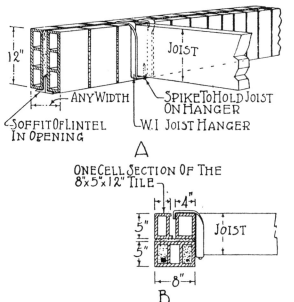

A

ONE CELL SECTION OF THE 8"x5"x12" TILE

B

Joist Hangers May Be Used with Various Types of Lintels to Keep Head of Window Opening Close to the Ceiling Line.

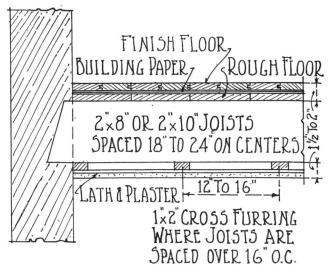

Total Depth of Floor Construction Taken as 10 Inches Where 2 by 6-Inch Joists Are Used; as 12 Inches Where 2 by 8-Inch Joists Are Used, and as 14 Inches Where 2 by 10-Inch Joists Are Used. Actually the Thickness Will Often Average About 1 Inch Less Than These Figures, Which Will Allow for the Leveling Up of Any Irregular Joist, or the Cross Stripping of Underfloor, so That the Finished Floor May Run in the Same Direction as the Underfloor.

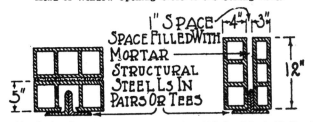

Lintels for Structural Shapes. Section "A" for 8-Inch Walls of 8 by 5 by 12-Inch Tile; Section "B" for 8-Inch Walls of 8 by 12 by 12-Inch Tile. The Size and Weight of Steel Shapes Required by Any Span and Loading May Be Figured from the Carnegie or Other Structural Steel Handbook. These Lintels Should Usually Have 12-Inch Bearing.

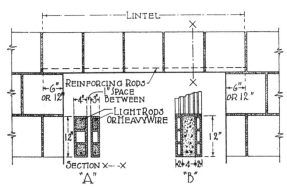

Section "A" for 8-Inch Walls of 8 by 12 by 12-Inch Tile; Section "B" for 4-Inch Walls of 4 by 12 by 12-Inch Tile and for Combining with Section "A" to Form Lintel for 12-Inch Wall. Lintels Made of Single Blocks Similar to Section "A" But 10 and 12 Inches in Thickness, Are Used for 10 and 12-Inch Walls, Respectively. All Lintels for Section "A" Type for Fairly Wide Openings, Particularly for 10 and 12-Inch Walls, Should Have One or Both of the Cells "T" Filled with Concrete, Reinforced with a Light Rod or Heavy Wire to Prevent Breakage in Handling.

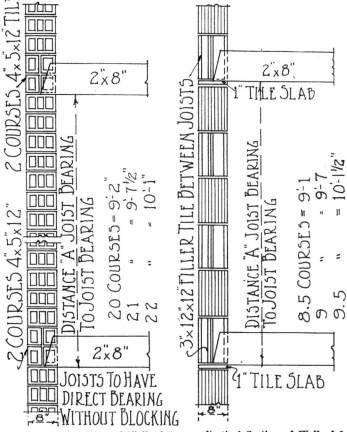
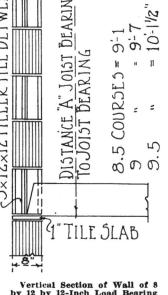

Vertical Section of Wall of 8 by 5 by 12-Inch Load Bearing Tile Laid on the Side.

Vertical Section of Wall of 8 by 12 by 12-Inch Load Bearing Tile Set on End.

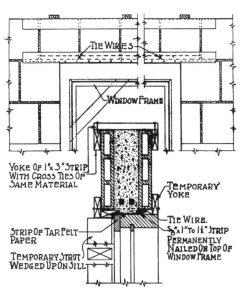

Details for Temporary Form Used for the Building of Lintels.

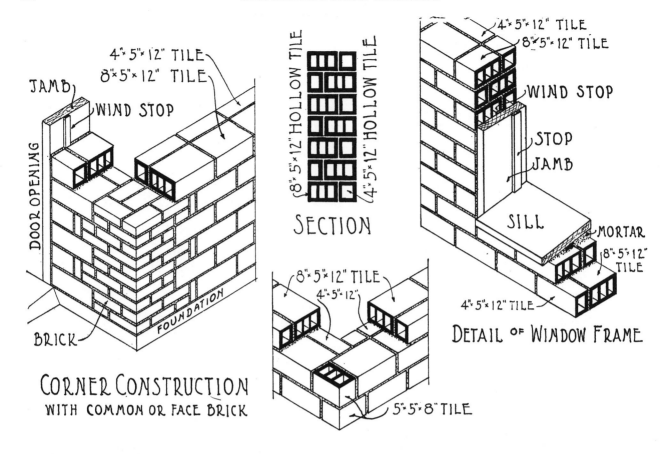

CORNER CONSTRUCTION
WITH COMMON OR FACE BRICK

DETAIL OF WINDOW FRAME

SECTION

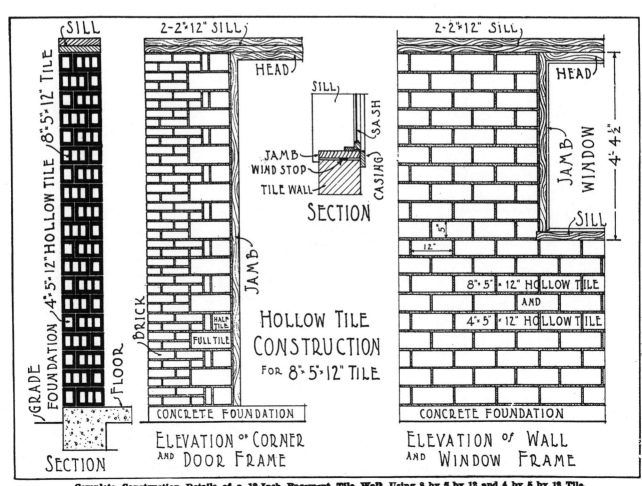

HOLLOW TILE
CONSTRUCTION
FOR 8"×5"×12" TILE

SECTION

ELEVATION OF CORNER
AND DOOR FRAME

ELEVATION OF WALL
AND WINDOW FRAME

Complete Construction Details of a 12-Inch Basement Tile Wall Using 8 by 5 by 12 and 4 by 5 by 12 Tile.

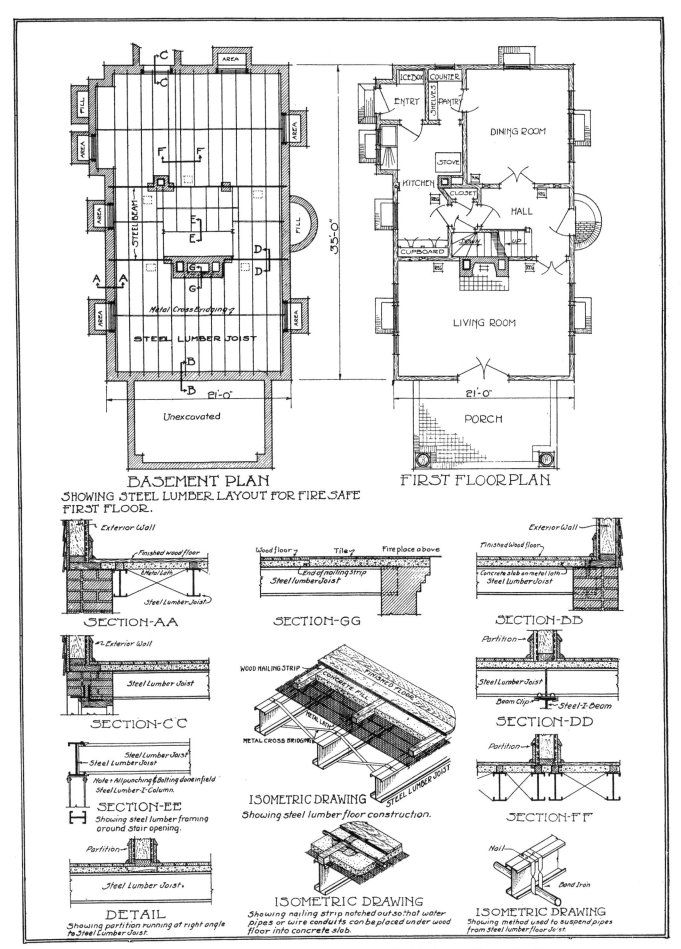

BASEMENT PLAN
SHOWING STEEL LUMBER LAYOUT FOR FIRE SAFE FIRST FLOOR.

FIRST FLOOR PLAN

SECTION-AA

SECTION-GG

SECTION-BB

SECTION-CC

ISOMETRIC DRAWING
Showing steel lumber floor construction.

SECTION-DD

SECTION-EE
Showing steel lumber framing around stair opening.

SECTION-FF

DETAIL
Showing partition running at right angle to Steel Lumber Joist.

ISOMETRIC DRAWING
Showing nailing strip notched out so that water pipes or wire conduits can be placed under wood floor into concrete slab.

ISOMETRIC DRAWING
Showing method used to suspend pipes from Steel lumber floor Joist.

Essentials of Steel Lumber Floor Construction as Used in Average Masonry Dwellings.

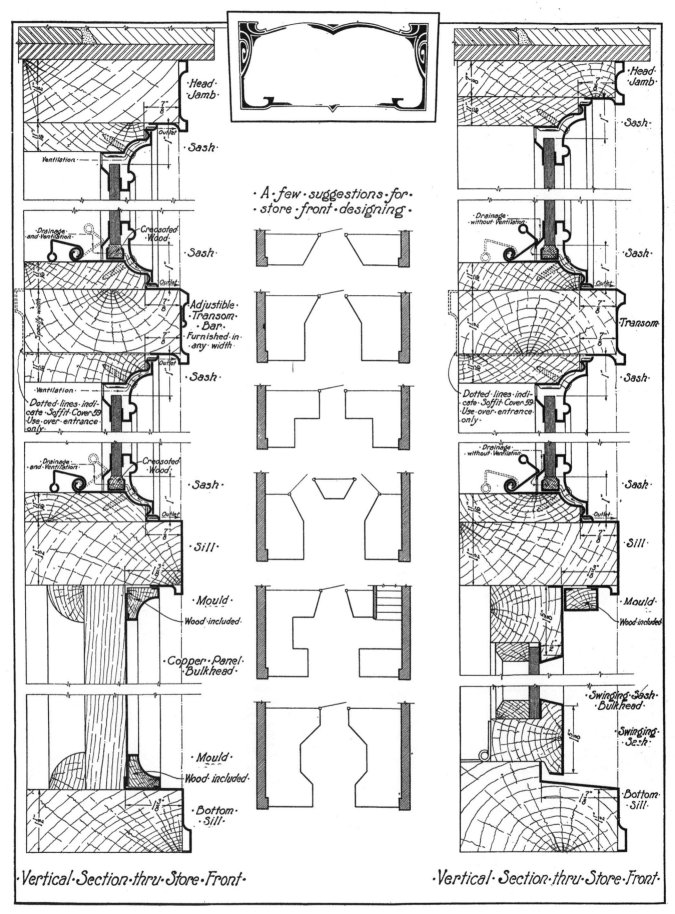

· A · few · suggestions · for ·
· store · front · designing ·

·Vertical·Section·thru·Store·Front·

·Vertical·Section·thru·Store·Front·

Floor Plans and Typical Details of Construction for Modern Display Windows for Stores.

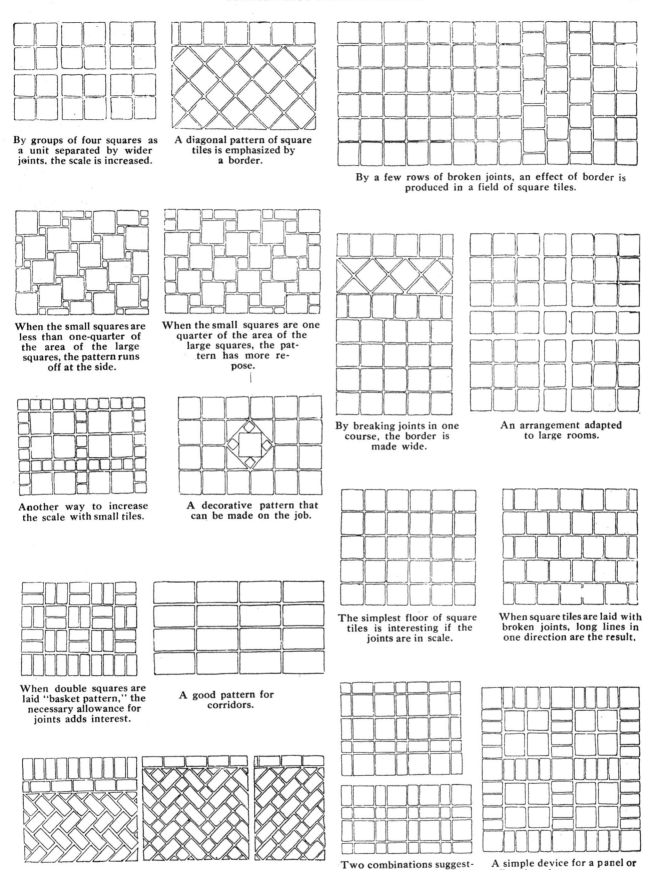

By groups of four squares as a unit separated by wider joints, the scale is increased.

A diagonal pattern of square tiles is emphasized by a border.

By a few rows of broken joints, an effect of border is produced in a field of square tiles.

When the small squares are less than one-quarter of the area of the large squares, the pattern runs off at the side.

When the small squares are one quarter of the area of the large squares, the pattern has more repose.

By breaking joints in one course, the border is made wide.

An arrangement adapted to large rooms.

Another way to increase the scale with small tiles.

A decorative pattern that can be made on the job.

The simplest floor of square tiles is interesting if the joints are in scale.

When square tiles are laid with broken joints, long lines in one direction are the result.

When double squares are laid "basket pattern," the necessary allowance for joints adds interest.

A good pattern for corridors.

Varieties of "herringbone."

Two combinations suggesting plaids.

A simple device for a panel or a floor for a large room.

SUGGESTIVE PATTERNS FOR TILE FLOORS.

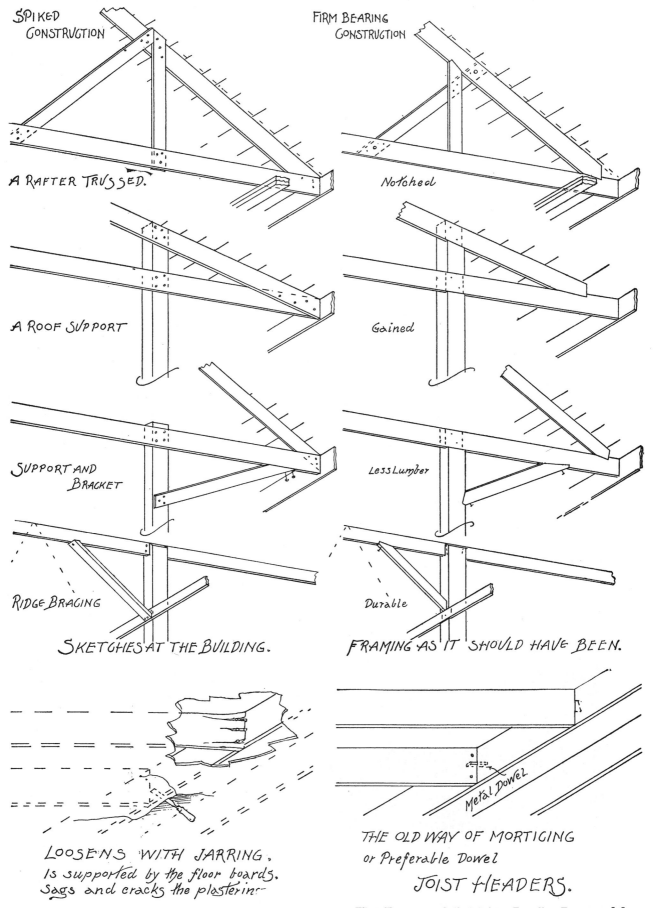

SPIKED CONSTRUCTION

FIRM BEARING CONSTRUCTION

A RAFTER TRUSSED.

Notched

A ROOF SUPPORT

Gained

SUPPORT AND BRACKET

Less Lumber

RIDGE BRACING

Durable

SKETCHES AT THE BUILDING.

FRAMING AS IT SHOULD HAVE BEEN.

LOOSENS WITH JARRING.
Is supported by the floor boards.
Sags and cracks the plastering.

THE OLD WAY OF MORTICING
or Preferable Dowel

Metal Dowel.

JOIST HEADERS.

What Happens to Spiked Joists; Doweling Recommended.

At the Left Is How Our Inspector Found the Work Being Done; at the Right the Better Way Is Shown.

GOOD AND BAD IN CARPENTRY WORK.

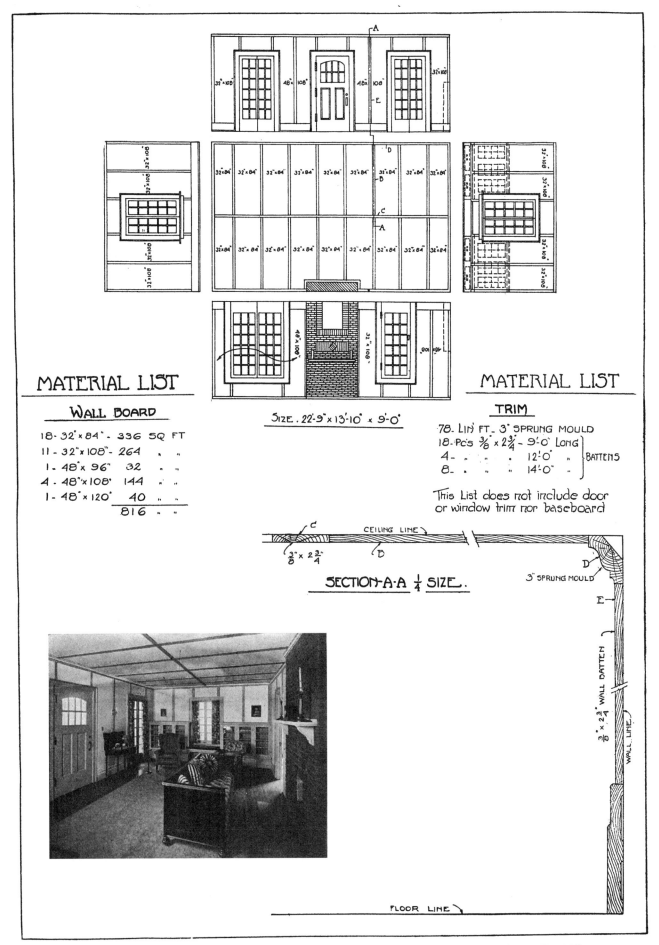

SIZE. 22'-9" x 13'-10" x 9'-0"

MATERIAL LIST

WALL BOARD

18 - 32" x 84" - 336 SQ FT
11 - 32" x 108" - 264 „ „
1 - 48" x 96" 32 „ „
4 - 48" x 108" 144 „ „
1 - 48" x 120" 40 „ „
816 „ „

MATERIAL LIST

TRIM

78 - LIN FT - 3" SPRUNG MOULD
18 - PC's 3/8 x 2 3/4 - 9'-0" LONG ⎫
4 - „ „ 12'-0" „ ⎬ BATTENS
8 - „ „ 14'-0" „ ⎭

This List does not include door or window trim nor baseboard

SECTION-A-A 1/4 SIZE.

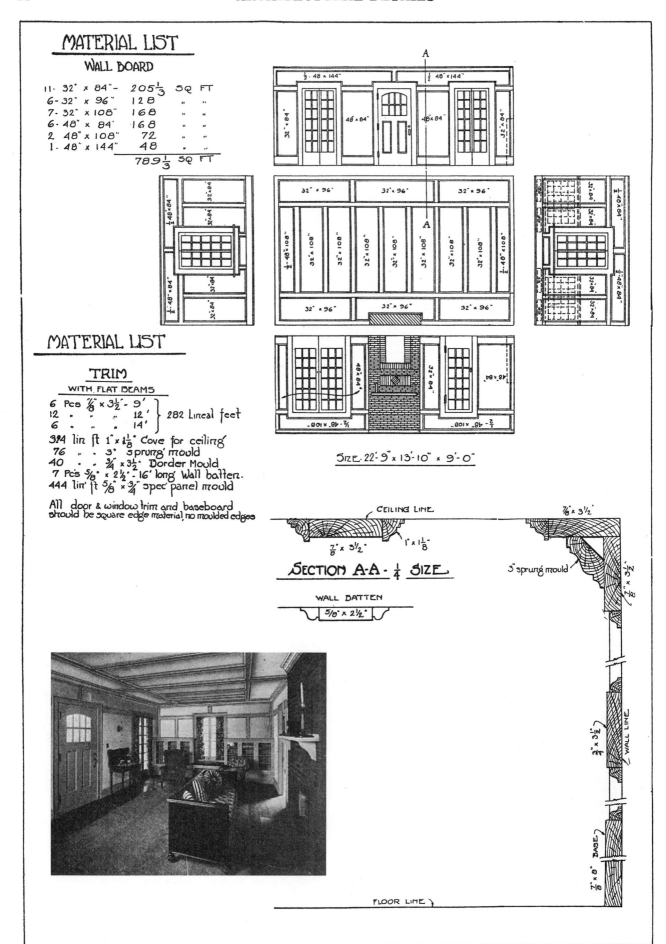

MATERIAL LIST

WALL BOARD

11 · 32" × 84" –	205⅓	SQ FT	
6 · 32" × 96"	128	"	"
7 · 32" × 108"	168	"	"
6 · 48" × 84"	168	"	"
2 · 48" × 108"	72	"	"
1 · 48" × 144"	48	"	"
	789⅓	SQ FT	

MATERIAL LIST

TRIM

WITH FLAT BEAMS

6 Pcs ⅞" × 3½" – 9'
12 " " – 12' } 282 Lineal feet
6 " " – 14'

324 lin' ft 1" × 1⅛" Cove for ceiling
76 " " 3" sprung mould
40 " " ¾" × 3½" Border Mould
7 Pcs ⅝" × 2½" – 16' long Wall batten.
444 lin' ft ⅝" × ¾" spec' panel mould

All door & window trim and baseboard
should be square edge material, no moulded edges

SIZE: 22'-9" × 13'-10" × 9'-0"

CEILING LINE ⅞ × 3½"
⅞" × 3½"   1" × 1⅛"
3" sprung mould
⅞ × 3½"

SECTION A-A - ¼ SIZE

WALL BATTEN
⅝" × 2½"

WALL LINE
¾" × 3½"

BASE
⅞" × 8"

FLOOR LINE

MATERIAL LIST
WALL BOARD

11- 32" x 84"   205⅓   SQ FEET
6 -32" x 96"   128   "   "
7 -32" x 108"   168   "   "
6 -48" x 84"   168   "   "
2 -48" x 108"   72   "   "
1 -48" x 144"   48   "   "

789⅓ SQ FT

MATERIAL LIST
TRIM
WITH BOX BEAM

76 Lin ft Half-Beam
124 "   " Full   "

324 - 7/8" x 4½"
124' 17/8" x 3¾" 545
76'. 17/8" x 17/8"
124' 7/8" x 3¾"
76 - 7/8" x 17/8"

40 Lin ft ¾" x 3½" Border Mould
4 - 5/8" x 2½" x 12'
2 "   "   " - 14' } Wall Batten
7 "   "   " - 16'
444 lin' ft 5/8" x ¾" Spec'- Panel Mould

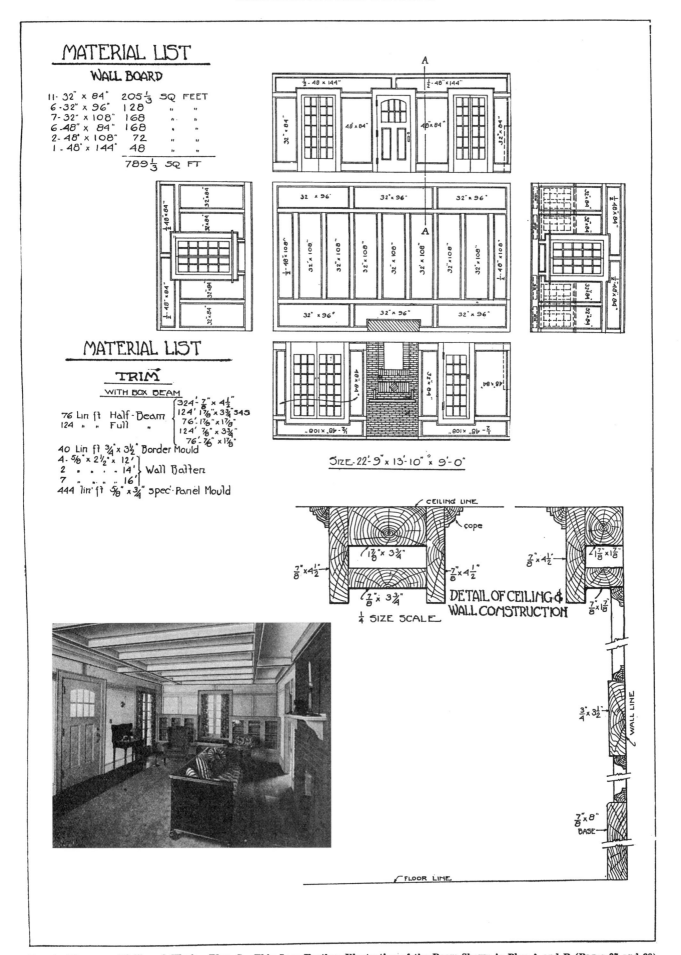

Size - 22'-9" x 13'-10" x 9'-0"

DETAIL OF CEILING & WALL CONSTRUCTION
¼ SIZE SCALE

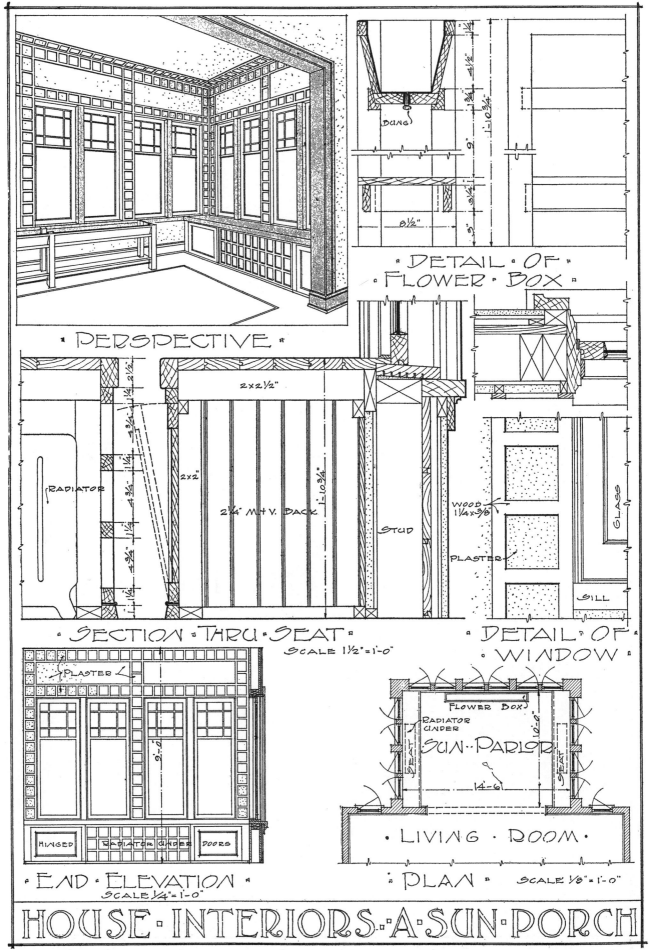

· PERSPECTIVE ·

DETAIL · OF ·
· FLOWER · BOX ·

BUNG

8½"

2 x 2½"

2 x 2"

2¼" M + V. BACK

RADIATOR

STUD

WOOD
1¼ x ⅜

PLASTER

GLASS

SILL

· SECTION · THRU · SEAT ·
SCALE 1½" = 1'-0"

· DETAIL · OF ·
· WINDOW ·

PLASTER

HINGED   RADIATOR UNDER   DOORS

· END · ELEVATION ·
SCALE ¼" = 1'-0"

FLOWER BOX
RADIATOR
UNDER
SEAT
SUN · PARLOR
SEAT
14'-6"
10'-0"

· LIVING · ROOM ·

· PLAN ·   SCALE ⅛" = 1'-0"

HOUSE · INTERIORS · A · SUN · PORCH

Perspective Sketch, Elevation, Plan and Construction Details of a Sun Parlor Finished in Lattice Style Suggesting the Outdoors.

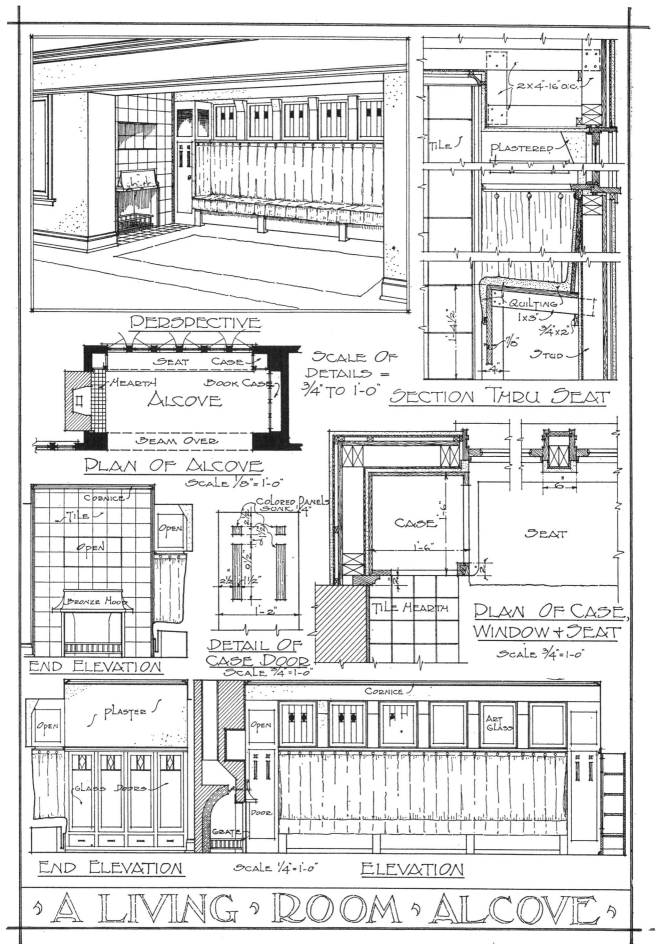

PERSPECTIVE

SCALE OF DETAILS = 3/4" TO 1'-0"

SECTION THRU SEAT

PLAN OF ALCOVE
Scale 1/8" = 1'-0"

DETAIL OF CASE DOOR
Scale 3/4" = 1'-0"

PLAN OF CASE, WINDOW & SEAT
Scale 3/4" = 1'-0"

END ELEVATION

END ELEVATION   Scale 1/4"=1'-0"   ELEVATION

A LIVING ROOM ALCOVE

Architect's Sketch Showing Details of Living Room Alcove, Including Comfortable Upholstered Seat with Art Glass Windows Above, Bookcases and Fireplace in Tile with Bronze Hood.

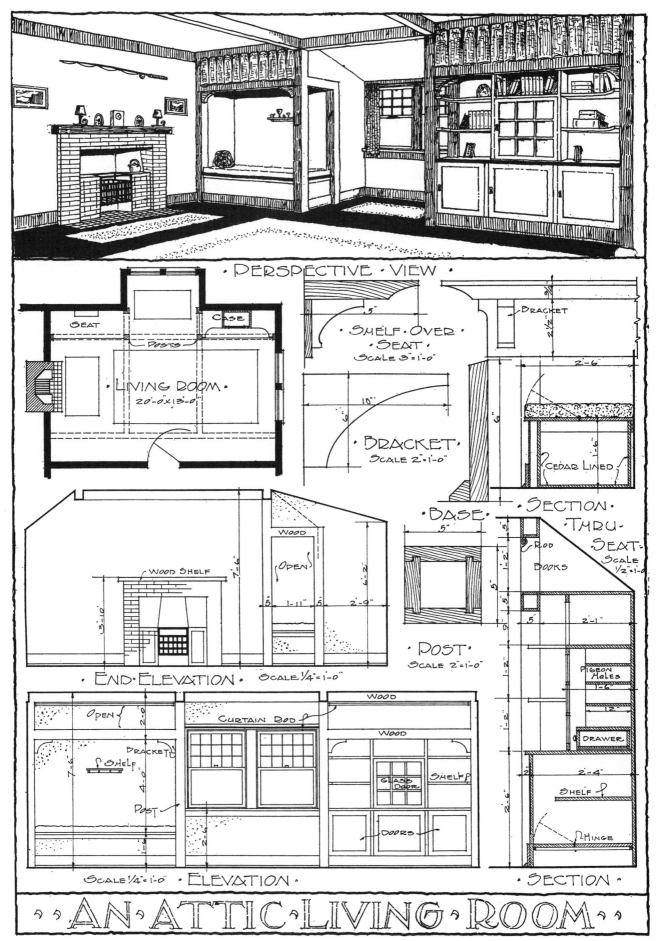

· PERSPECTIVE · VIEW ·

SEAT   CASE

POSTS

· LIVING ROOM ·
20'-0" X 13'-0"

· SHELF · OVER ·
· SEAT ·
SCALE 3"=1'-0"

· BRACKET ·
SCALE 2"=1'-0"

BRACKET

CEDAR LINED

· SECTION ·
· THRU ·
· SEAT ·
SCALE ½"=1'-0"

· BASE ·

WOOD SHELF

WOOD

OPEN

· END · ELEVATION ·   SCALE ¼"=1'-0"

· POST ·
SCALE 2"=1'-0"

ROD

BOOKS

PIGEON HOLES

DRAWER

SHELF

OPEN

SHELF

BRACKET

POST

CURTAIN ROD

WOOD

WOOD

GLASS DOOR

SHELF

DOORS

HINGE

SCALE ¼"=1'-0"   · ELEVATION ·

· SECTION ·

· AN · ATTIC · LIVING · ROOM ·

Sketch, Plan, Elevations and Construction Details of an Attic Living Room.

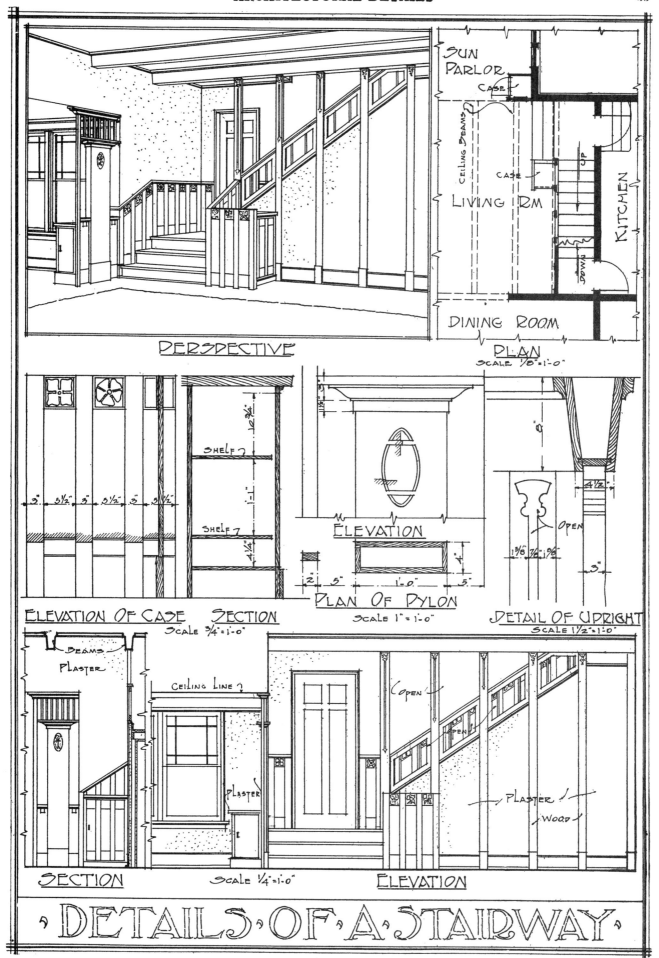

PERSPECTIVE

SUN PARLOR
CASE
CEILING BEAMS
CASE
LIVING RM
UP
KITCHEN
DOWN
DINING ROOM

PLAN
SCALE 1/8"=1'-0"

SHELF
12 3/4"
1'-1"
SHELF
4 1/4"
3" 5 1/2" 3" 5 1/2" 3" 5 1/2"

ELEVATION OF CASE   SECTION
SCALE 3/4"=1'-0"

ELEVATION
PLAN OF PYLON
SCALE 1"=1'-0"
2" 5" 1'-0" 5"

4 1/2"
OPEN
1 5/8" 7/8" 1 5/8"
3"

DETAIL OF UPRIGHT
SCALE 1 1/2"=1'-0"

BEAMS
PLASTER
CEILING LINE
PLASTER
OPEN
OPEN
PLASTER
WOOD

SECTION   SCALE 1/4"=1'-0"   ELEVATION

DETAILS OF A STAIRWAY

Perspective Sketch, Floor Plan and Details of Open Stairway Going Up Out of a Living Room. A Design of Considerable Originality.

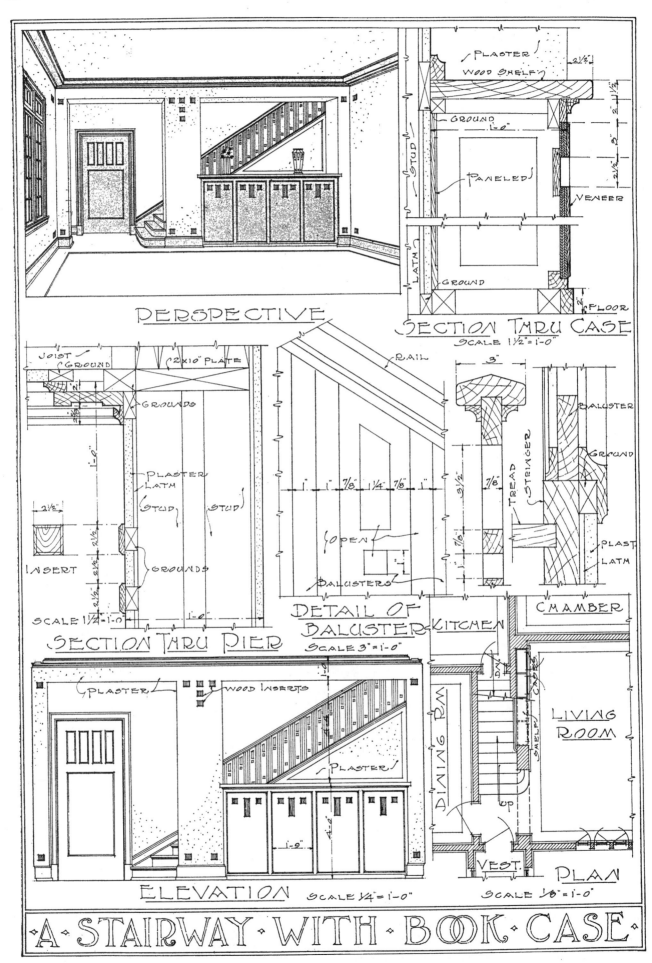

PERSPECTIVE

SECTION THRU CASE
SCALE 1½"=1-0"

SECTION THRU PIER
SCALE 1½"=1-0

DETAIL OF BALUSTER
SCALE 3"=1-0"

ELEVATION   SCALE ¼"=1-0"

PLAN   SCALE ⅛"=1-0"

A · STAIRWAY · WITH · BOOK · CASE

Perspective Sketch, Elevation, Plan and Scale Details of Semi-Open Stair Handled in the Modern Straight Line Style.

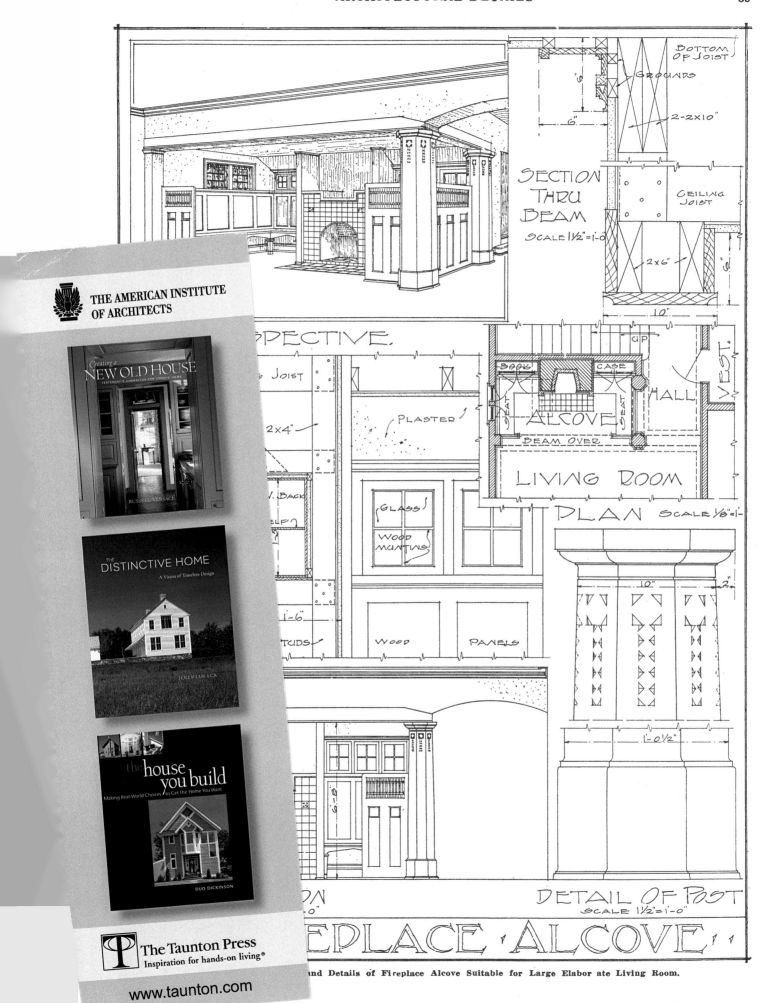

SECTION THRU BEAM
SCALE 1½"=1-0

BOTTOM OF JOIST
GROUNDS
2-2x10"
CEILING JOIST
2x6"

PLAN SCALE ⅛"=1-

UP
BOOKS   CASE
SEAT   ALCOVE   SEAT   HALL
BEAM OVER
LIVING ROOM
VEST.

DETAIL OF POST
SCALE 1½"=1-0

PERSPECTIVE.

PLASTER
2x4"
W. BACK
GLASS
WOOD MUNTING
WOOD PANELS
STUDS

FIREPLACE ALCOVE

and Details of Fireplace Alcove Suitable for Large Elaborate Living Room.

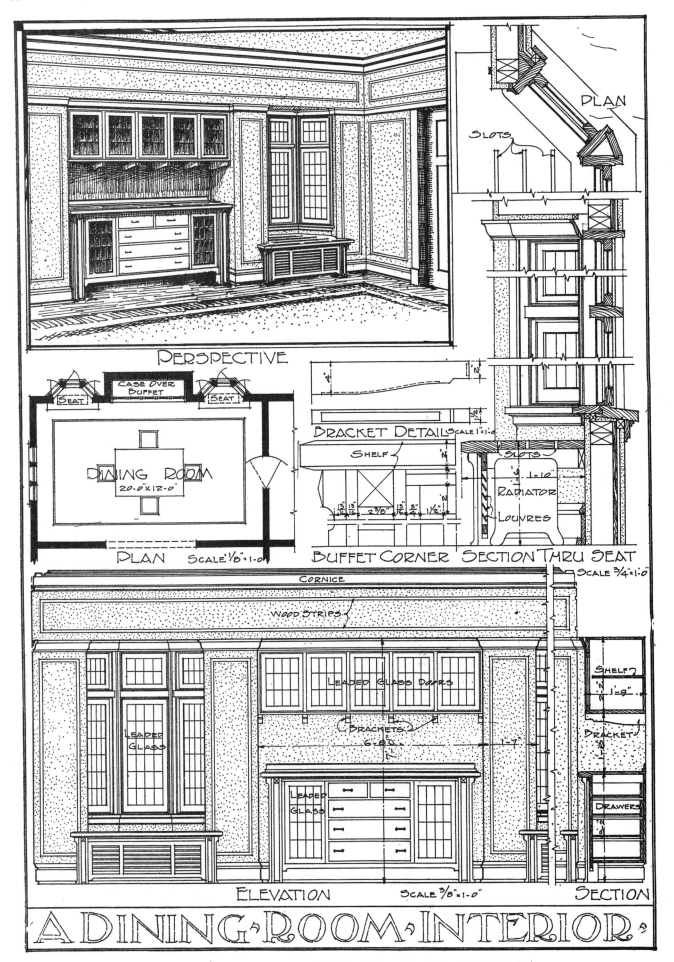

PERSPECTIVE

CASE OVER BUFFET

SEAT   SEAT

DINING ROOM
20'-0" x 12'-0"

PLAN   SCALE ⅛"=1'-0"

BRACKET DETAIL SCALE 1"=1'-0"

SHELF

PLAN

SLOTS

SHELF

SLOTS

RADIATOR

LOUVRES

BUFFET CORNER   SECTION THRU SEAT

SCALE ¾"=1'-0"

CORNICE

WOOD STRIPS

LEADED GLASS DOORS

LEADED GLASS

BRACKETS
6'-0"

LEADED GLASS

SHELF

BRACKET

DRAWERS

ELEVATION   SCALE ⅜"=1'-0"   SECTION

A·DINING·ROOM·INTERIOR·

Sketch, Floor Plans, Elevations and Details of Interesting Dining Room Interior.

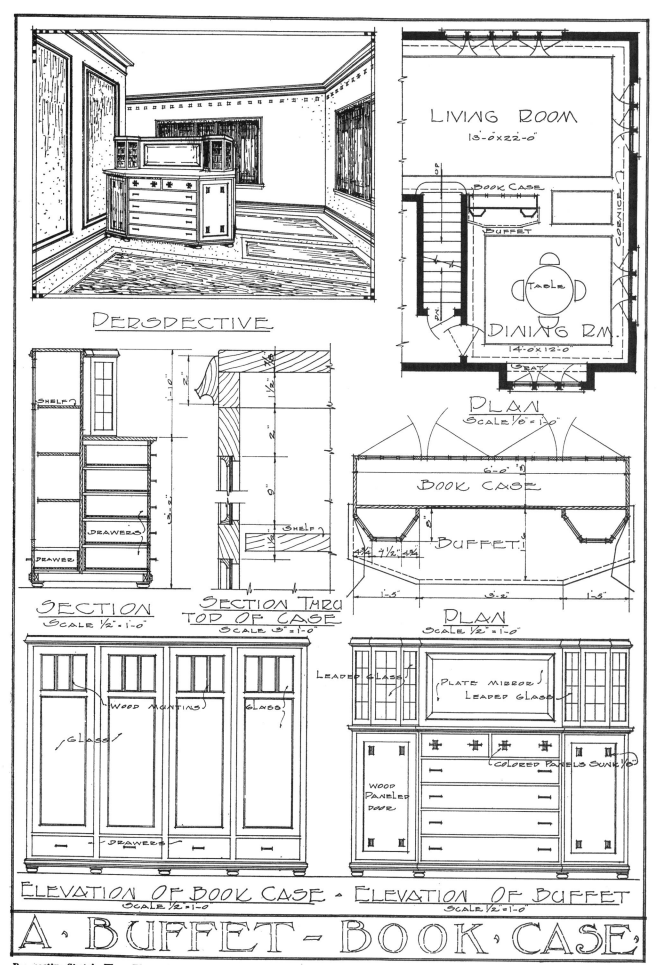

PERSPECTIVE

LIVING ROOM
13'-0"x22'-0"

BOOK CASE
BUFFET

TABLE

DINING RM.
14'-0"x12'-0"

SEAT

PLAN
SCALE 1/8"=1'-0"

SHELF

SECTION
SCALE 1/2"=1'-0"

SHELF

DRAWERS
DRAWER

SECTION THRU
TOP OF CASE
SCALE 3"=1'-0"

6'-0"

BOOK CASE

BUFFET

4¾" 7½" 4¾"

1'-5"   3'-2"   1'-5"

PLAN
SCALE 1/2"=1'-0"

LEADED GLASS

PLATE MIRROR
LEADED GLASS

WOOD MUNTINS

GLASS

GLASS

WOOD
PANELED
DOOR

COLORED PANELS SUNK ⅛"

DRAWERS

ELEVATION OF BOOK CASE
SCALE 1/2"=1'-0"

ELEVATION OF BUFFET
SCALE 1/2"=1'-0"

A · BUFFET - BOOK · CASE ·

Perspective Sketch, Floor Plan, Elevation and Details of a Combined Buffet and Book Case, Arranged to Form a Half Partition Between
a Dining Room and a Living Room.

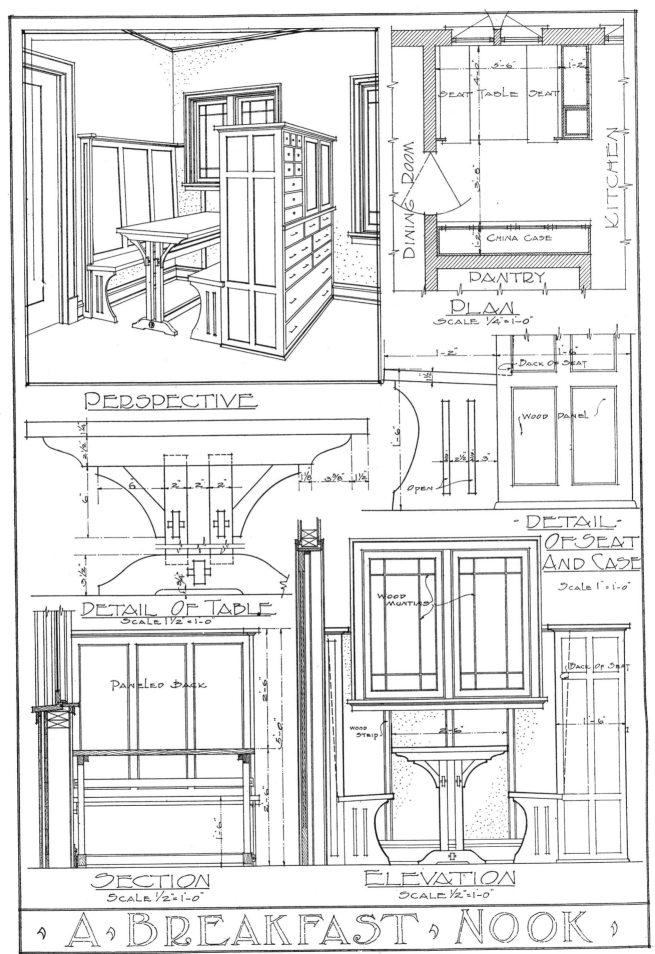

PERSPECTIVE

PLAN
SCALE ¼"=1'-0"

DINING ROOM

Seat   Table   Seat

5'-6"   1'-2"

3'-8"

China Case

KITCHEN

PANTRY

Back of Seat

1'-2"   1'-6"

Wood Panel

1'-6"

Open

- DETAIL -
OF SEAT
AND CASE
Scale 1"=1'-0"

DETAIL OF TABLE
Scale 1½"=1'-0"

SECTION
Scale ½"=1'-0"

Paneled Back

5'-0"

2'-6"

2'-6"

1'-6"

ELEVATION
Scale ½"=1'-0"

Wood Muntins

Wood Strip

2'-6"

Back of Seat

1'-6"

- A - BREAKFAST - NOOK -

Architect's Drawing Giving Perspective Sketch, Floor Plan and Details of a Very Interesting Breakfast Alcove Formed by Kitchen Cabinet.

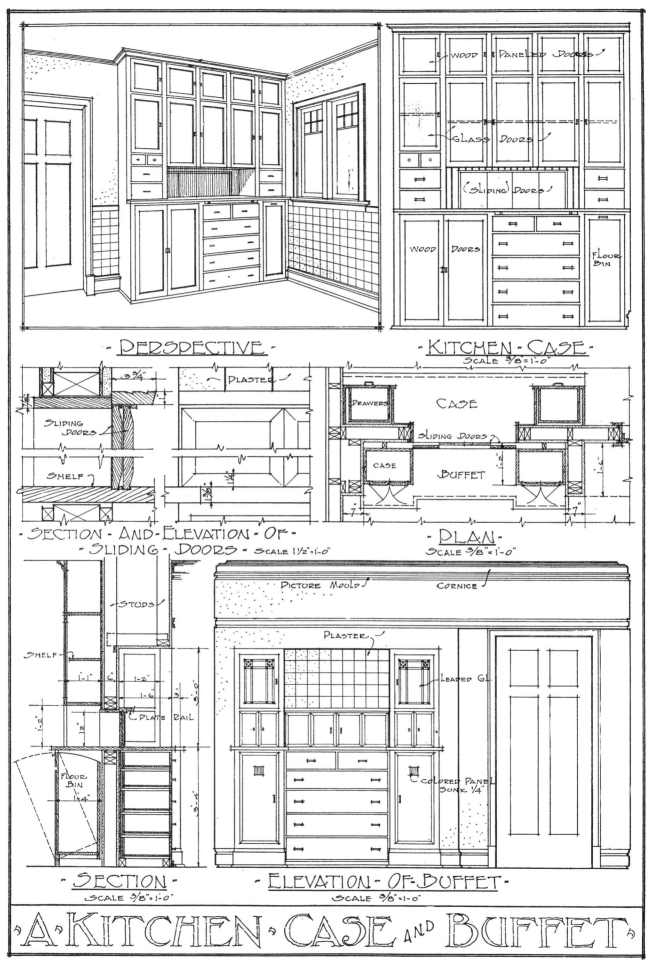

- PERSPECTIVE -

- KITCHEN - CASE -
SCALE 3/8"=1'-0"

WOOD PANELED DOORS

GLASS DOORS

(SLIDING) DOORS

WOOD DOORS

FLOUR BIN

PLASTER

SLIDING DOORS

SHELF

CASE

DRAWERS

SLIDING DOORS

CASE

BUFFET

- SECTION - AND - ELEVATION - OF -
- SLIDING - DOORS - SCALE 1½"=1'-0"

- PLAN -
SCALE 3/8"=1'-0"

STUDS

SHELF

PLATE RAIL

FLOUR BIN

PICTURE MOULD

CORNICE

PLASTER

LEADED GL.

COLORED PANEL
SUNK ¼"

- SECTION -
SCALE 3/8"=1'-0"

- ELEVATION - OF - BUFFET -
SCALE 3/8"=1'-0"

A KITCHEN CASE AND BUFFET

Details of a Commodious Cabinet and Sideboard to Be Built Into the Wall Between the Dining Room and the Kitchen.

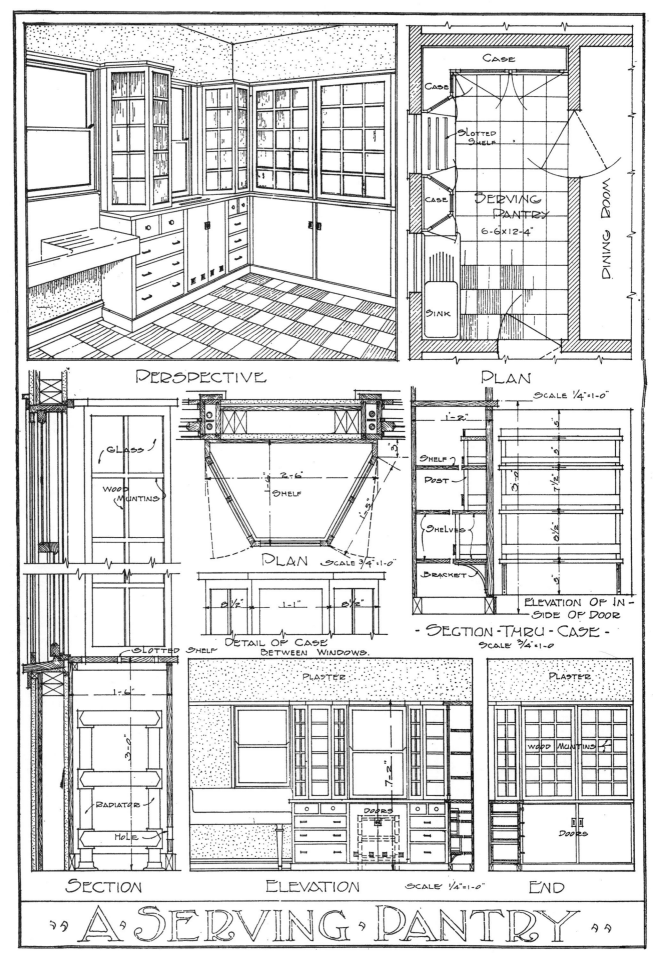

PERSPECTIVE

PLAN

CASE

CASE

SLOTTED SHELF

CASE

SERVING PANTRY
6'-6"x12'-4"

DINING ROOM

SINK

SCALE ¼"=1'-0"

GLASS

WOOD MUNTINS

2'-6"
SHELF

PLAN   SCALE ¾"=1'-0"

0½"   1'-1"   0½"

DETAIL OF CASE
BETWEEN WINDOWS.

1'-2"

SHELF

POST

SHELVES

BRACKET

ELEVATION OF IN-
SIDE OF DOOR
- SECTION · THRU · CASE -
SCALE ¾"=1'-0"

SLOTTED SHELF

1'-4"

3'-0"

RADIATOR

HOLE

SECTION

PLASTER

7'-2"

DOORS

ELEVATION   SCALE ¼"=1'-0"

PLASTER

WOOD MUNTINS

DOORS

END

A SERVING PANTRY

Perspective Sketch, Plan and Details of a Well Equipped Serving Pantry.

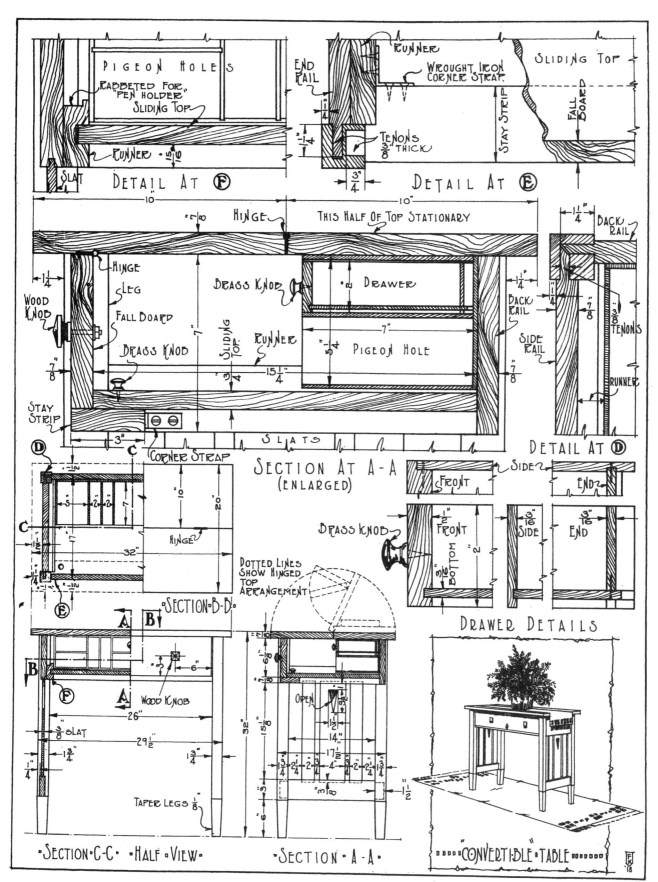

Perspective Sketch and Working Drawing Showing Construction of an Ingenious Table Desk

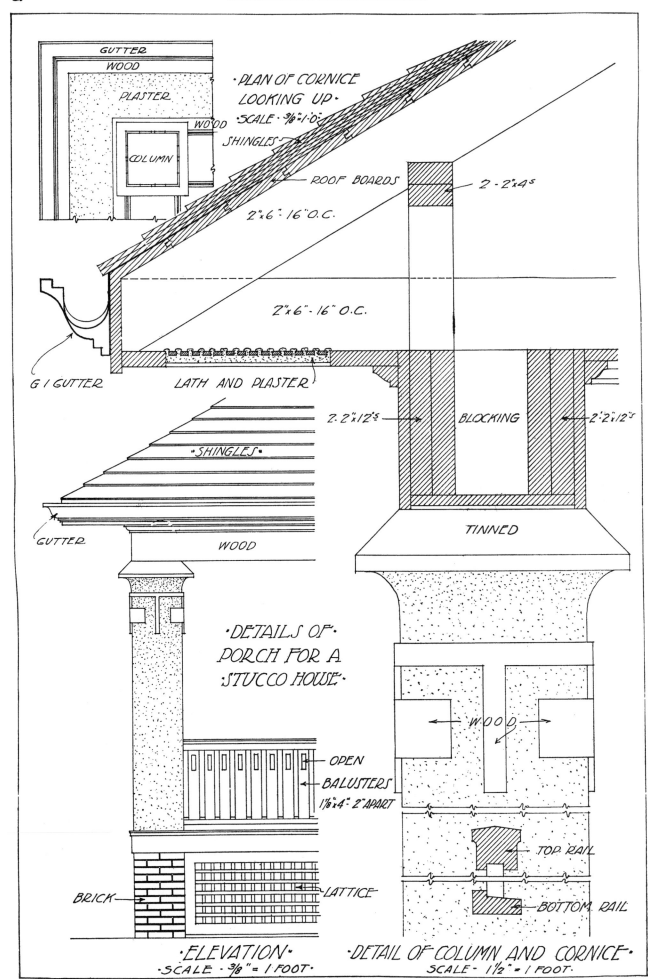

GUTTER

WOOD

PLASTER

WOOD

COLUMN

·PLAN OF CORNICE
LOOKING UP·
·SCALE · 3/8"·1'·0"·

SHINGLES

ROOF BOARDS

2"x6"· 16"O.C.

2-2"x4's

2"x6"· 16" O.C.

G I GUTTER

LATH AND PLASTER

2·2"x12's

BLOCKING

2·2"x12's

TINNED

·SHINGLES·

GUTTER

WOOD

·DETAILS OF·
PORCH FOR A
·STUCCO HOUSE·

W·O·O·D

OPEN

BALUSTERS
1⅛"x4"· 2"APART

TOP RAIL

BRICK

LATTICE

BOTTOM RAIL

·ELEVATION·
·SCALE · 3/8" = 1 FOOT·

·DETAIL OF COLUMN AND CORNICE·
·SCALE· 1½" = 1 FOOT·

Design and Details of Modern Style Stucco Porch.

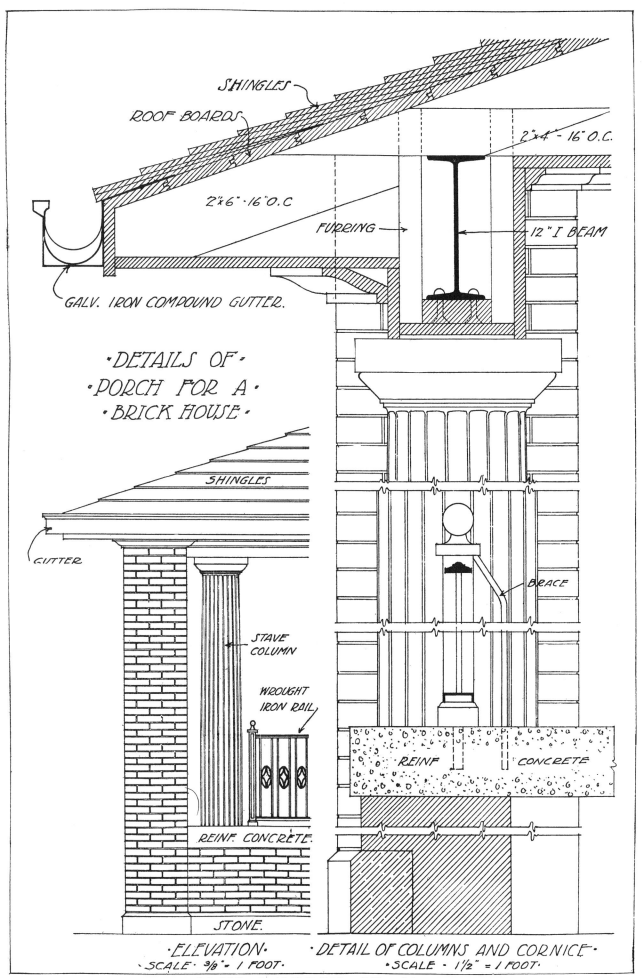

SHINGLES

ROOF BOARDS

2"x4" - 16" O.C.

2"x6" · 16"O.C

FURRING

12" I BEAM

GALV. IRON COMPOUND GUTTER.

·DETAILS OF·
·PORCH FOR A·
·BRICK HOUSE·

SHINGLES

GUTTER.

STAVE
COLUMN

BRACE

WROUGHT
IRON RAIL

REINF   CONCRETE

REINF. CONCRETE.

STONE.

·ELEVATION·
·SCALE · 3/8" = 1 FOOT·

·DETAIL OF COLUMNS AND CORNICE·
·SCALE · 1 1/2" = 1 FOOT·

Colonial Porch with Both Brick and Stave Columns.

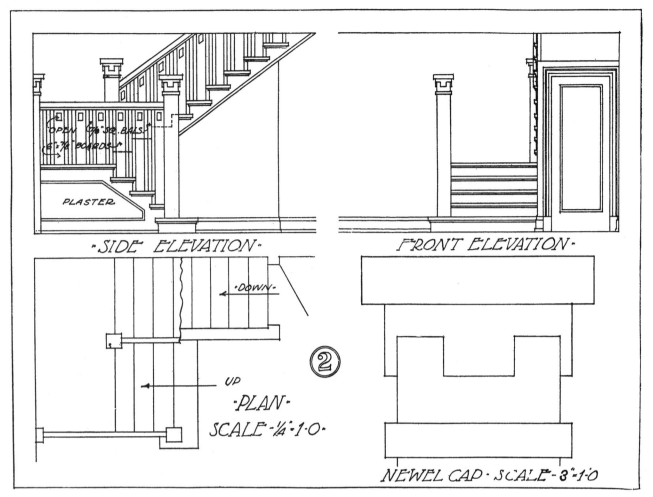

·SIDE ELEVATION·

·FRONT ELEVATION·

OPEN G⅞"SQ. BALS"
6"×⅞" BOARDS·

PLASTER

·DOWN·

UP

②

·PLAN·
SCALE ·¼·=·1·0·

NEWEL CAP · SCALE · 3"=1·0

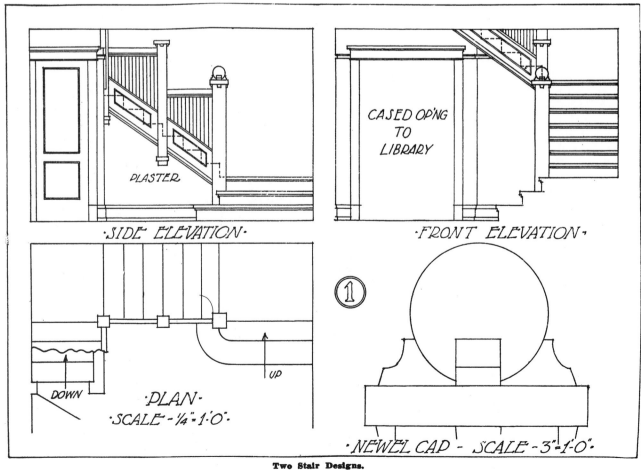

PLASTER

·SIDE ELEVATION·

CASED OP'NG
TO
LIBRARY

·FRONT ELEVATION·

①

DOWN

UP

·PLAN·
·SCALE ·¼"=·1·0·

·NEWEL CAP · SCALE · 3"=1·0·

Two Stair Designs.

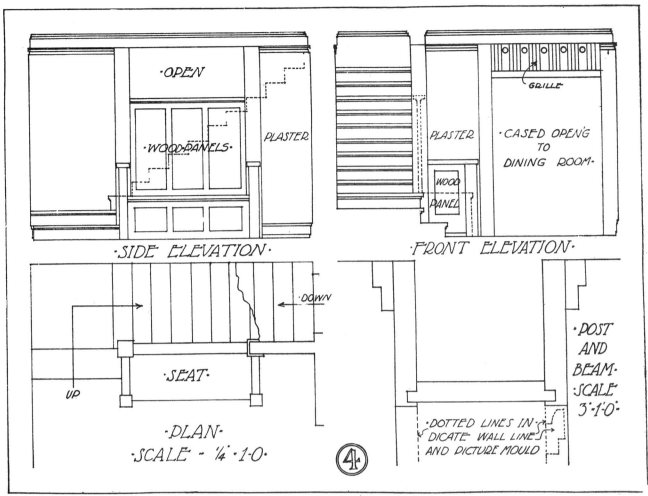

·SIDE ELEVATION·

·OPEN·

·WOOD·PANELS·   PLASTER

·FRONT ELEVATION·

GRILLE

PLASTER   ·CASED OPEN'G
                    TO
WOOD   DINING ROOM·
PANEL

DOWN

·SEAT·

UP

·PLAN·
·SCALE - ¼'·1·0·

④

·POST
AND
BEAM·
·SCALE·
3·1·0·

·DOTTED LINES IN·
DICATE· WALL LINES·
AND PICTURE MOULD·

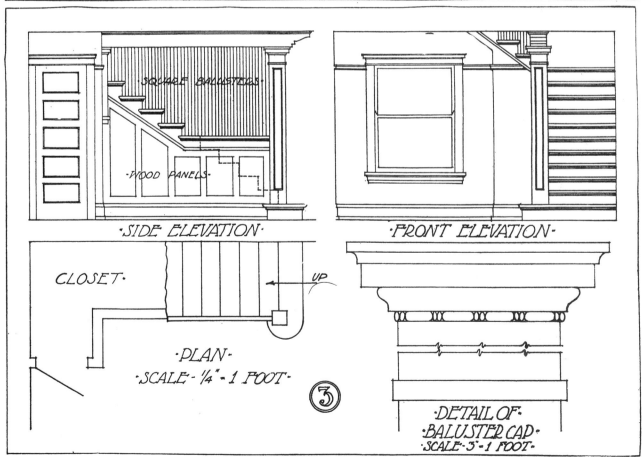

·SIDE ELEVATION·

SQUARE BALUSTERS

·WOOD PANELS·

·FRONT ELEVATION·

CLOSET·

UP

·PLAN·
·SCALE· ¼" · 1 FOOT·

③

·DETAIL OF·
·BALUSTER CAP·
·SCALE· 3'·1 FOOT·

Two Stair Designs.

Corner Trellis and Flower Pot Shelf.

Arch Trellis Over a Window.

Lattice Ornament for Wall.

A Pergola Entry.

A Trellis and Seat Entry.

VINE TRELLISES AND ORNAMENTAL FEATURES.

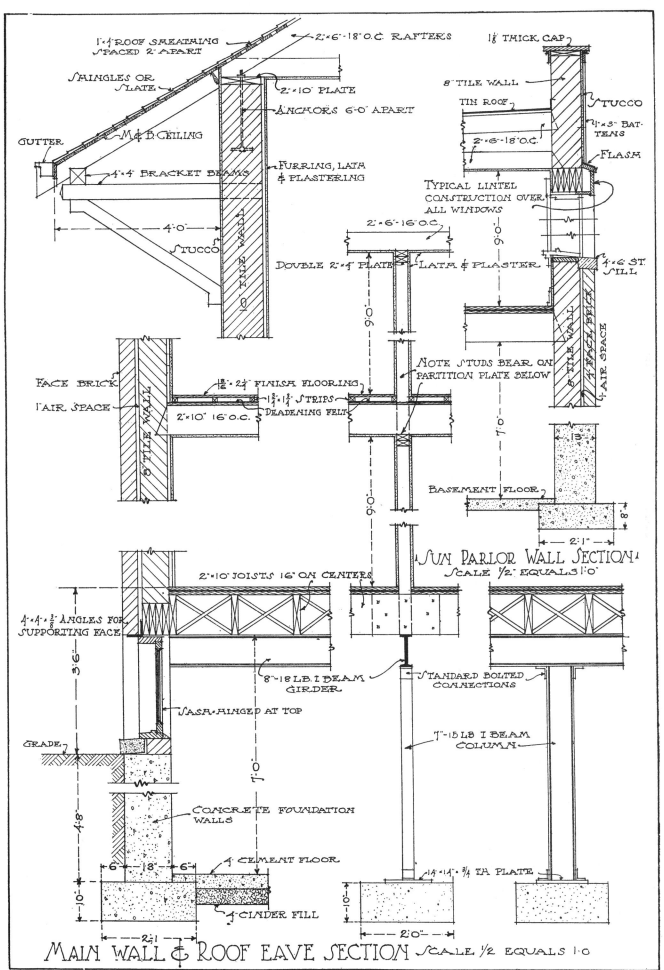

MAIN WALL & ROOF EAVE SECTION Scale ½ Equals 1:0

How to Fasten Wood Rafters and Plate to Tile Wall, and How to Seat Joists on Tile.

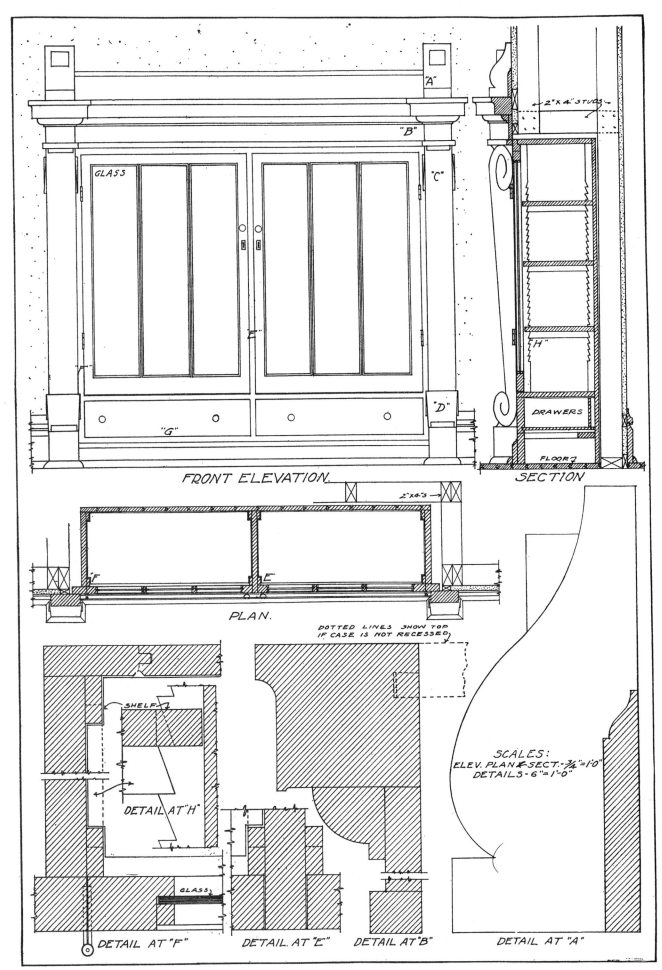

FRONT ELEVATION.

SECTION

PLAN.

GLASS

"A"

"B"

"C"

"D"

"E"

"G"

2"X4" STUDS

"H"

DRAWERS

FLOOR

2"X4"'S

DOTTED LINES SHOW TOP
IF CASE IS NOT RECESSED

SHELF

DETAIL AT "H"

GLASS

DETAIL AT "F"

DETAIL AT "E"

DETAIL AT "B"

DETAIL AT "A"

SCALES:
ELEV. PLAN & SECT.- ¾"=1'-0"
DETAILS- 6"=1'-0"

Built-In Colonial Book Case—Recessed (See Opposite Page).

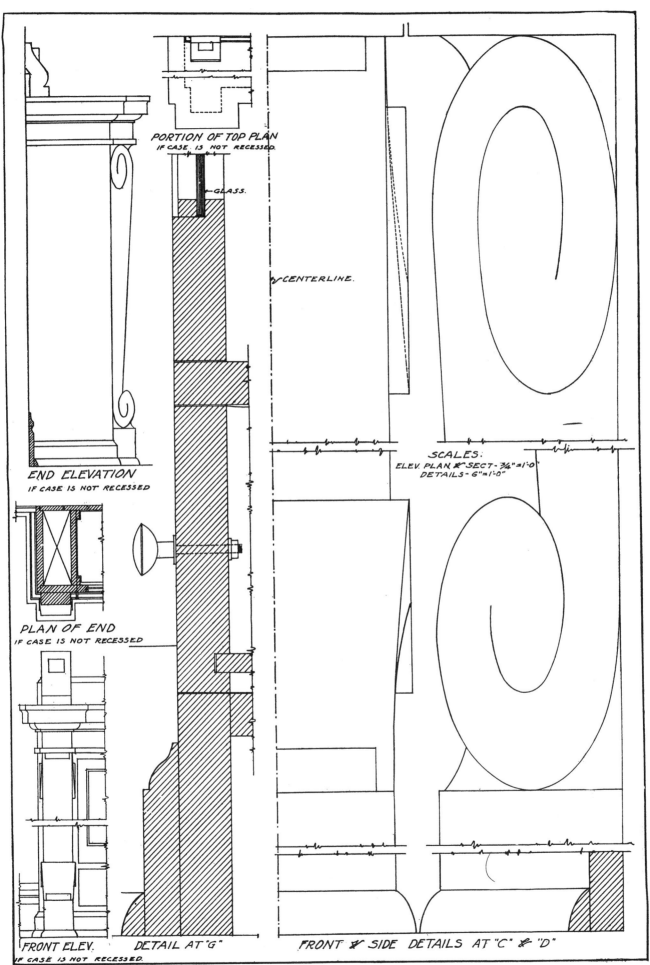

PORTION OF TOP PLAN
IF CASE IS NOT RECESSED.

GLASS.

CENTERLINE.

END ELEVATION
IF CASE IS NOT RECESSED

PLAN OF END
IF CASE IS NOT RECESSED

SCALES:
ELEV. PLAN & SECT-3/4"=1'-0"
DETAILS-6"=1'-0"

FRONT ELEV.
IF CASE IS NOT RECESSED.

DETAIL AT "G"

FRONT & SIDE DETAILS AT "C" & "D"

Arrangement of Book Case to Project Into Room (See Opposite Page).

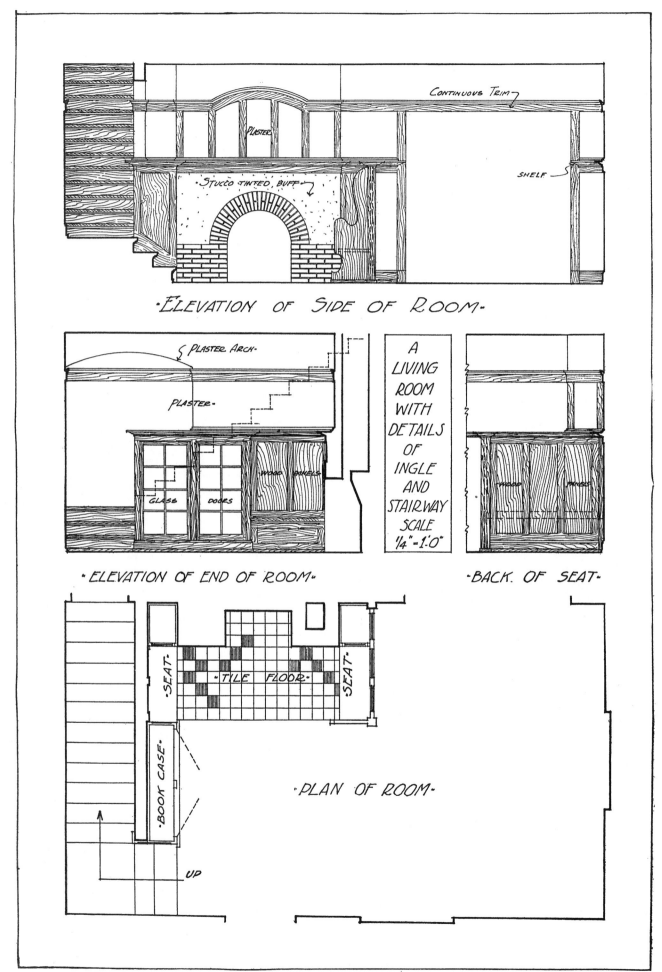

·ELEVATION OF SIDE OF ROOM·

CONTINUOUS TRIM

PLASTER

STUCCO TINTED, BUFF

SHELF

·ELEVATION OF END OF ROOM·

PLASTER ARCH·

PLASTER·

GLASS   DOORS

WOOD PANELS

A LIVING ROOM WITH DETAILS OF INGLE AND STAIRWAY SCALE 1/4"=1'·0"

·BACK OF SEAT·

WOOD PANELS

·PLAN OF ROOM·

BOOK CASE

·SEAT·   ·TILE FLOOR·   ·SEAT·

UP

Living Room, with Ingle, Built-In Case and Stair (See Opposite Page for Details).

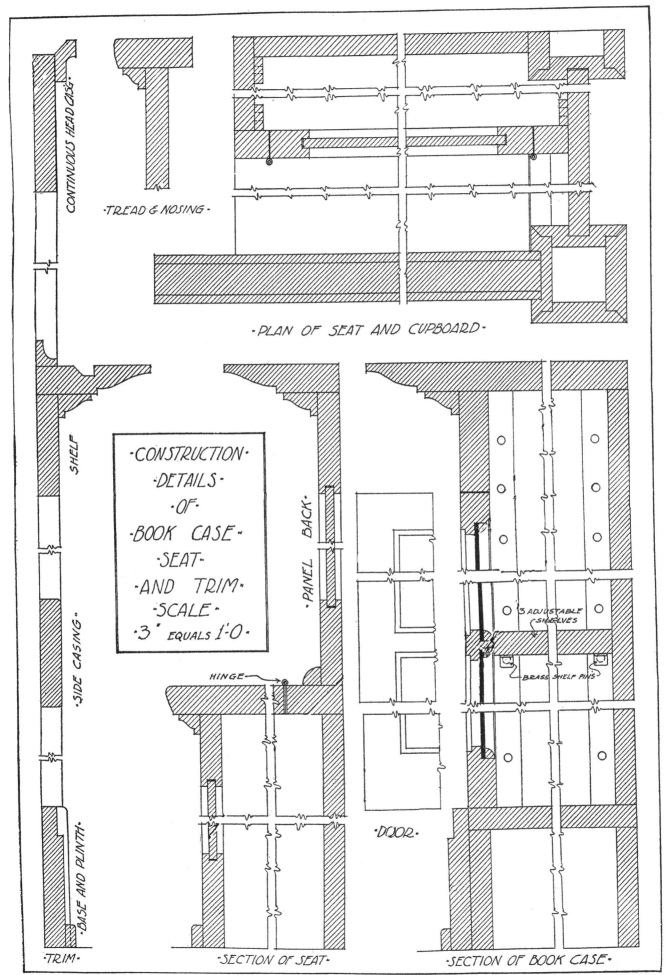

·CONTINUOUS HEAD CAS'G·

·TREAD & NOSING·

·PLAN OF SEAT AND CUPBOARD·

·SHELF

·CONSTRUCTION·
·DETAILS·
·OF·
·BOOK CASE·
·SEAT·
·AND TRIM·
·SCALE·
·3" EQUALS 1'·0·

·PANEL BACK·

·SIDE CASING·

·BASE AND PLINTH·

HINGE

·DOOR·

3 ADJUSTABLE SHELVES

BRASS SHELF PINS

·TRIM·

·SECTION OF SEAT·

·SECTION OF BOOK CASE·

Details of Built-In Case, Seat, Etc., Used in Living Room Design on Opposite Page.

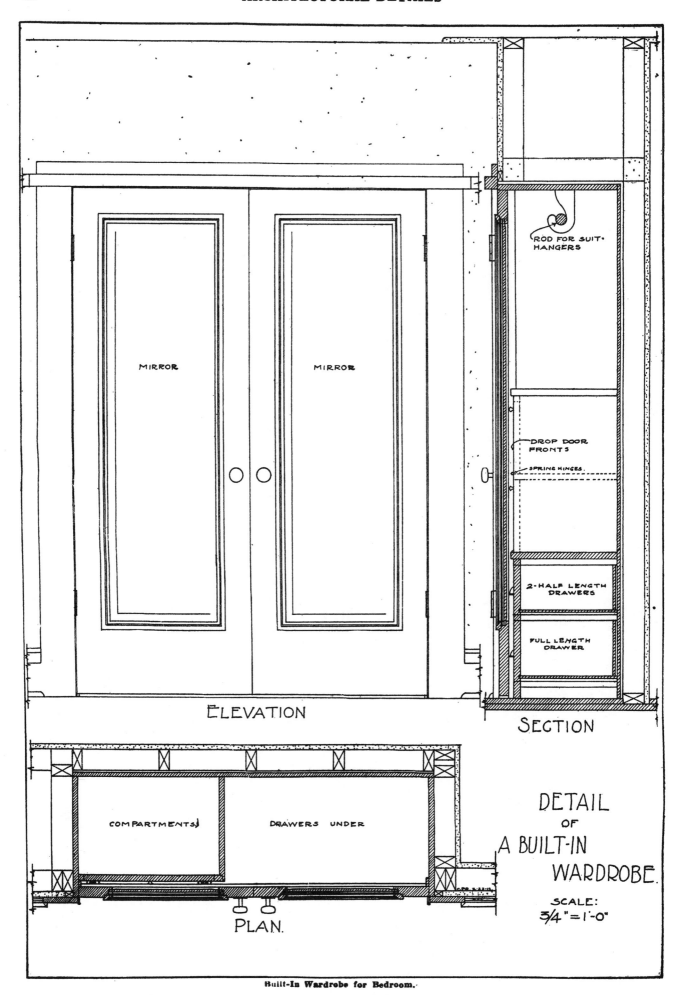

MIRROR

MIRROR

ROD FOR SUIT-
HANGERS

DROP DOOR
FRONTS

SPRING HINGES.

2-HALF LENGTH
DRAWERS

FULL LENGTH
DRAWER

ELEVATION

SECTION

COMPARTMENTS

DRAWERS UNDER

DETAIL
OF
A BUILT-IN
WARDROBE

SCALE:
3/4"=1'-0"

PLAN.

Built-In Wardrobe for Bedroom.

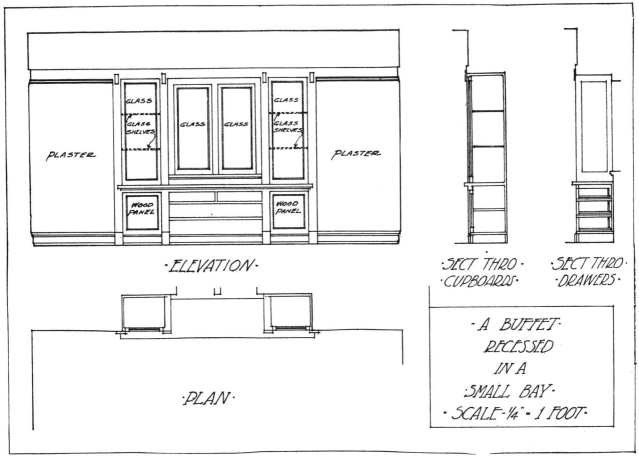

Side Board Set Into Wall.

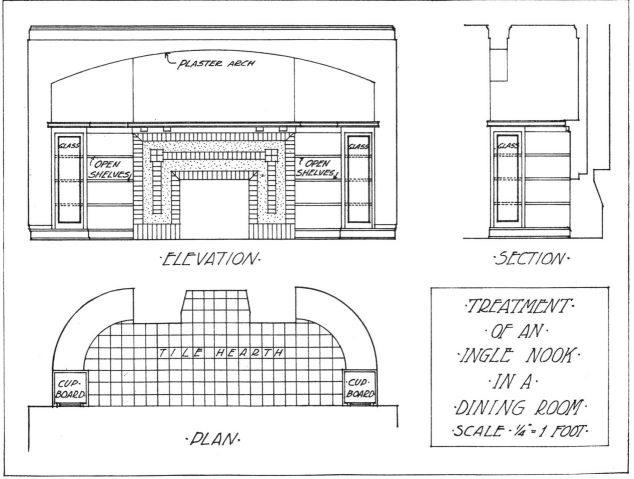

Curved Ingle Nook with Open Shelves.

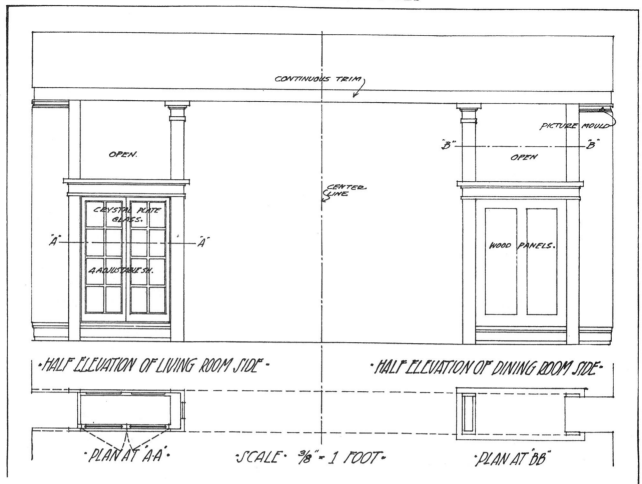

CONTINUOUS TRIM

PICTURE MOULD

CENTER LINE

OPEN.

"B"   OPEN   "B"

"A"   "A"

CRYSTAL PLATE GLASS.

A. ADJUSTABLE SH.

WOOD PANELS.

·HALF ELEVATION OF LIVING ROOM SIDE·   ·HALF ELEVATION OF DINING ROOM SIDE·

·PLAN AT "A·A"·   ·SCALE· ⅜" = 1 FOOT·   ·PLAN AT "BB"

Scale Drawings of China Closet Colonnade Between Dining and Living Rooms

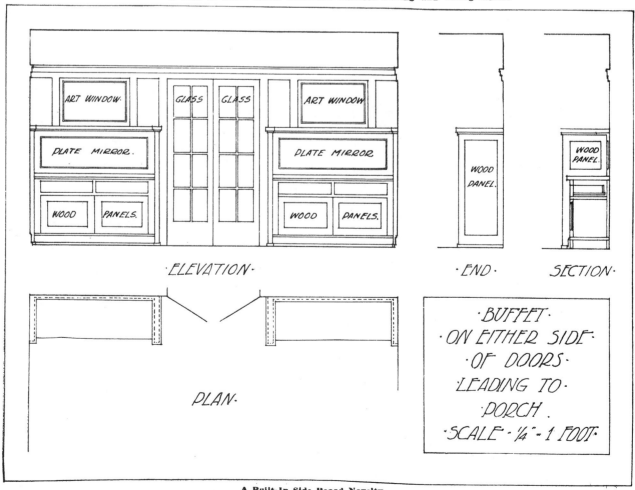

ART WINDOW.   GLASS   GLASS   ART WINDOW

PLATE MIRROR.   PLATE MIRROR

WOOD   PANELS.   WOOD   PANELS.

WOOD PANEL.   WOOD PANEL.

·ELEVATION·   ·END·   ·SECTION·

·PLAN·

·BUFFET·
·ON EITHER SIDE·
·OF DOORS·
·LEADING TO·
·PORCH·
·SCALE· ¼" = 1 FOOT·

A Built-In Side Board Novelty.

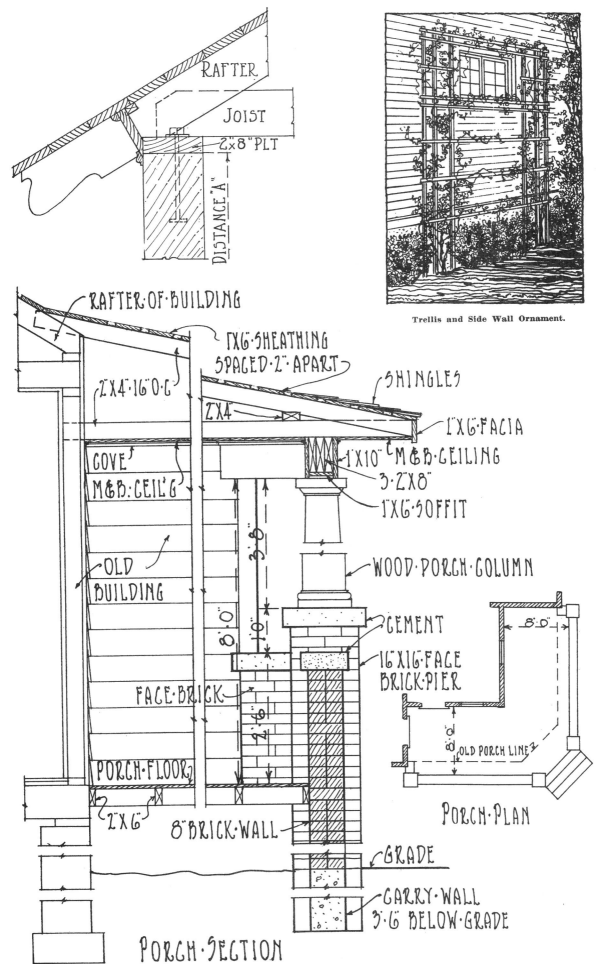

RAFTER

JOIST

2×8"·PLT

DISTANCE "A"

Trellis and Side Wall Ornament.

RAFTER·OF·BUILDING

1×6·SHEATHING SPACED·2"·APART

2×4·16"·O·C

SHINGLES

2×4

1"×6·FACIA

COVE M&B·CEIL'G

1×10"·M&B·CEILING

3·2"×8"

1×6·SOFFIT

OLD BUILDING

WOOD·PORCH·COLUMN

3'-8"

8'-0"

6'-0"

CEMENT

FACE·BRICK

16"×16"·FACE BRICK·PIER

8'-0"

2'-0"

PORCH·FLOOR

2×6

8"·BRICK·WALL

OLD·PORCH·LINE

8'-0"

PORCH·PLAN

GRADE

CARRY·WALL 3'·6"·BELOW·GRADE

PORCH·SECTION

How to Build on a New Brick Porch, Showing Details of a Modernized Porch Suggested as a Substitute for the Old Porch.

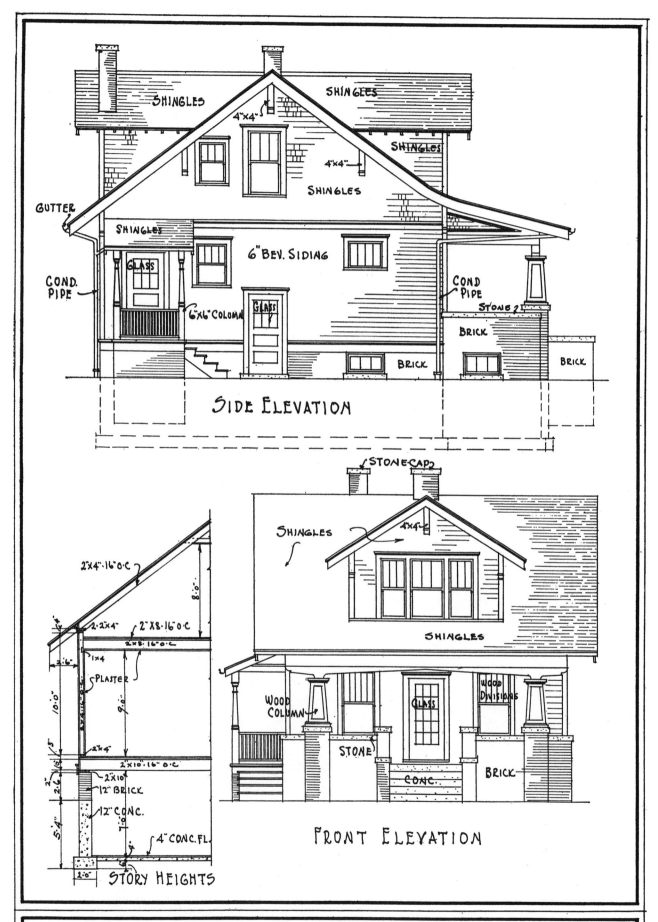

SHINGLES
SHINGLES
4"x4"
SHINGLES
SHINGLES
4"x4"
SHINGLES
GUTTER
6" BEV. SIDING
SHINGLES
GLASS
COND. PIPE
COND PIPE
STONE
6"x6" COLUMN
GLASS
BRICK
BRICK
BRICK

SIDE ELEVATION

STONE CAP
SHINGLES
4"x4"
SHINGLES

2"x4"-16"O.C.
8'-0"
2-2"x4"
2"x8-16"O.C.
2"x8-16"O.C.
1"x4
PLASTER
2'-6"
10'-0"
9'-0"
2"x4"
3"
2"x10-16"O.C.
2'-6"
2'-0"
2"x10
12" BRICK
7'-0"
12" CONC.
5'-4"
4" CONC. FL.
1'-0"

WOOD COLUMN
GLASS
WOOD DIVISIONS
STONE
CONC.
BRICK

STORY HEIGHTS

FRONT ELEVATION

PLANS OF SIX ROOM ONE AND ONE HALF STORY RESIDENCE
SCALE ⅛ = ONE FOOT
SHEET NO 1

Front and Side Elevations and Wall Section ⅛ Inch to the Foot of Pretty Little Six-Room Home

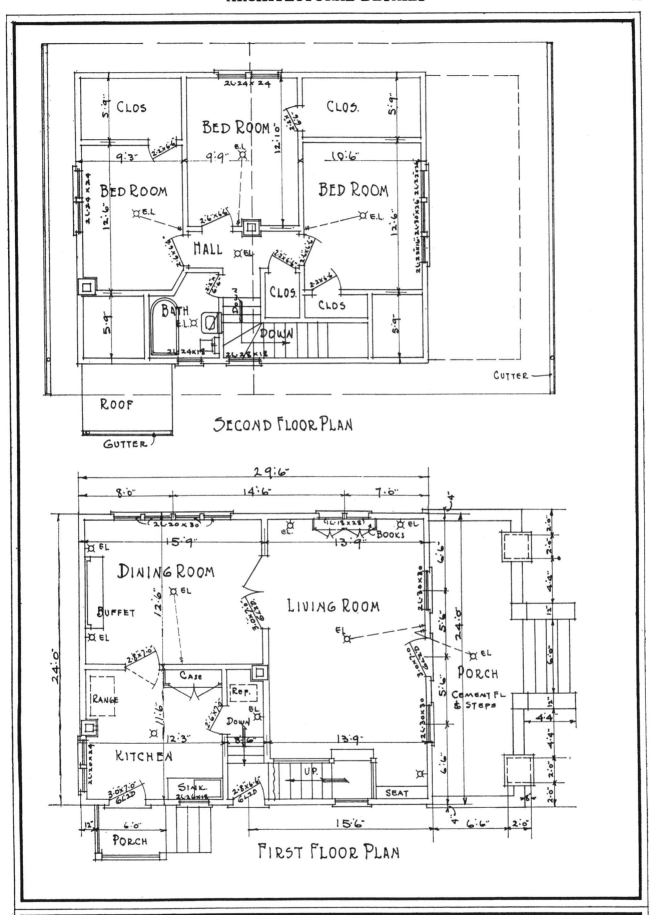

SECOND FLOOR PLAN

FIRST FLOOR PLAN

PLANS OF SIX ROOM ONE AND ONE HALF STORY RESIDENCE

SCALE 1/8" = ONE FOOT   SHEET NO. 2.

First and Second Floor Plans of Pretty Little Six-Room Home.

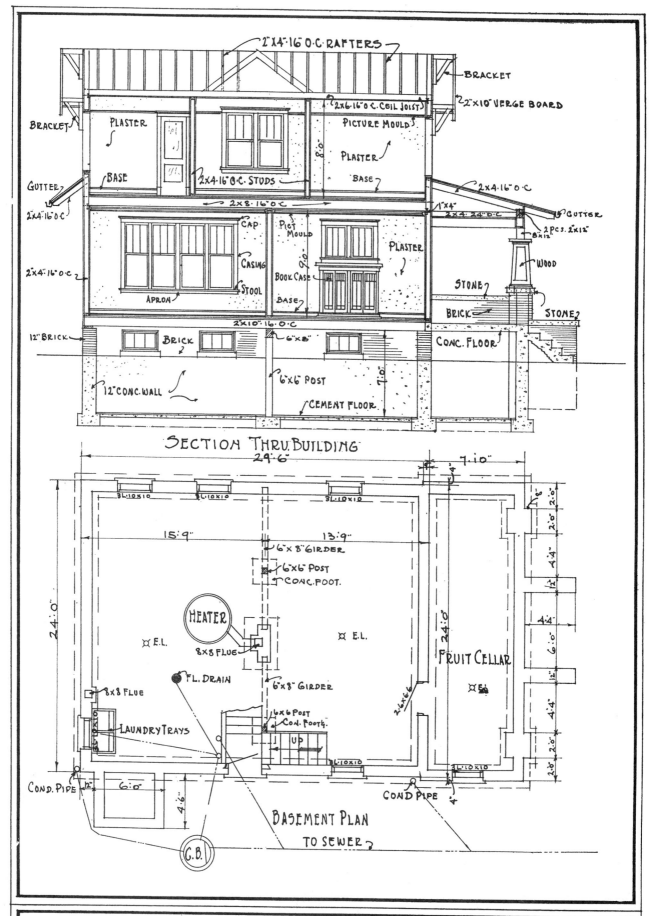

SECTION THRU BUILDING

BASEMENT PLAN

PLANS OF SIX ROOM ONE AND ONE HALF STORY RESIDENCE

SCALE ⅛ = ONE FOOT   SHEET NO 3.

Basement Plan and Section Thru Building Showing Construction ⅛ Inch to the Foot of Pretty Little Six-Room Home.

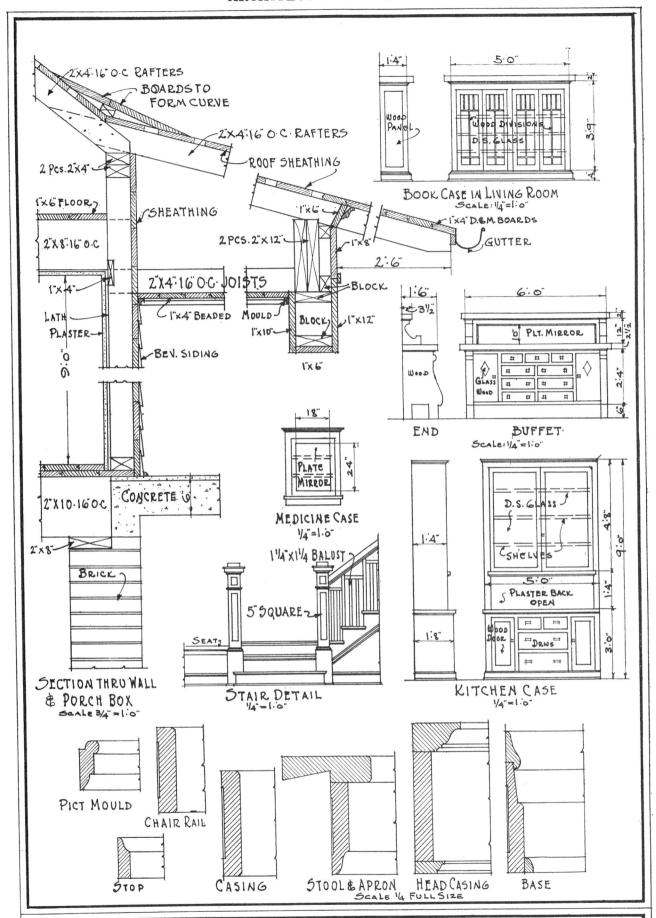

2"x4'16" O.C RAFTERS
BOARDS TO FORM CURVE
2"x4' 16" O.C. RAFTERS
ROOF SHEATHING
2 Pcs. 2"x4"
1"x6" FLOOR
SHEATHING
2"x8" 16" O.C.
1"x4"
LATH
PLASTER
9'·0"
BEV. SIDING
2"X4" 16" O.C. JOISTS
1"x4" BEADED   MOULD
1"x10"
1"x6"
1"x6"
2 PCS. 2"x12"
1"x8"
2'·6"
BLOCK
BLOCK
1"x12"
CONCRETE 9"
2"X10· 16" O.C
2"x8"
BRICK

SECTION THRU WALL & PORCH BOX
Scale 3/4" = 1'·0"

BOOK CASE IN LIVING ROOM
Scale 1/4" = 1'·0"
1'·4"   5'·0"
WOOD PANEL
WOOD DIVISIONS
D.S. GLASS
3'·9"
1"x4" D.&M. BOARDS
GUTTER

1'·6"
3 1/2"
WOOD
6'·0"
PLT. MIRROR
GLASS WOOD
END   BUFFET
Scale 1/4" = 1'·0"

18"
PLATE MIRROR
24"
MEDICINE CASE
1/4" = 1'·0"

1 1/4" x 1 1/4" BALUST.
5" SQUARE
SEAT
STAIR DETAIL
1/4" = 1'·0"

1'·4"
1'·8"
KITCHEN CASE
1/4" = 1'·0"
D.S. GLASS
SHELVES
4'·8"
9'·0"
5'·0"
PLASTER BACK OPEN
1'·4"
WOOD DOOR
DRWS
3'·0"

PICT MOULD
CHAIR RAIL
STOP
CASING
STOOL & APRON
Scale 1/4 FULL SIZE
HEAD CASING
BASE

PLANS OF SIX ROOM ONE AND ONE HALF STORY RESIDENCE
SCALE AS NOTED ABOVE   SHEET NO 4

Details of Inside Trim and of Wall Construction, Pretty Little Six-Room Home.

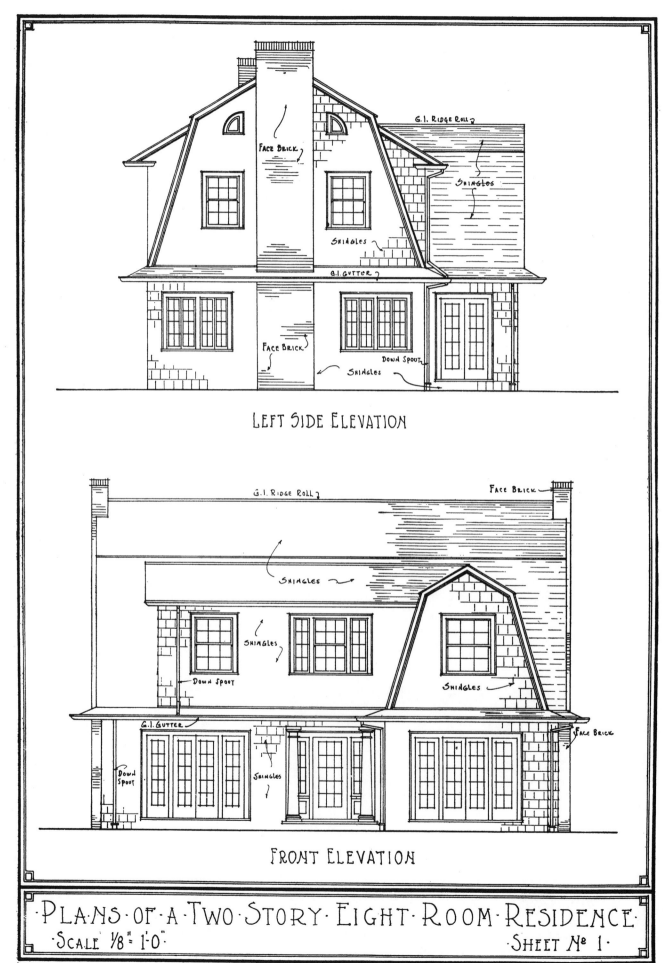

G.I. RIDGE ROLL

FACE BRICK

SHINGLES

SHINGLES

G.I. GUTTER

FACE BRICK

DOWN SPOUT

SHINGLES

LEFT SIDE ELEVATION

G.I. RIDGE ROLL

FACE BRICK

SHINGLES

SHINGLES

DOWN SPOUT

DOWN SPOUT

SHINGLES

FACE BRICK

G.I. GUTTER

DOWN SPOUT

SHINGLES

FRONT ELEVATION

PLANS OF A TWO STORY EIGHT ROOM RESIDENCE

SCALE ⅛" = 1'-0"

SHEET № 1

Front and Side Elevations, Scale ½ Inch Equals One Foot, of Dutch Colonial Residence.

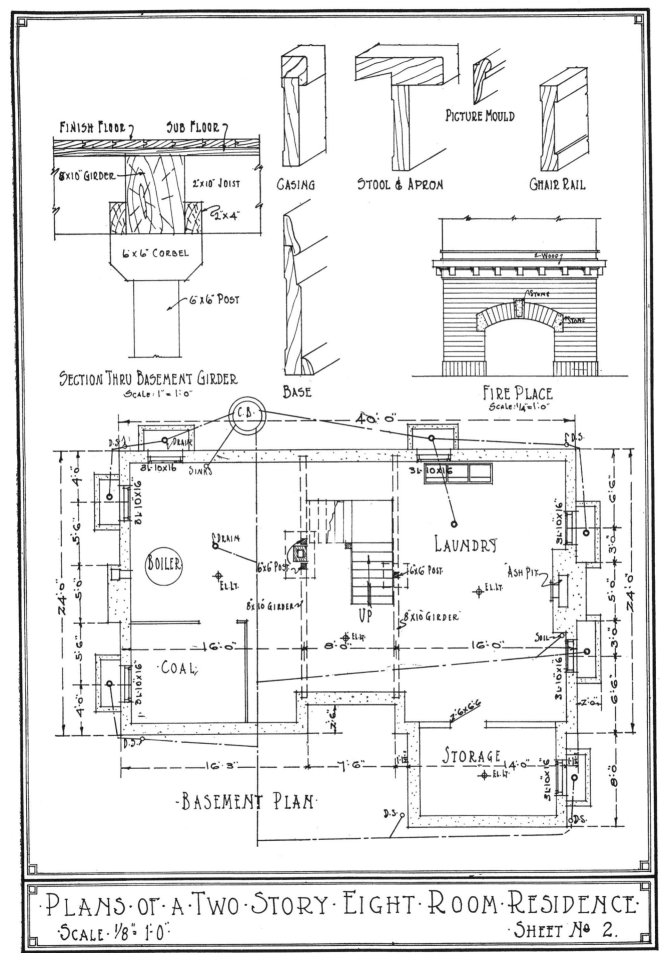

FINISH FLOOR   SUB FLOOR

8"x10" GIRDER   2"x10" JOIST

2"x4"

6"x6" CORBEL

6"x6" POST

SECTION THRU BASEMENT GIRDER
Scale: 1" = 1'-0"

CASING

STOOL & APRON

PICTURE MOULD

CHAIR RAIL

BASE

FIRE PLACE
Scale: 1/4" = 1'-0"

C.B.

40'-0"

D.S.   DRAIN   D.S.

3'-10x16   SINKS   3'-10x16

8'10x16

BOILER   DRAIN   LAUNDRY   3'-10x16

EL.LT.   6x6 POST   6x6 POST   ASH PIT   SOIL

8"x10" GIRDER   UP   EL.LT.   8x10 GIRDER   3'-10x16

16'-0"   EL.LT.   16'-0"

COAL   2'6x6'6

STORAGE   EL.LT.   3'-10x16

D.S.

16'-3"   7'-6"   4'-0"   8'-0"

-BASEMENT PLAN-

D.S.   D.S.

24'-0"   4'-0"   5'-6"   5'-0"   5'-6"   4'-0"

6'-6"   3'-0"   5'-0"   3'-0"   6'-6"   24'-0"

PLANS·OF·A·TWO·STORY·EIGHT·ROOM·RESIDENCE·
SCALE·1/8"=1'0"   SHEET Nº 2.

Basement Plan and Details, 1/2-, 1/4- and 1-Inch Scales, of Dutch Colonial Residence.

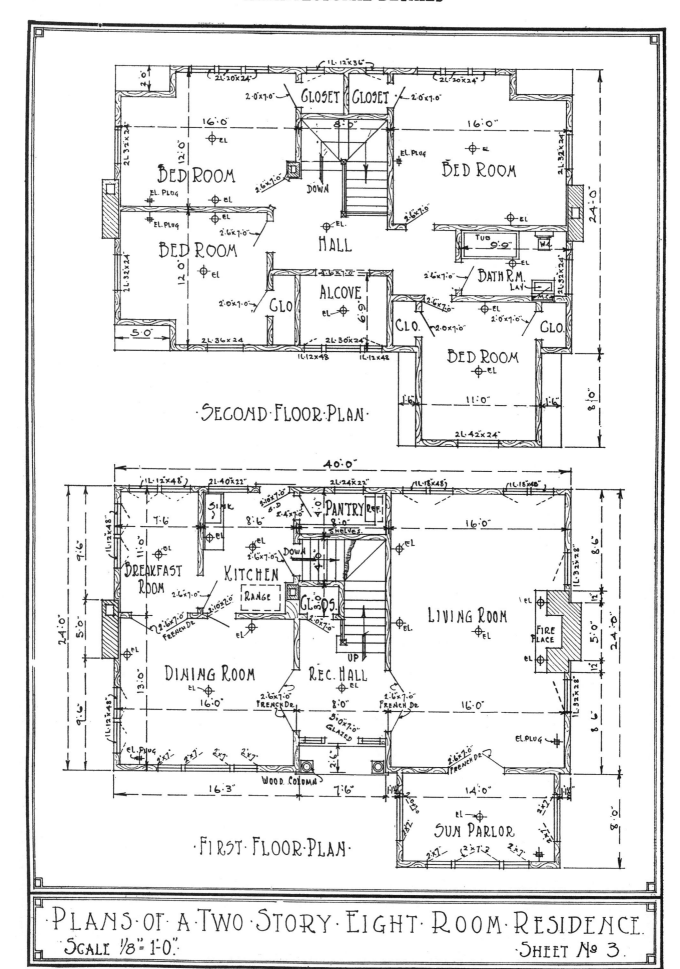

SECOND·FLOOR·PLAN·

FIRST·FLOOR·PLAN·

PLANS·OF·A·TWO·STORY·EIGHT·ROOM·RESIDENCE.
SCALE 1/8"=1'-0".   SHEET N⁰ 3.

First and Second Floor Plan of Dutch Colonial Residence.

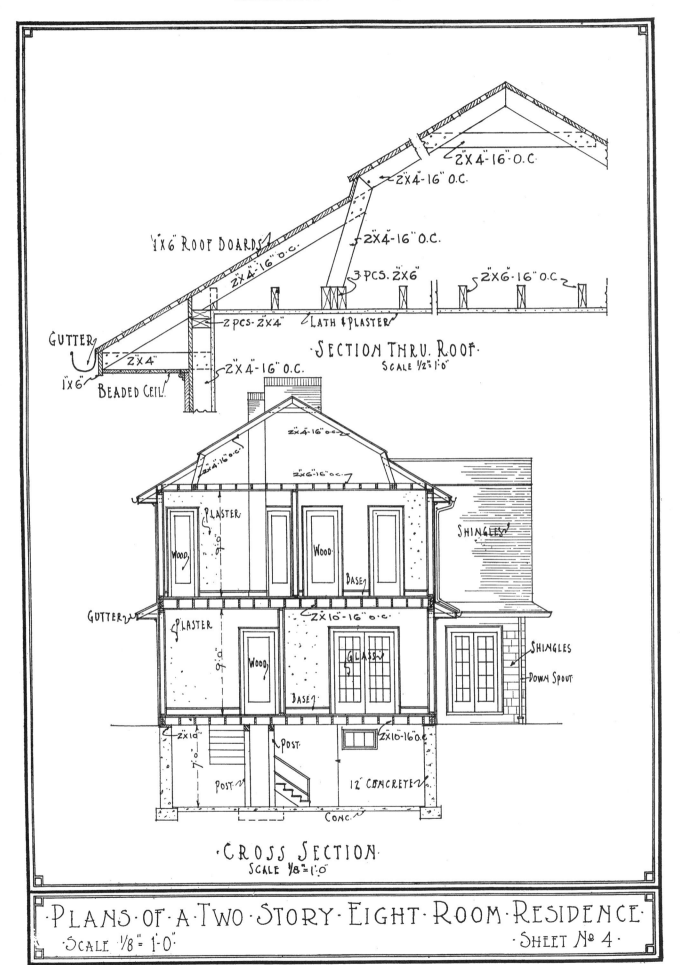

SECTION THRU. ROOF.
Scale ½"=1'·0"

·CROSS·SECTION·
Scale ⅛"=1'·0"

·PLANS·OF·A·TWO·STORY·EIGHT·ROOM·RESIDENCE·
·Scale ⅛"=1'·0"·   · Sheet № 4 ·

Section and Construction Detail, Drawn to ⅛- and ½-Inch Scales, of Dutch Colonial Residence.

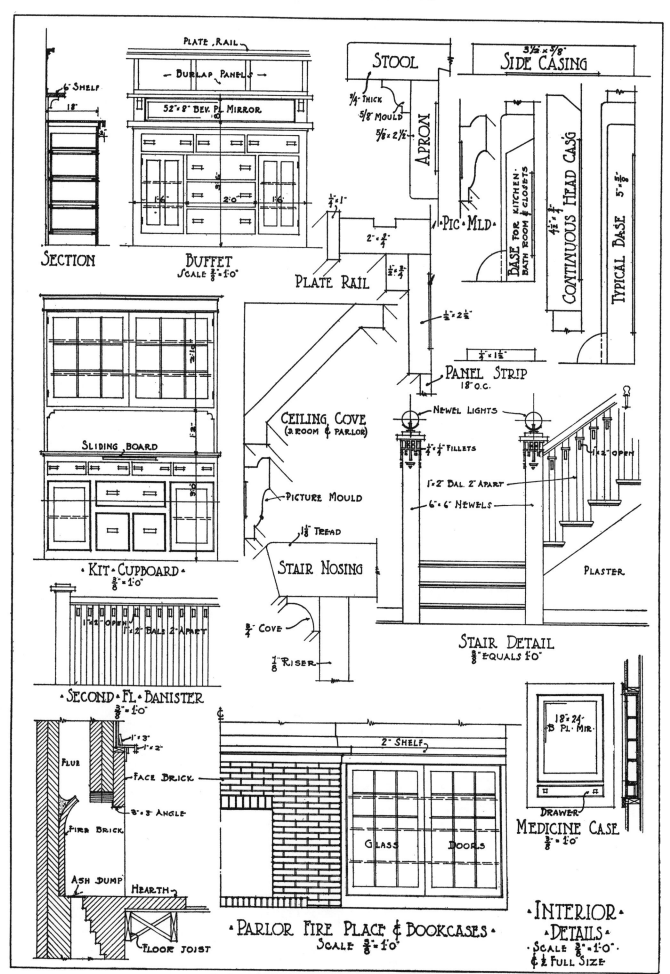

Typical Interior Details of Southern Style Residence.

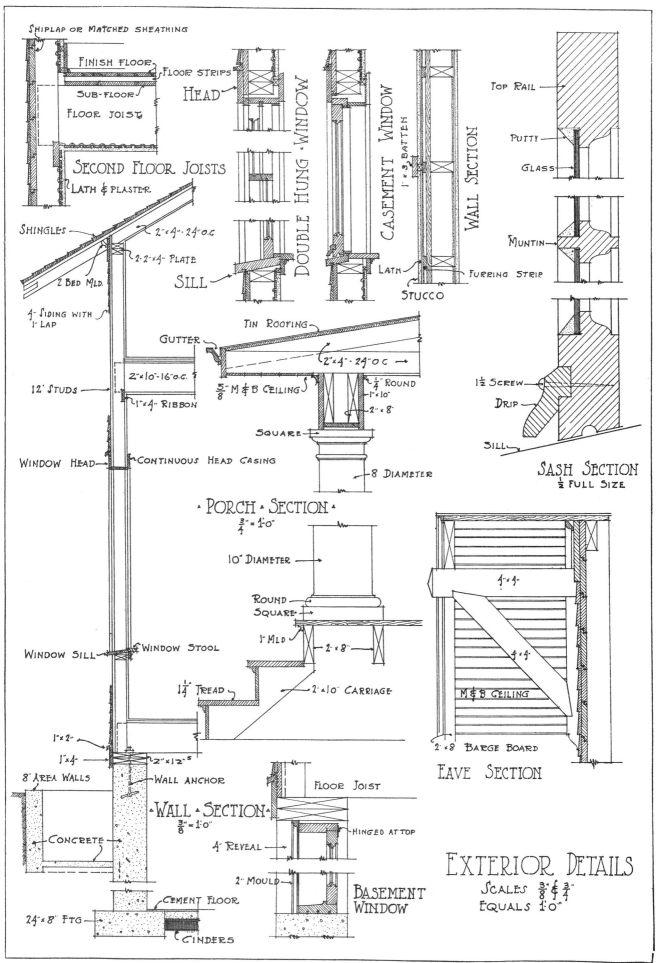

SHIPLAP OR MATCHED SHEATHING
FINISH FLOOR
FLOOR STRIPS
SUB-FLOOR
HEAD
FLOOR JOIST
SECOND FLOOR JOISTS
LATH & PLASTER

SHINGLES
2"x4"-24"O.C
2-2"x4" PLATE
2 BED MLD.
4" SIDING WITH 1" LAP

DOUBLE HUNG WINDOW
SILL

CASEMENT WINDOW
1"x3" BATTEN
LATH
STUCCO

WALL SECTION
FURRING STRIP

TOP RAIL
PUTTY
GLASS
MUNTIN
1½ SCREW
DRIP
SILL

SASH SECTION
½ FULL SIZE

TIN ROOFING
GUTTER
2"x4"-24"O.C
12" STUDS
2"x10"-16"o.c.
1"x4" RIBBON
⅝ M&B CEILING
¼ ROUND
1"x10"
2"x8"
SQUARE
8" DIAMETER

WINDOW HEAD
CONTINUOUS HEAD CASING

• PORCH • SECTION •
¾" = 1'-0"

10" DIAMETER
ROUND
SQUARE
1" MLD
2"x8"

4"x4"
4"x4"
M&B CEILING
2"x8" BARGE BOARD

EAVE SECTION

WINDOW SILL
WINDOW STOOL
1¼" TREAD
2"x10" CARRIAGE

1"x2"
1"x4"
2"x12"-5

8" AREA WALLS
WALL ANCHOR

• WALL • SECTION •
⅜" = 1'-0"

CONCRETE

FLOOR JOIST
HINGED AT TOP
4" REVEAL
2" MOULD

BASEMENT WINDOW

CEMENT FLOOR
24"x8" FTG
CINDERS

EXTERIOR DETAILS
SCALES ⅜ & ¾
EQUALS 1'-0"

Exterior Details of Construction, to Scale, of Southern Style Residence.

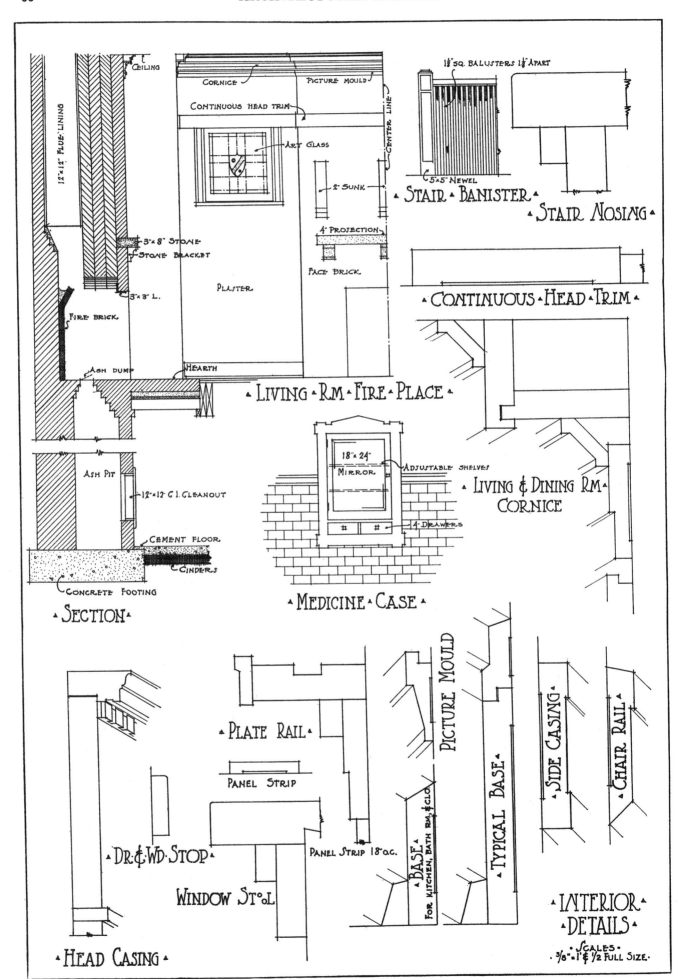

Complete Details of Interior Finish for Compact Residence.

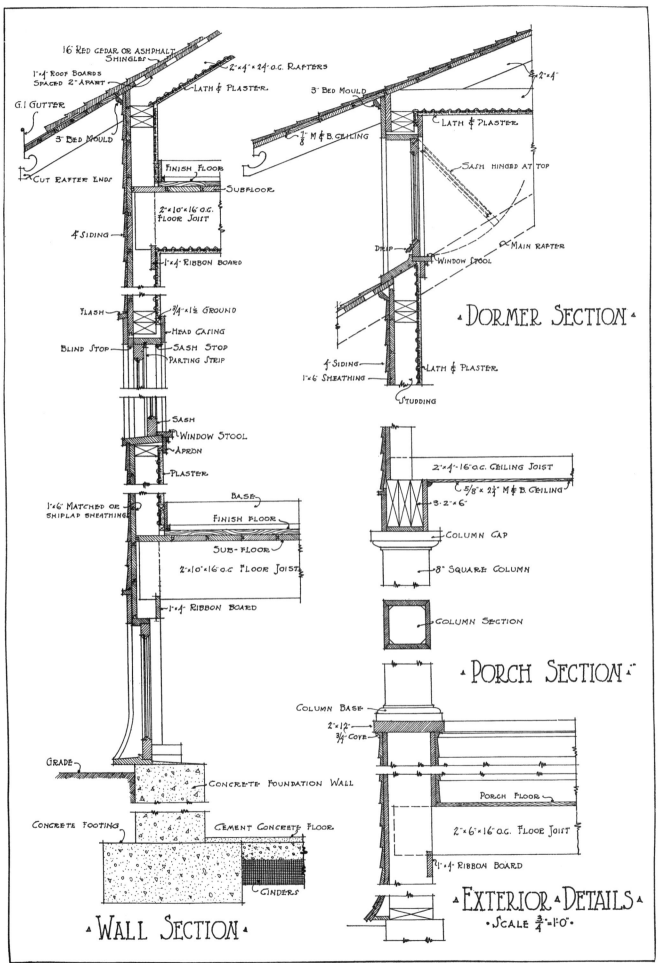

16" RED CEDAR OR ASHPHALT SHINGLES

2"×4"×24" O.C. RAFTERS

1"×4" ROOF BOARDS SPACED 2" APART

LATH & PLASTER

G.I. GUTTER

3" BED MOULD

3" BED MOULD

2"×4"

LATH & PLASTER

7/8" M & B. CEILING

CUT RAFTER ENDS

FINISH FLOOR

SUBFLOOR

SASH HINGED AT TOP

4" SIDING

2"×10"×16" O.C. FLOOR JOIST

1"×4" RIBBON BOARD

DRIP

MAIN RAFTER

WINDOW STOOL

· DORMER · SECTION ·

FLASH

3/4"×1½" GROUND

HEAD CASING

BLIND STOP

SASH STOP

PARTING STRIP

4" SIDING

LATH & PLASTER

1"×6" SHEATHING

STUDDING

SASH

WINDOW STOOL

APRON

PLASTER

2"×4"×16" O.C. CEILING JOIST

5/8"×2½" M & B. CEILING

3-2"×6"

1"×6" MATCHED OR SHIPLAP SHEATHING

BASE

FINISH FLOOR

SUB-FLOOR

2"×10"×16" O.C. FLOOR JOIST

COLUMN CAP

8" SQUARE COLUMN

COLUMN SECTION

1"×4" RIBBON BOARD

· PORCH · SECTION ·

COLUMN BASE

2"×12"

3/4" COVE

GRADE

CONCRETE FOUNDATION WALL

PORCH FLOOR

CONCRETE FOOTING

CEMENT CONCRETE FLOOR

2"×6"×16" O.C. FLOOR JOIST

CINDERS

1"×4" RIBBON BOARD

· WALL · SECTION ·

· EXTERIOR · DETAILS ·
· SCALE ¾"=1'0" ·

Exterior Details of Construction, to Scale, of Compact Residence.

Built-in Furniture--Some Interesting Designs

ONE of the charms of the interior of any home is the furniture which is built into it. The dressers, seats, bookcases more than half solve the problem of furnishing it.

Furniture that is built to fit the place it is in, is far more decorative and more comfortable than detached pieces could be in the same place. Not only is space saved by this means, but a keynote is given for the rest of the fittings in the home, which, unless it is utterly disregarded, will tend to keep the furnishings of the room in harmony.

Large Kitchen Cupboard, Lighted at Center by Casement Window.

Kitchen Cupboard of Generous Dimensions.

Dining Room Buffet.

Book Cases and Book Shelves.

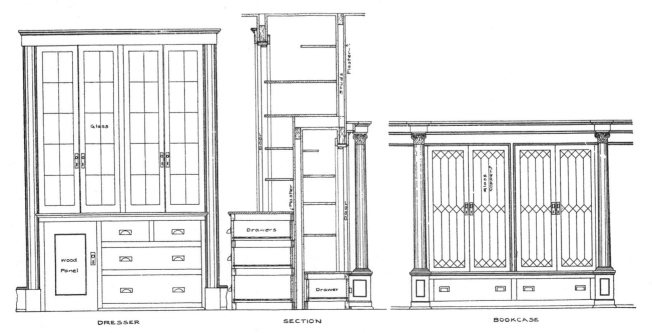

DRESSER   SECTION   BOOKCASE

Kitchen Dresser on One Side of Partition, Library Book Case on Other.

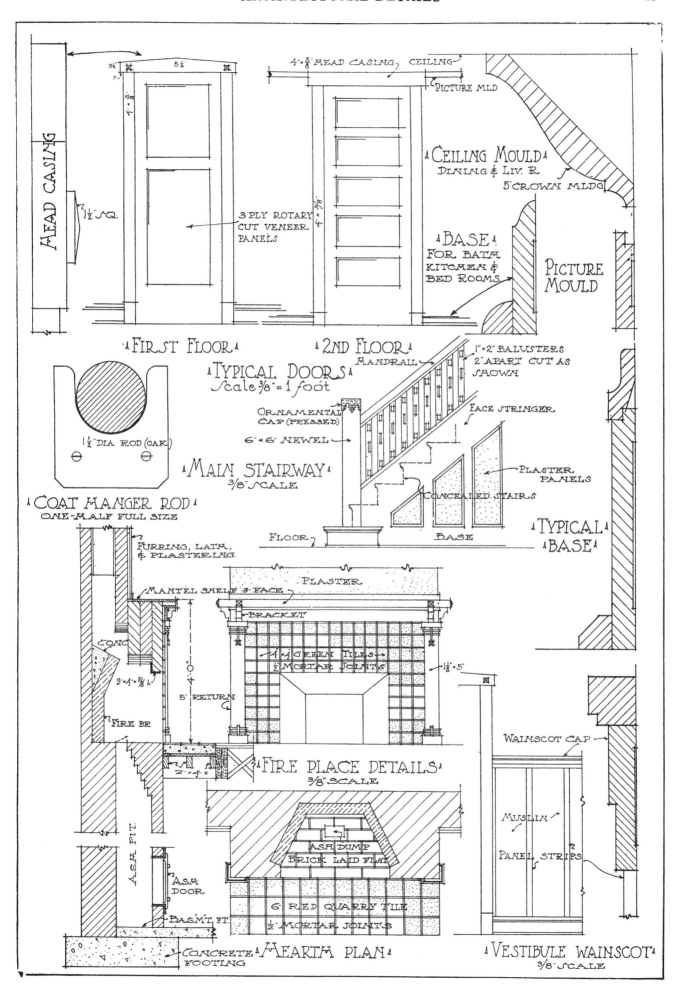

Details of Interior Finish of Brick and Stucco Finished Tile House.

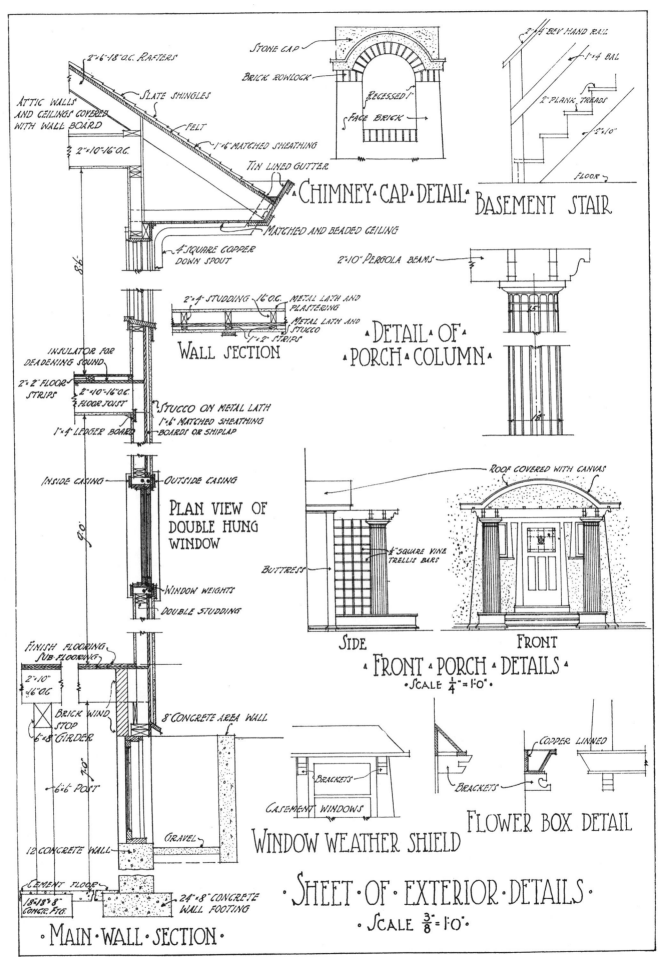

CHIMNEY·CAP·DETAIL

BASEMENT STAIR.

WALL SECTION

DETAIL·OF·PORCH·COLUMN

PLAN VIEW OF DOUBLE HUNG WINDOW

FRONT·PORCH·DETAILS
·SCALE ¼"= 1'·0"

WINDOW WEATHER SHIELD

FLOWER BOX DETAIL

·MAIN·WALL·SECTION·

SHEET·OF·EXTERIOR·DETAILS·
·SCALE ⅜"= 1'·0"·

Exterior Details of Construction, to Scale, of Cement Plaster Residence.

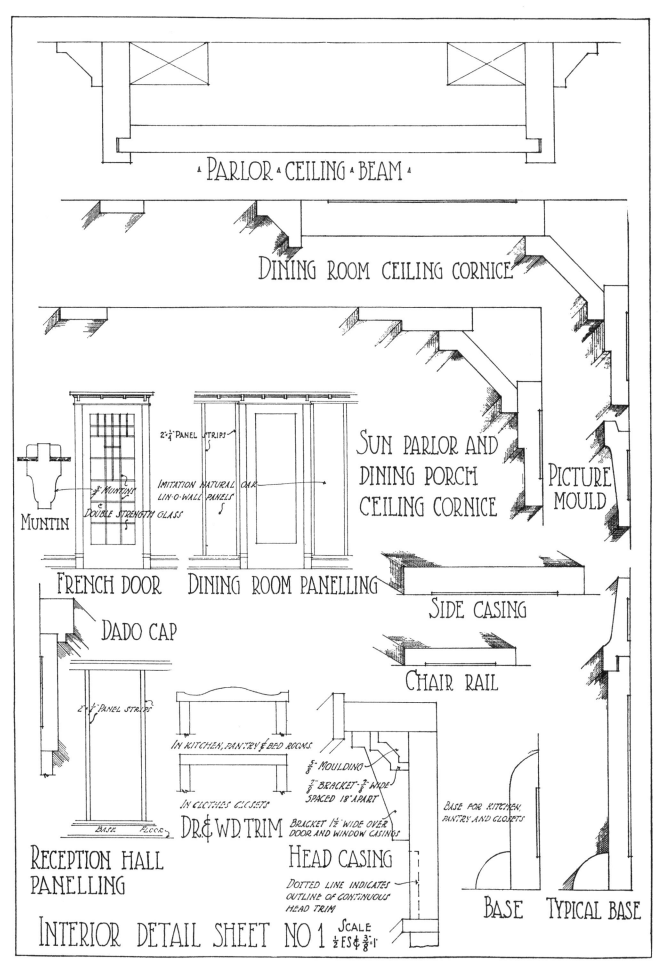

· PARLOR · CEILING · BEAM ·

DINING ROOM CEILING CORNICE

2·¼" PANEL STRIPS

IMITATION NATURAL OAK
LIN·O·WALL PANELS

SUN PARLOR AND
DINING PORCH
CEILING CORNICE

PICTURE
MOULD

MUNTIN

¾" MUNTINS
&
DOUBLE STRENGTH GLASS

MUNTIN

FRENCH DOOR

DINING ROOM PANELLING

SIDE CASING

DADO CAP

CHAIR RAIL

2·¼" PANEL STRIPS

IN KITCHEN, PANTRY & BED ROOMS.

IN CLOTHES CLOSETS

BASE   FLOOR

RECEPTION HALL
PANELLING

DR.& WD. TRIM

⅝" MOULDING

⅞" BRACKET - ⅞" WIDE
SPACED 18" APART

BRACKET 1½" WIDE OVER
DOOR AND WINDOW CASINGS

HEAD CASING

DOTTED LINE INDICATES
OUTLINE OF CONTINUOUS
HEAD TRIM

BASE FOR KITCHEN,
PANTRY AND CLOSETS

BASE   TYPICAL BASE

INTERIOR DETAIL SHEET NO 1   SCALE
½ F·S & ⅜"=1'

Details of Interior Finish, to Scale for Cement Plaster Residence.

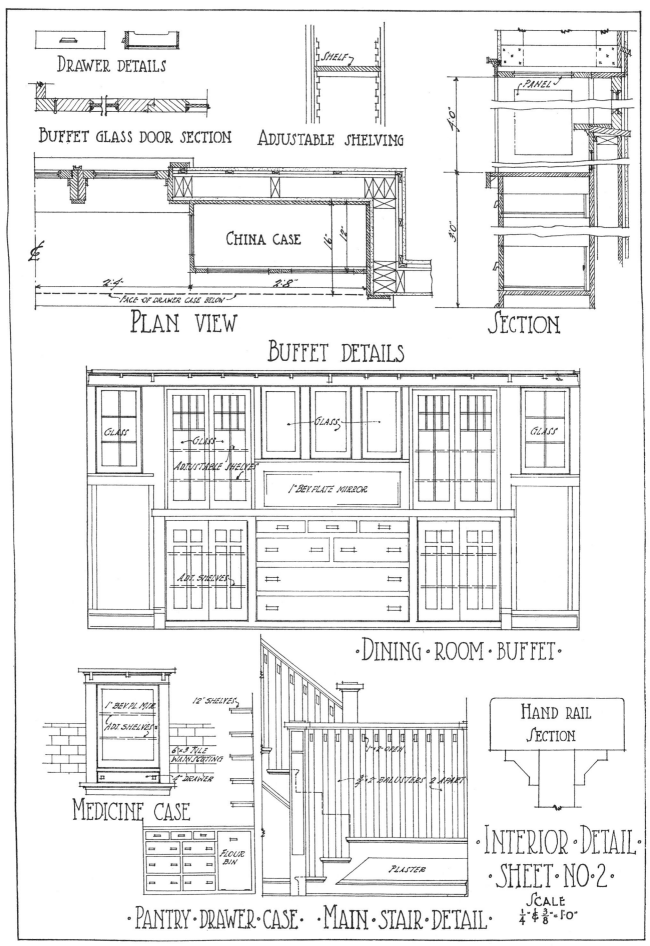

DRAWER DETAILS

BUFFET GLASS DOOR SECTION   ADJUSTABLE SHELVING

SHELF

PLAN VIEW

CHINA CASE

FACE OF DRAWER CASE BELOW

2:4   2:8

SECTION

PANEL

BUFFET DETAILS

GLASS

GLASS   GLASS   GLASS

ADJUSTABLE SHELVES

1" BEV. PLATE MIRROR

A.DJ. SHELVES

·DINING·ROOM·BUFFET·

MEDICINE CASE

1" BEV. PL. M'R.
ADJ. SHELVES
6"x3" TILE WAINSCOTING
4" DRAWER

12" SHELVES

·PANTRY·DRAWER·CASE·

FLOUR BIN

·MAIN·STAIR·DETAIL·

PLASTER

1"x2" OPEN
2"x2" BALUSTERS 2" APART

HAND RAIL SECTION

·INTERIOR·DETAIL·
·SHEET·NO·2·

SCALE
¼" & ⅜" = 1'-0"

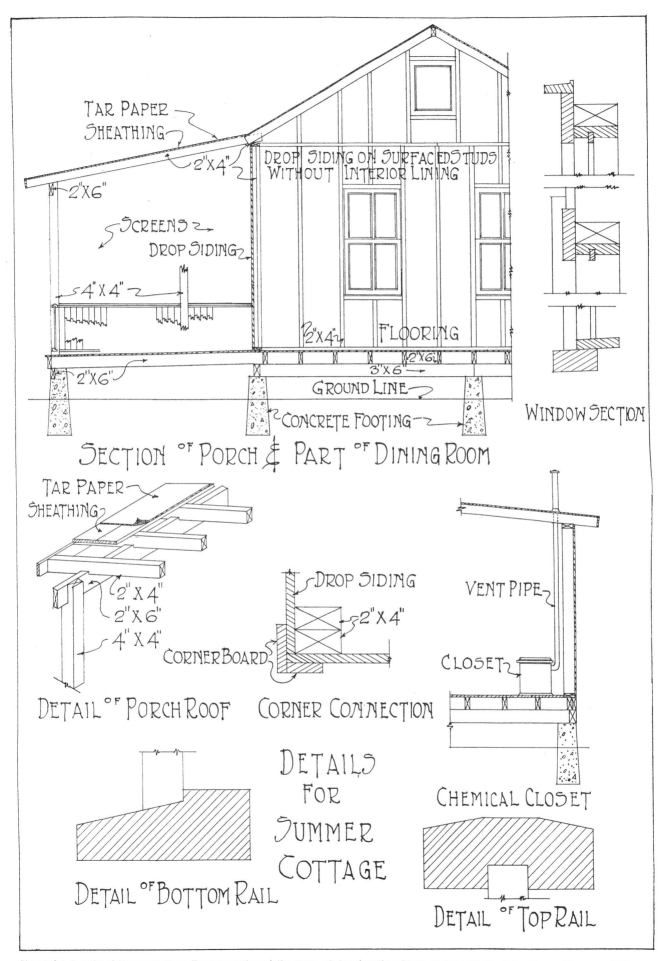

TAR PAPER SHEATHING

2"X4"

2"X6"

SCREENS

DROP SIDING

4"X4"

DROP SIDING ON SURFACED STUDS WITHOUT INTERIOR LINING

FLOORING

2"X4"

2"X6"

3"X6"

2"X6"

GROUND LINE

CONCRETE FOOTING

SECTION OF PORCH & PART OF DINING ROOM

WINDOW SECTION

TAR PAPER SHEATHING

2"X4"
2"X6"
4"X4"

DETAIL OF PORCH ROOF

DROP SIDING

2"X4"

CORNER BOARD

CORNER CONNECTION

VENT PIPE

CLOSET

CHEMICAL CLOSET

DETAILS FOR SUMMER COTTAGE

DETAIL OF BOTTOM RAIL

DETAIL OF TOP RAIL

Structural Details of Frame Cottage Representative of the Type of Construction Most Commonly Used in Frame Summer Cottages.

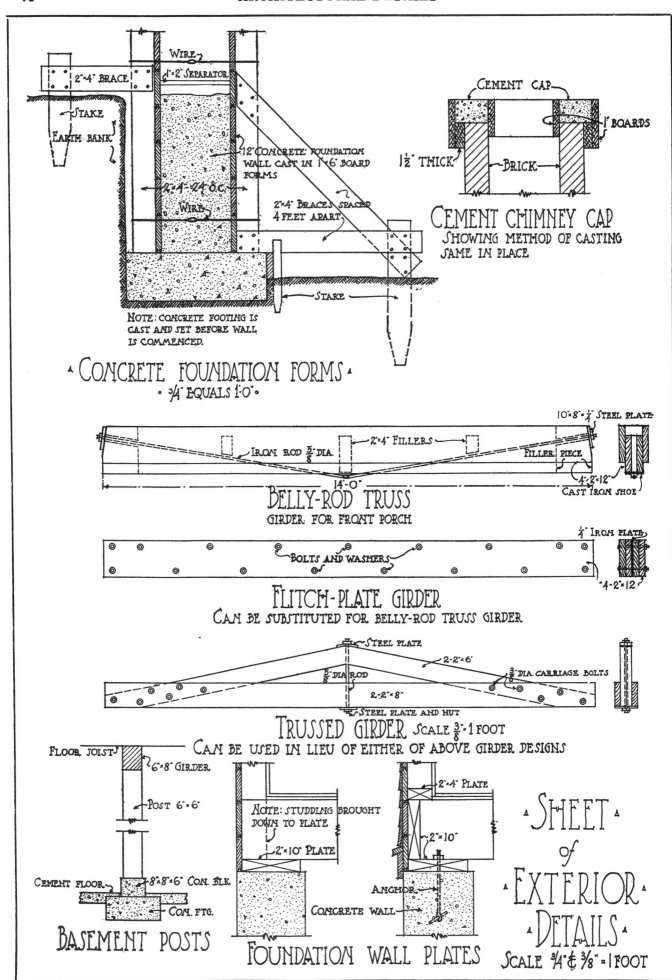

WIRE

1"x2" SEPARATOR

2"x4" BRACE

STAKE

EARTH BANK

12" CONCRETE FOUNDATION WALL CAST IN 1"x6" BOARD FORMS

2-1"-24" O.C.

WIRE

2"x4" BRACES SPACED 4 FEET APART

STAKE

NOTE: CONCRETE FOOTING IS CAST AND SET BEFORE WALL IS COMMENCED.

· CONCRETE FOUNDATION FORMS ·
· ¾" EQUALS 1'-0" ·

CEMENT CAP

1½" THICK

1" BOARDS

BRICK

CEMENT CHIMNEY CAP
SHOWING METHOD OF CASTING SAME IN PLACE

10"x8"x¼" STEEL PLATE

IRON ROD ⅝" DIA.

2"x4" FILLERS

FILLER PIECE

14'-0"

4"x2"x12

CAST IRON SHOE

BELLY-ROD TRUSS
GIRDER FOR FRONT PORCH

¼" IRON PLATE

BOLTS AND WASHERS

4-2"x12

FLITCH-PLATE GIRDER
CAN BE SUBSTITUTED FOR BELLY-ROD TRUSS GIRDER

STEEL PLATE

2-2"x6

⅝" DIA ROD

¾" DIA. CARRIAGE BOLTS

2-2"x8"

STEEL PLATE AND NUT

TRUSSED GIRDER SCALE ⅜"=1 FOOT
CAN BE USED IN LIEU OF EITHER OF ABOVE GIRDER DESIGNS

FLOOR JOIST

6"x8" GIRDER

POST 6"x6"

CEMENT FLOOR

8"x8"x6" CON. BLK.

CON. FTG.

BASEMENT POSTS

NOTE: STUDDING BROUGHT DOWN TO PLATE

2"x10" PLATE

2"x4" PLATE

2"x10"

ANCHOR

CONCRETE WALL

FOUNDATION WALL PLATES

· SHEET · of · EXTERIOR · DETAILS ·
SCALE ¾" & ⅜" = 1 FOOT

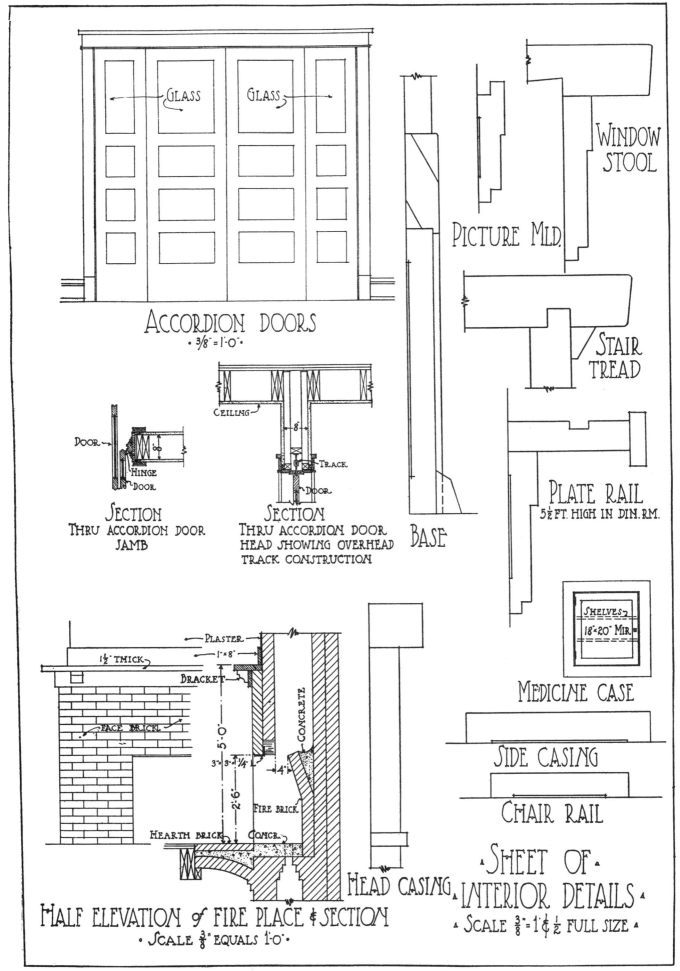

GLASS   GLASS

ACCORDION DOORS
· 3/8" = 1'-0" ·

WINDOW STOOL

PICTURE MLD.

STAIR TREAD

CEILING

DOOR

HINGE
DOOR

SECTION
THRU ACCORDION DOOR
JAMB

TRACK
DOOR

SECTION
THRU ACCORDION DOOR
HEAD SHOWING OVERHEAD
TRACK CONSTRUCTION

BASE

PLATE RAIL
5½ FT. HIGH IN DIN. RM.

SHELVES
18"×20" MIR.

MEDICINE CASE

PLASTER

1½" THICK

1"×8"

BRACKET

CONCRETE

FACE BRICK

5'-0"

3" 3" 1¼"

4"

2'-6"

FIRE BRICK

HEARTH BRICK   CONCR.

CONCR.

HEAD CASING

SIDE CASING

CHAIR RAIL

HALF ELEVATION of FIRE PLACE & SECTION
· SCALE 3/8" EQUALS 1'-0" ·

SHEET OF
INTERIOR DETAILS
· SCALE 3/8" = 1' & ½ FULL SIZE ·

Interior Details of Prize Farm House.

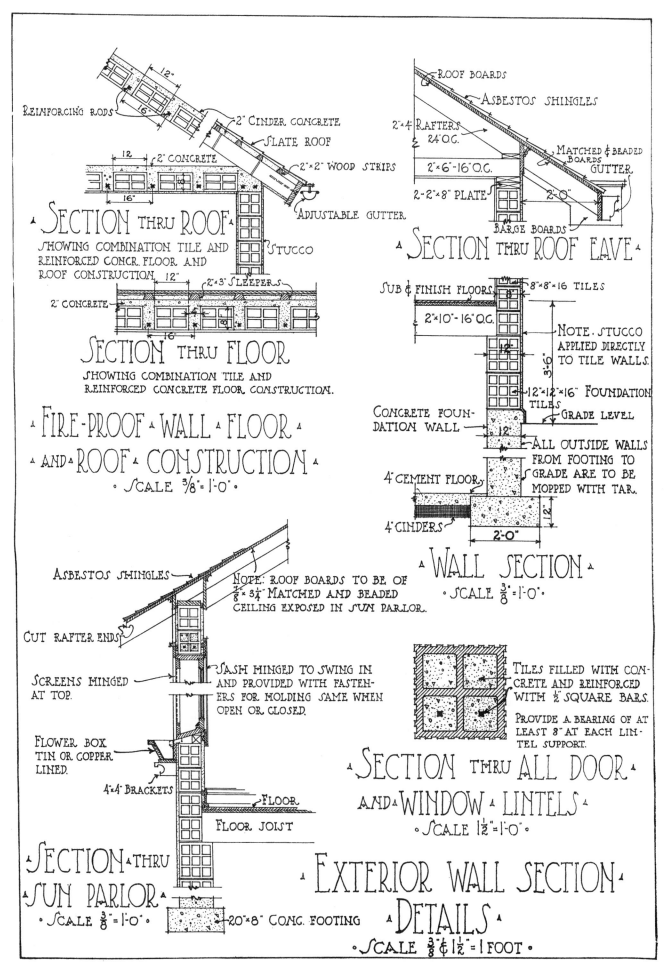

REINFORCING RODS
12"
16"
2" CINDER CONCRETE
SLATE ROOF
2"x 2" WOOD STRIPS
12
2" CONCRETE
16"
ADJUSTABLE GUTTER
STUCCO

SECTION THRU ROOF
SHOWING COMBINATION TILE AND
REINFORCED CONCR. FLOOR AND
ROOF CONSTRUCTION.

12"
2"x 3" SLEEPERS
2" CONCRETE
16"

SECTION THRU FLOOR
SHOWING COMBINATION TILE AND
REINFORCED CONCRETE FLOOR CONSTRUCTION.

**FIRE-PROOF WALL FLOOR
AND ROOF CONSTRUCTION**
SCALE 3/8" = 1'-0"

ROOF BOARDS
ASBESTOS SHINGLES
2"x 4" RAFTERS 24" O.C.
2"x 6"- 16" O.C.
MATCHED & BEADED BOARDS
GUTTER
2-2"x 8" PLATE
2'-0"
BARGE BOARDS

SECTION THRU ROOF EAVE

SUB & FINISH FLOORS
8"x 8"x 16 TILES
2"x 10"- 16" O.C.
12"
3'-6"
NOTE. STUCCO APPLIED DIRECTLY TO TILE WALLS.
12"x 12"x 16" FOUNDATION TILES
CONCRETE FOUNDATION WALL
GRADE LEVEL
12"
ALL OUTSIDE WALLS FROM FOOTING TO GRADE ARE TO BE MOPPED WITH TAR.
4" CEMENT FLOOR
4" CINDERS
12"
2'-0"

WALL SECTION
SCALE 3/8" = 1'-0"

ASBESTOS SHINGLES
NOTE: ROOF BOARDS TO BE OF 7/8" x 3 1/4" MATCHED AND BEADED CEILING EXPOSED IN SUN PARLOR.
CUT RAFTER ENDS
SCREENS HINGED AT TOP.
SASH HINGED TO SWING IN AND PROVIDED WITH FASTENERS FOR HOLDING SAME WHEN OPEN OR CLOSED.
FLOWER BOX TIN OR COPPER LINED.
4"x 4" BRACKETS
FLOOR
FLOOR JOIST

SECTION THRU SUN PARLOR
SCALE 3/8" = 1'-0"
20"x 8" CONC. FOOTING

TILES FILLED WITH CONCRETE AND REINFORCED WITH 1/2" SQUARE BARS.
PROVIDE A BEARING OF AT LEAST 8" AT EACH LINTEL SUPPORT.

SECTION THRU ALL DOOR AND WINDOW LINTELS
SCALE 1 1/2" = 1'-0"

EXTERIOR WALL SECTION DETAILS
SCALE 3/8" & 1 1/2" = 1 FOOT

Construction Details of Hollow Tile Residence.

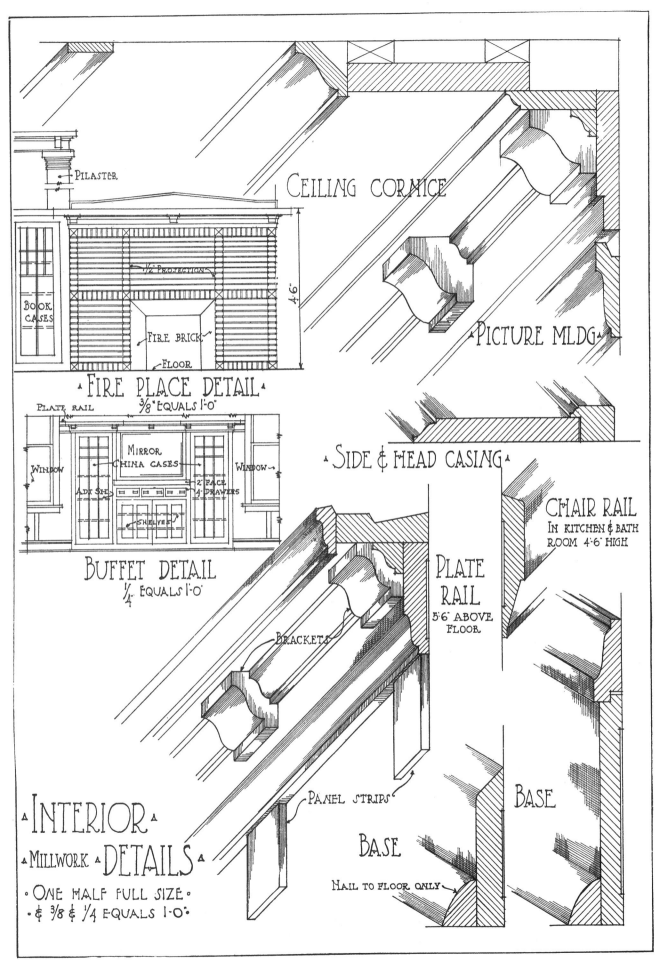

CEILING CORNICE

PILASTER

½" PROTECTION

4'-6"

BOOK CASES

FIRE BRICK

FLOOR

▲ FIRE PLACE DETAIL ▲
⅜" EQUALS 1'-0"

PICTURE MLDG.

PLATE RAIL

MIRROR
CHINA CASES

WINDOW

A DISH

2" FACE
4 DRAWERS

WINDOW

SHELVES

BUFFET DETAIL
¼ EQUALS 1'-0"

▲ SIDE & HEAD CASING ▲

CHAIR RAIL
IN KITCHEN & BATH
ROOM 4'-6" HIGH

PLATE RAIL
5'-6" ABOVE
FLOOR

BRACKETS

PANEL STRIPS

BASE

▲ INTERIOR ▲
▲ MILLWORK ▲ DETAILS ▲
• ONE HALF FULL SIZE •
• & ⅜ & ¼ EQUALS 1'-0" •

BASE

NAIL TO FLOOR ONLY

Details of Interior Finish in Modern Fireproof Residence.

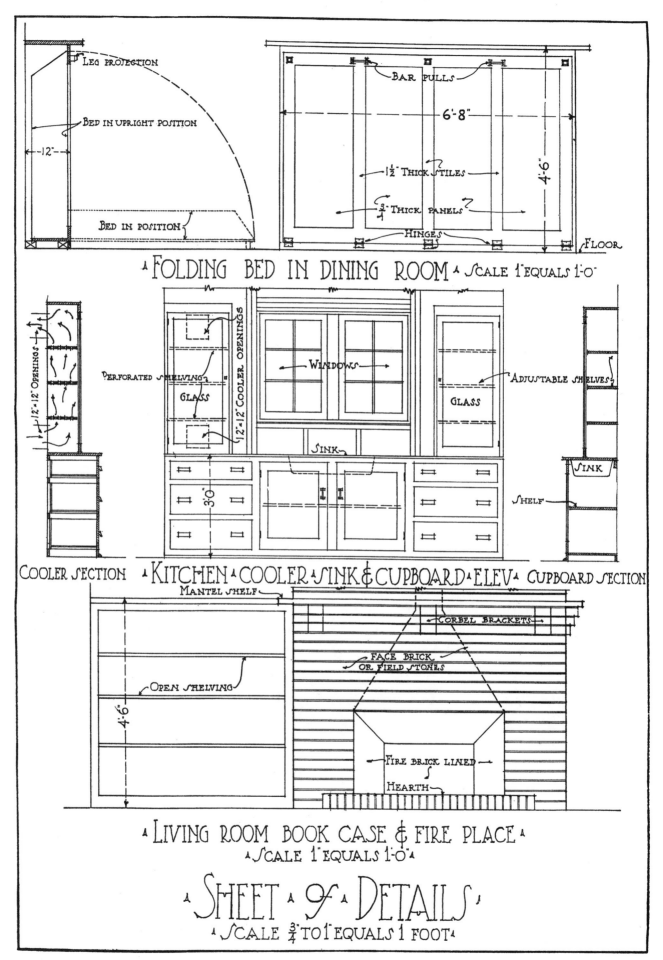

Leg projection

Bed in upright position

—12"—

Bed in position

Bar pulls

6'-8"

4'-6"

1½" Thick Stiles

¾" Thick panels

Hinges

Floor

⌃ FOLDING BED IN DINING ROOM ⌃ Scale 1" equals 1'-0"

12"×12" Openings

Perforated Shelving

Glass

12"×12" Cooler openings

Windows

Glass

Adjustable Shelves

Sink

3'-0"

Sink

Shelf

Cooler Section ⌃ KITCHEN ⌃ COOLER ⌃ SINK & CUPBOARD ⌃ ELEV ⌃ Cupboard Section

Mantel Shelf

Corbel Brackets

Face Brick
or Field Stones

Open Shelving

4'-6"

Fire Brick lined

Hearth

⌃ LIVING ROOM BOOK CASE & FIRE PLACE ⌃
⌃ Scale 1" equals 1'-0" ⌃

⌃ SHEET ⌃ of ⌃ DETAILS ⌃
⌃ Scale ¾" to 1" equals 1 foot ⌃

Details of Interior Finish of Summer Bungalow.

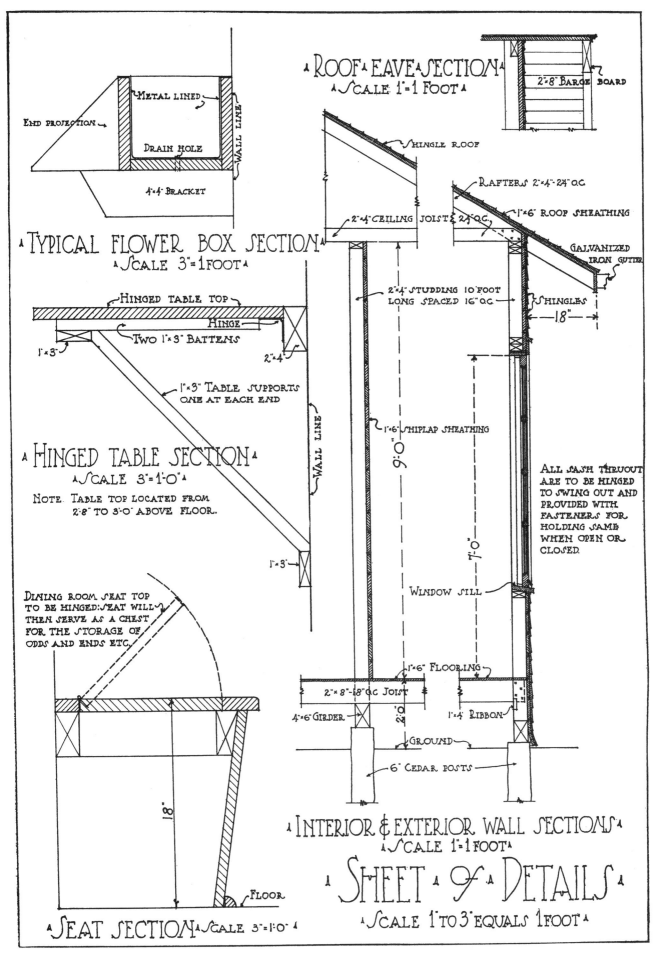

Details of Construction of Summer Bungalow.

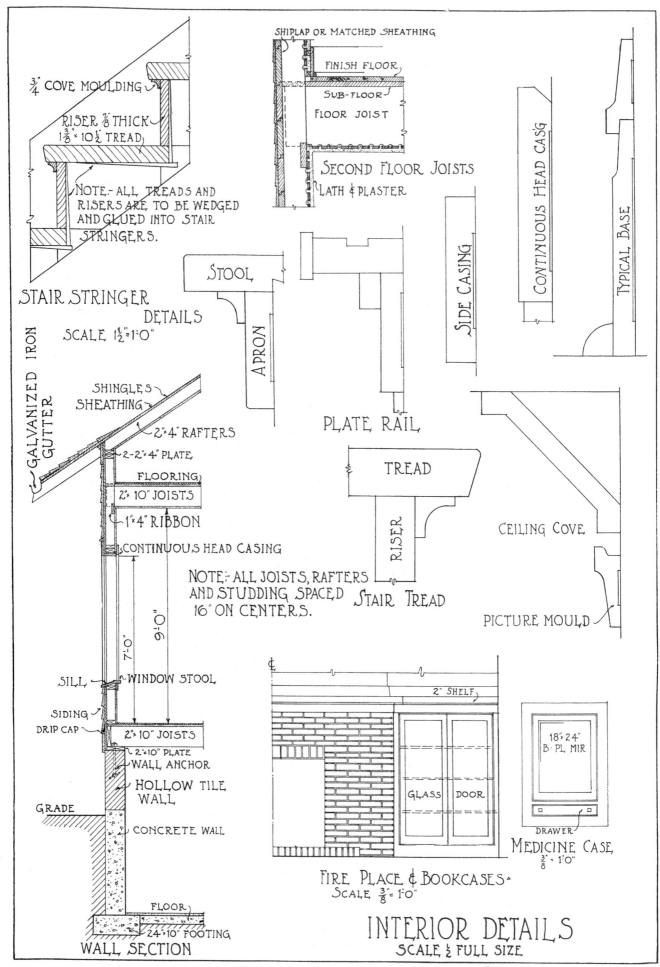

¾" COVE MOULDING

RISER ⅞" THICK

1⅜" × 10½" TREAD

NOTE:- ALL TREADS AND RISERS ARE TO BE WEDGED AND GLUED INTO STAIR STRINGERS.

STAIR STRINGER DETAILS
SCALE 1½"=1'0"

SHIPLAP OR MATCHED SHEATHING

FINISH FLOOR

SUB-FLOOR

FLOOR JOIST

Second Floor Joists
LATH & PLASTER

STOOL

APRON

PLATE RAIL

SIDE CASING

CONTINUOUS HEAD CASG

TYPICAL BASE

GALVANIZED IRON GUTTER

SHINGLES

SHEATHING

2"×4" RAFTERS

2-2"×4" PLATE

FLOORING

2"×10" JOISTS

1"×4" RIBBON

CONTINUOUS HEAD CASING

NOTE:- ALL JOISTS, RAFTERS AND STUDDING SPACED 16" ON CENTERS.

TREAD

RISER

STAIR TREAD

CEILING COVE

PICTURE MOULD

9'0"

7'0"

SILL

WINDOW STOOL

SIDING

DRIP CAP

2"×10" JOISTS

2"×10" PLATE

WALL ANCHOR

HOLLOW TILE WALL

GRADE

CONCRETE WALL

2" SHELF

GLASS   DOOR

18"×24" B. PL. MIR

DRAWER

MEDICINE CASE
¾" = 1'0"

FIRE PLACE & BOOKCASES
SCALE ⅜" = 1'0"

FLOOR

24"×10" FOOTING

WALL SECTION

INTERIOR DETAILS
SCALE ½ FULL SIZE

Details of Inside Trim and of Construction Used in Model Nine-Room Farm House.

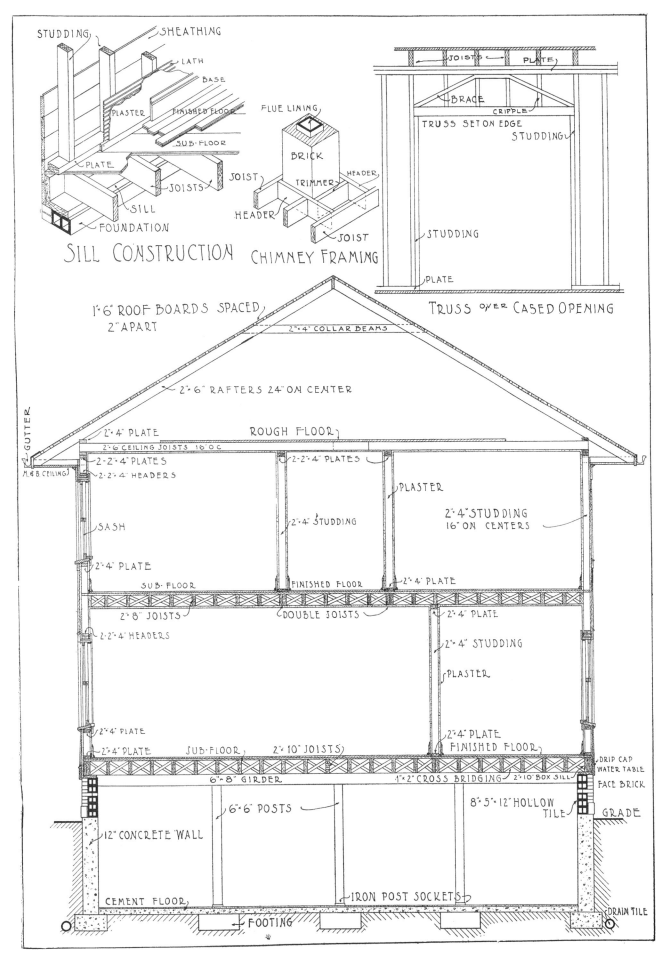

SILL CONSTRUCTION   CHIMNEY FRAMING

STUDDING / SHEATHING / LATH / BASE / PLASTER / FINISHED FLOOR / SUB-FLOOR / PLATE / JOISTS / SILL / FOUNDATION

FLUE LINING / BRICK / TRIMMER / HEADER / JOIST / HEADER / JOIST

TRUSS over CASED OPENING

JOISTS / PLATE / BRACE / CRIPPLE / TRUSS SET ON EDGE / STUDDING / STUDDING / PLATE

1"×6" ROOF BOARDS SPACED 2" APART

2"×4" COLLAR BEAMS

2"×6" RAFTERS 24" ON CENTER

ROUGH FLOOR

2"×4" PLATE

2"×6" CEILING JOISTS 16" O C

GUTTER

M. & B. CEILING

2-2"×4" PLATES

2-2"×4" HEADERS

2-2"×4" PLATES

2"×4" STUDDING

PLASTER

2"×4" STUDDING 16" ON CENTERS

SASH

2"×4" PLATE

SUB-FLOOR

FINISHED FLOOR

2"×4" PLATE

2"×8" JOISTS

DOUBLE JOISTS

2"×4" PLATE

2-2"×4" HEADERS

2"×4" STUDDING

PLASTER

2"×4" PLATE

2"×4" PLATE

2"×4" PLATE

FINISHED FLOOR

SUB-FLOOR

2"×10" JOISTS

1"×2" CROSS BRIDGING

2"×10" BOX SILL

DRIP CAP

WATER TABLE

FACE BRICK

6"×8" GIRDER

8"×5"×12" HOLLOW TILE

GRADE

6"×6" POSTS

12" CONCRETE WALL

CEMENT FLOOR

IRON POST SOCKETS

FOOTING

DRAIN TILE

Construction Details of Modern Farm House of Frame.

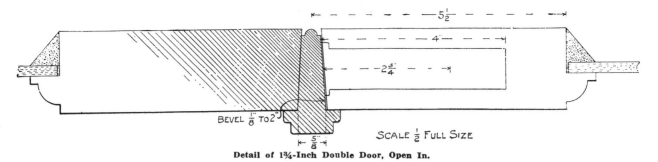

Detail of 1¾-Inch Double Door, Open In.

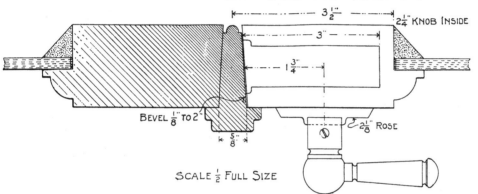

Detail of 1¾-Inch Double Door, Open Out.

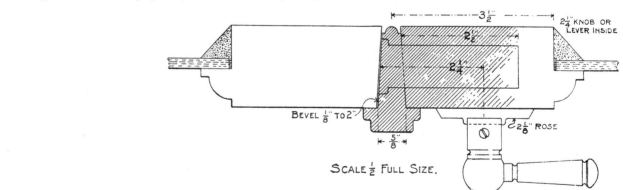

Detail of 1¾-Inch Double Door, Open In, on Which the Narrowest Cylinder Front Door Lock Can be Used.

Detail of 1¾-Inch Double Door, Open Out, on Which the Narrowest Cylinder Front Door Lock Can be Used.

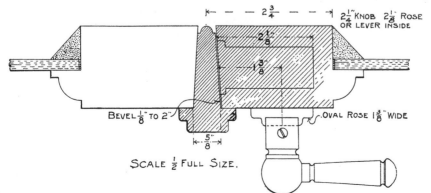

Detail of 1¾-Inch Double French Window, Open In, Bit Key or Thumb Bolt Lock.

STANDARD DETAILS FOR BUILDERS' HARDWARE.

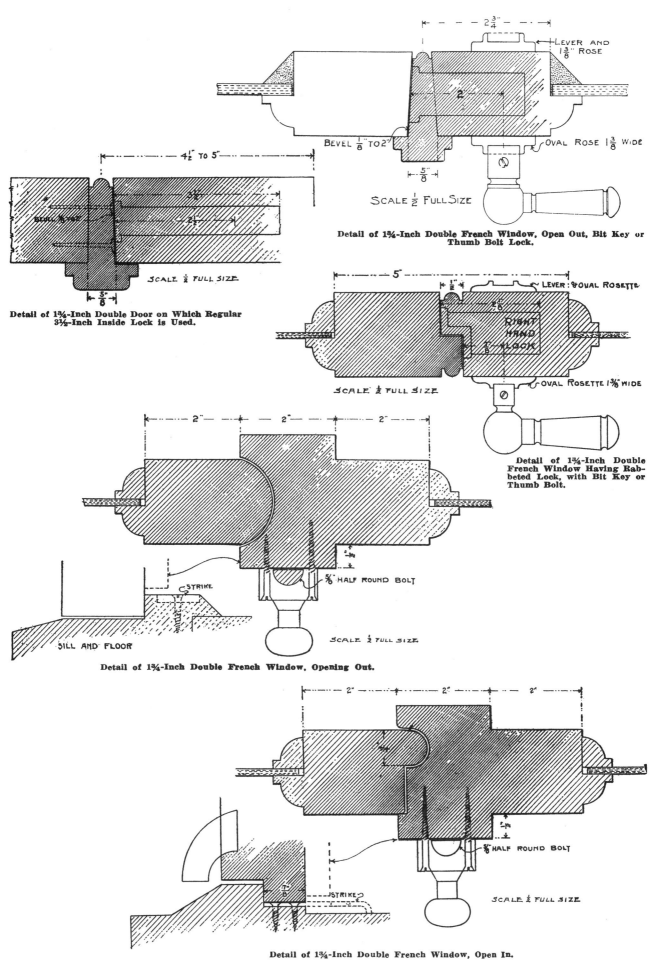

Detail of 1¾-Inch Double French Window, Open Out, Bit Key or Thumb Bolt Lock.

Detail of 1¾-Inch Double Door on Which Regular 3½-Inch Inside Lock is Used.

Detail of 1¾-Inch Double French Window Having Rabbeted Lock, with Bit Key or Thumb Bolt.

Detail of 1¾-Inch Double French Window, Opening Out.

Detail of 1¾-Inch Double French Window, Open In.

STANDARD DETAILS FOR BUILDERS' HARDWARE.

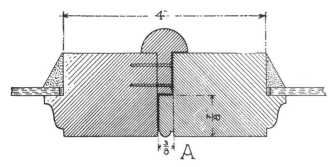

Section Thru Meeting Rails of Pair of Inward Opening Casements. Note T-Astragal on Outside to Keep Out the Rain.

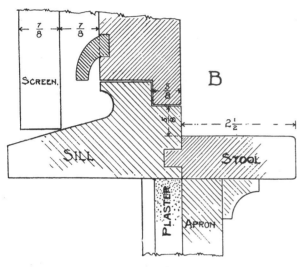

Section Thru Sill—Warranted Proof Even Against Driving Rain. Note That Standard Flush Bolt Requires Sill Rabbet to be at Least ⅝ Inch.

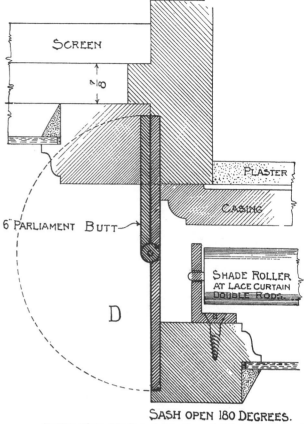

SASH OPEN 180 DEGREES.

Section Thru Window Jamb—Use of 6-Inch Parliament Butts Permits Opening 180 Degrees.

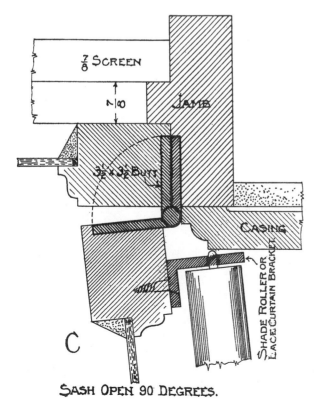

SASH OPEN 90 DEGREES.

Section Thru Window Jamb, Flush with Plaster.

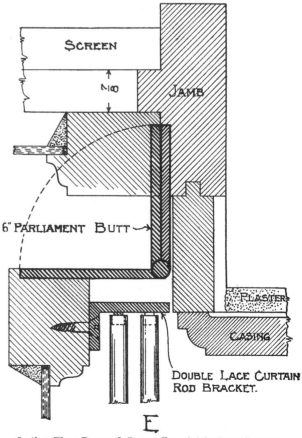

Section Thru Recessed Jamb—Use of 6-Inch Parliament Butts Gives Room for Curtain Rod Brackets.

Details of Inward Opening Casements. All Details Half Full Size.

STANDARD DETAILS FOR BUILDERS' HARDWARE.

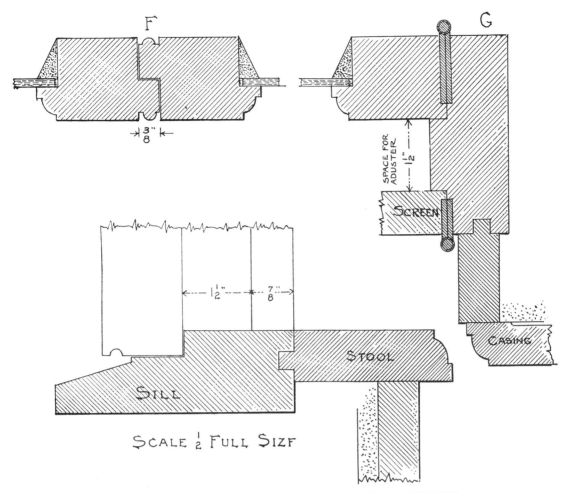

STANDARD DETAIL FOR OPEN OUT CASEMENT WINDOWS

"F," Section Thru Meeting Rails of Double Casements, Showing ⅜-Inch Rabbet to Fit Standard Mortise Turn-buckle. "G," Section Thru Jamb, Showing 1½ Inch Space Necessary for Standard Adjusters.

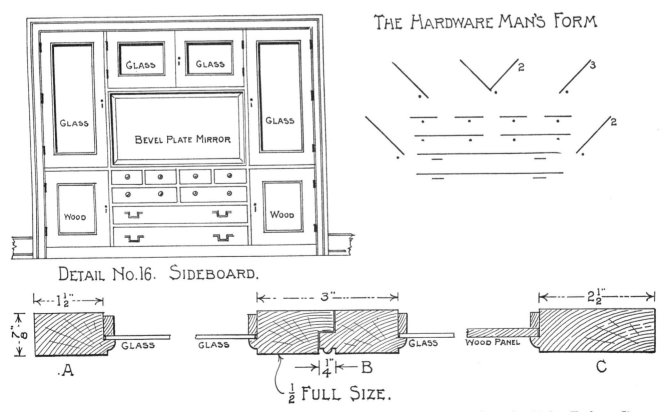

DETAIL No. 16. SIDEBOARD.   THE HARDWARE MAN'S FORM

Diagram Illustrating Correct Detailing for Sideboard, and Hardware Trimmer's Short Hand Form for Listing Hardware Items.

STANDARD DETAILS FOR BUILDERS' HARDWARE.

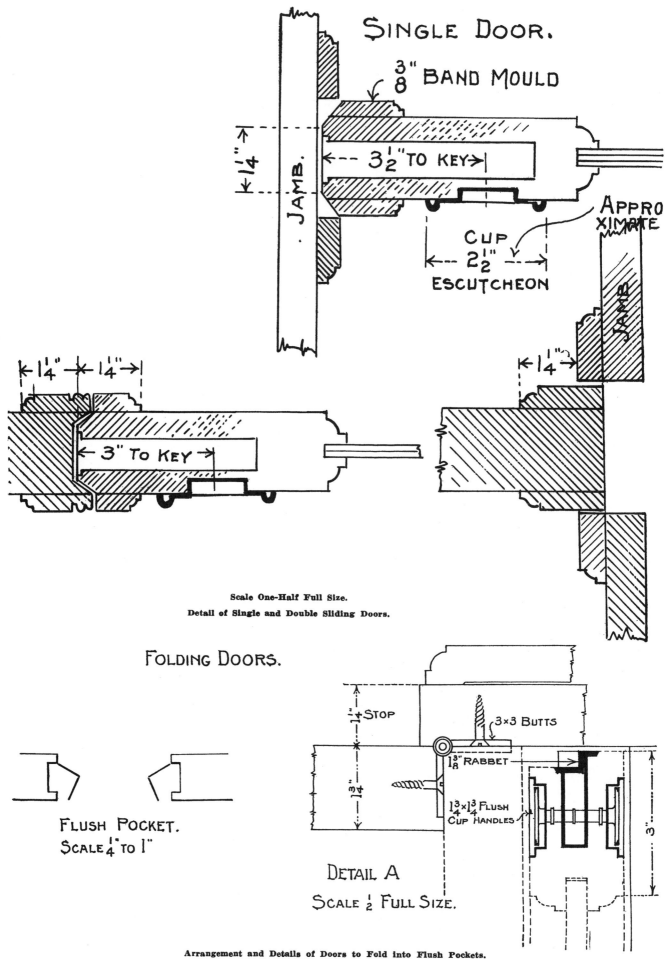

SINGLE DOOR.

$\frac{3}{8}$" BAND MOULD

JAMB.

$1\frac{1}{4}$"

$3\frac{1}{2}$" TO KEY

CUP
$2\frac{1}{2}$"
ESCUTCHEON

APPROXIMATE

JAMB

$1\frac{1}{4}$"

$1\frac{1}{4}$" $1\frac{1}{4}$"

3" TO KEY

Scale One-Half Full Size.
Detail of Single and Double Sliding Doors.

FOLDING DOORS.

$\frac{1}{4}$" STOP

3×3 BUTTS

$1\frac{3}{8}$" RABBET

$1\frac{3}{4}$"

$1\frac{3}{4}×1\frac{3}{4}$ FLUSH
CUP HANDLES

3"

FLUSH POCKET.
SCALE $\frac{1}{4}$" TO 1"

DETAIL A
SCALE $\frac{1}{2}$ FULL SIZE.

Arrangement and Details of Doors to Fold into Flush Pockets.
STANDARD DETAILS FOR BUILDERS' HARDWARE.

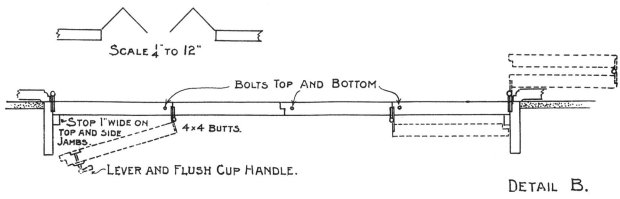

SCALE ¼" TO 12"

BOLTS TOP AND BOTTOM

STOP 1" WIDE ON TOP AND SIDE JAMBS

4 x 4 BUTTS.

LEVER AND FLUSH CUP HANDLE.

DETAIL B.

SCALE 1" TO 12"

Arrangement for Accordion or Four Fold Doors Showing Only Proper Way.

Accordion Folding Doors

THERE is nothing in the building line which puzzles the millmen, the carpenter, and the hardware man so much as accordion folding partitions.

The manufacturers of accordion hangers should treat more fully on this subject. They should place in the hands of the architects full descriptive matter, also half size or full size drawings with hardware in place. Then the architects can show the carpenter how it is done and also show the hardware man what items he has to furnish to make a perfect workmanlike job.

Doors should never be made thinner than 1¾ inches, because a lock knob and flush cup handle cannot be applied in doors thinner than 1¾ inches.

The detail below shows six full width doors and two half width doors.

Here you have a sliding door proposition because the hanging of the doors forces you to it. You must supply a hanger for the door farthest from the half door, and a hanger for every second door from this.

You can readily see that the track is full width of the opening. You must use a sliding door lock with the regular flush cup escutcheons. You should use four flush extension bolts at the bottom. You cannot use flush bolts at the top because you cannot apply the strikes or keepers to the top jamb; *there is a slot in the top jamb.*

You can omit the use of the bottom bolts, but it is not good practice, because the doors will buckle and you have no other method of keeping the doors rigid at the bottom when same are closed.

If you wish to use eight full width doors and two half width doors you must use the same number of hangers as shown in the detail, but these two extra inner doors must be treated to operate same as regular pair of hinged doors with a soffit closing up the slot in the top jamb and bolts, lock, knob and flush cup handle.

Now, to obtain a good workmanlike job of folding partition doors, the writer suggests the use of the adjustable hanging strip as shown in detail to left.

If the doors shrink the flush bolts can be shot into their keepers. All makers of hardware furnish keepers or strikes with oblong holes in them (because they know doors will shrink), hence the strikes or keepers need not be moved.

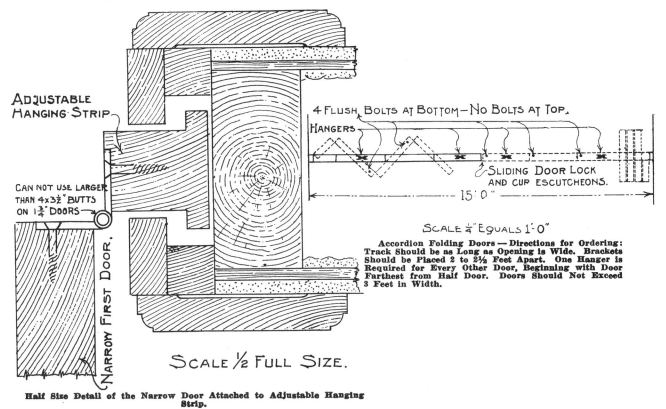

ADJUSTABLE HANGING STRIP

CAN NOT USE LARGER THAN 4x3½" BUTTS ON 1¾" DOORS

NARROW FIRST DOOR.

SCALE ½ FULL SIZE.

4 FLUSH BOLTS AT BOTTOM—NO BOLTS AT TOP.

HANGERS

SLIDING DOOR LOCK AND CUP ESCUTCHEONS.

15' 0"

SCALE ¼" EQUALS 1' 0"

Accordion Folding Doors — Directions for Ordering: Track Should be as Long as Opening is Wide. Brackets Should be Placed 2 to 2½ Feet Apart. One Hanger is Required for Every Other Door, Beginning with Door Farthest from Half Door. Doors Should Not Exceed 3 Feet in Width.

Half Size Detail of the Narrow Door Attached to Adjustable Hanging Strip.

STANDARD DETAILS FOR BUILDERS' HARDWARE.

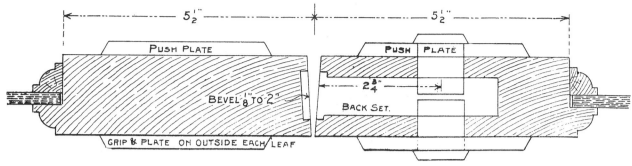

DOUBLE DOORS OPEN OUT

Detail of Double Doors to Open Out. Note That Edges Are Beveled, Not Rounded.

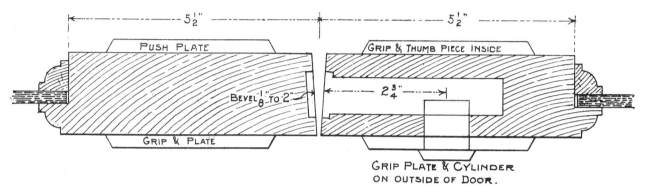

GRIP PLATE & CYLINDER
ON OUTSIDE OF DOOR.

Detail of Double Doors to Open Out—for Schools, Churches, Theaters and Loft Buildings.

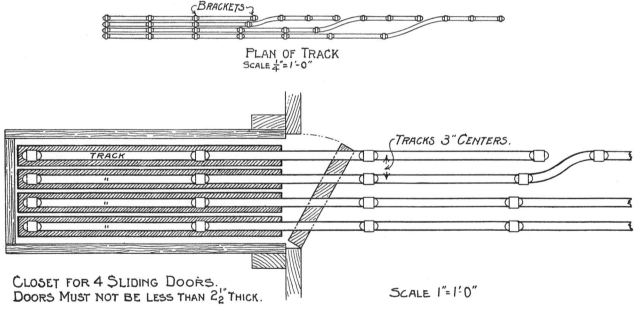

Plan View of Tracks for Four-Door School House Partition Heavy Enough to Carry Blackboard Panels; with Detail View of Pocket for Doors to Slide Back Into.

School-Room Partition Doors

ARRANGEMENT OF PARTITION DOORS HEAVY ENOUGH TO CARRY BLACKBOARD PANEL

WE show herewith, in the bottom detail, four sliding doors, all of which slide back into one pocket.

You will notice that this scheme is to take the place of accordion folding doors, dividing a large room into two or more smaller rooms.

This is especially desirable if these partition doors are required for additional blackboard space.

This device is in common use in the Chicago public schools, and is being installed in many of the schools in the larger cities. The accordion folding doors are much lower in price; but price does not count when a perfect up-to-date device is wanted.

Any number of doors can be used. If you have the space for a pocket in the opposite wall you can slide some of the doors into same.

If it is desired to hide these doors, a panel can be placed in front of the doors when same are back into the pocket.

This panel can be hung on invisible hinges and a very satisfactory job is obtained.

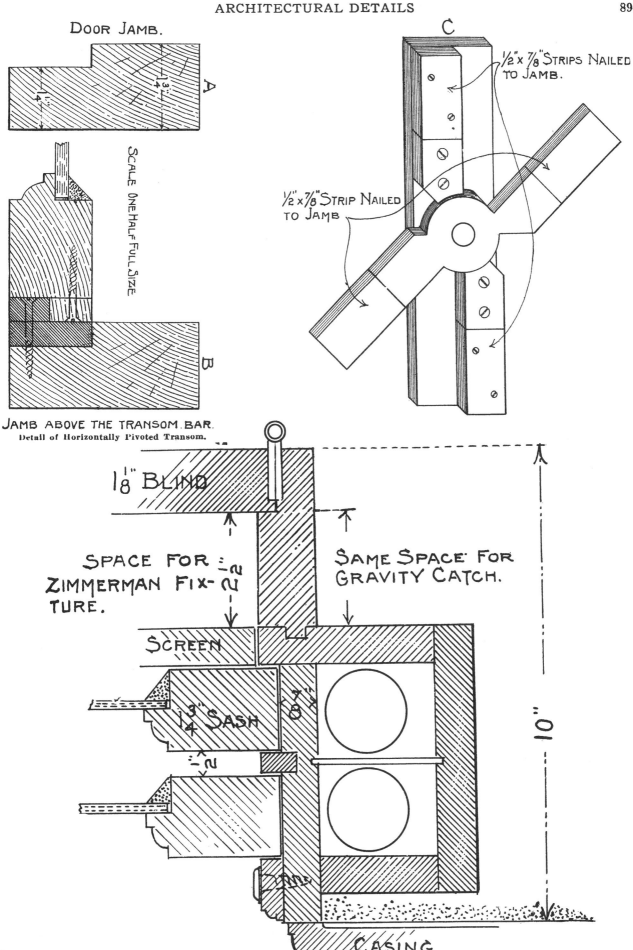

Door Jamb.

Scale One Half Full Size.

Jamb above the transom. bar.
Detail of Horizontally Pivoted Transom.

½" x ⅞" Strips Nailed to Jamb.

½" x ⅞" Strip Nailed to Jamb.

1⅛" Blind

Space for Zimmerman Fixture.

Same Space for Gravity Catch.

Screen

1¾" Sash

10' 0"

Casing

Detail of Outside Blinds for 10-Inch Wall. Note That There Must be a Space of at Least 2½ Inches Between Screen and Blind for Zimmerman or Gravity Fixtures; Scale One-Half Full Size.

STANDARD DETAILS FOR BUILDERS' HARDWARE.

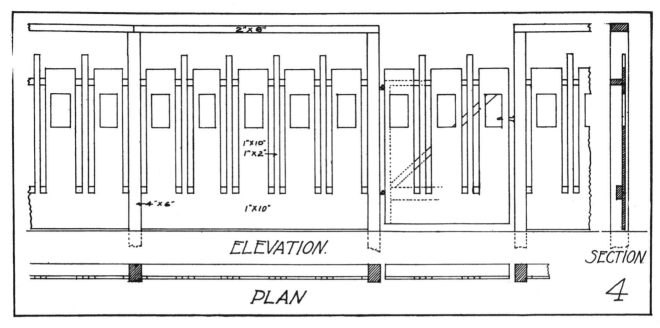

ELEVATION.

SECTION.

PLAN

4

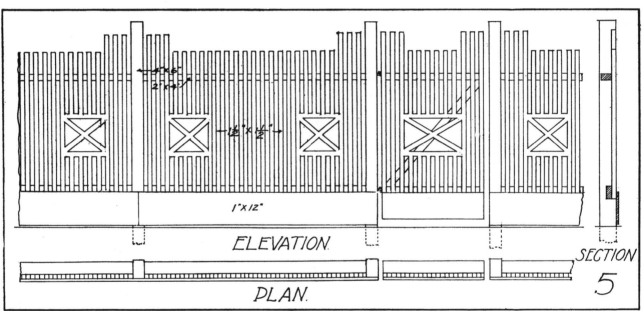

ELEVATION.

SECTION

PLAN.

5

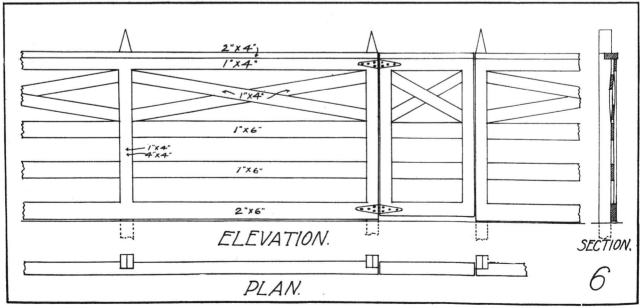

ELEVATION.

SECTION.

PLAN.

6

Ornamental Gates and Fences.

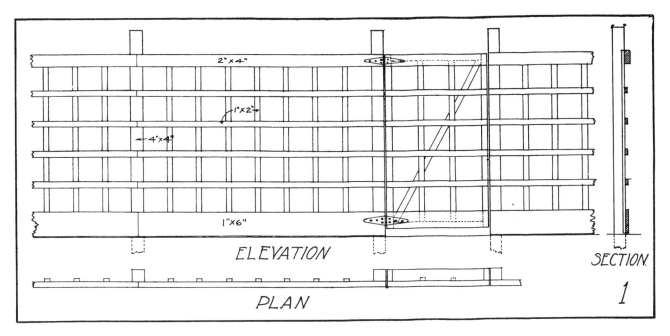

2"x4"

1"x2"

4"x4"

1"x6"

ELEVATION

PLAN

SECTION.

1

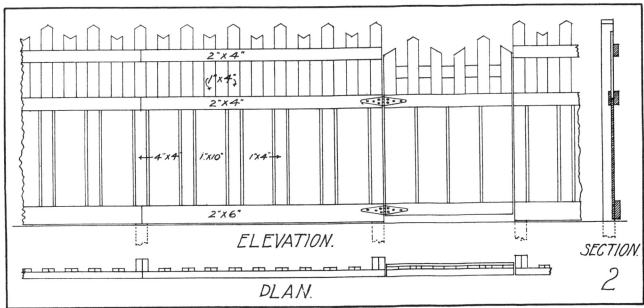

2"x4"

1"x4"

2"x4"

4"x4" 1"x10" 1"x4"

2"x6"

ELEVATION.

DLAN.

SECTION.

2

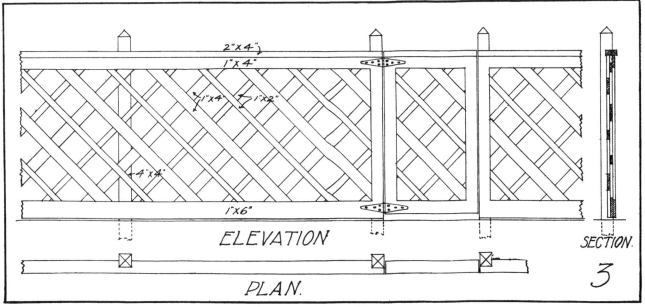

2"x4"

1"x4"

1"x4" 1"x2"

4"x4"

1"x6"

ELEVATION

PLAN.

SECTION.

3

Ornamental Gates and Fences.

Sun Parlor and Sleeping Porch Modernize Old Homes

THERE are few houses that were built before sun parlors and sleeping porches came into demand that cannot be remodeled so as to have these modern features. The cost of the additional rooms is more than gained by the satisfaction they give the owner and the increase in the value of the house, should it be sold.

In designing a sun parlor, or a sun parlor and sleeping porch, first consider the type of architecture of the house and place the addition where it will most improve the dwelling. The addition here shown was placed at the side of the house, at the front. This is constructed of face brick, set on a concrete foundation, with a stucco strip below the sleeping porch windows. Details of the construction are given in the section.

The floor plan of the sun parlor, or living porch, calls for a tile floor, but any material suitable or wanted by the owner can be substituted. The glazed doors leading from the living room to the porch also can be changed into any other desirable type, or left out altogether.

In this design the roof line was extended out over the porch to conform to that of the rest of the building. That is a feature that should not be overlooked—to so design and build the addition that it will not appear as an addition, but apparently will be a part of the original construction.

As has been said, this design is susceptible to many alterations. For instance, the living porch here shown can be transformed into an outdoor dining porch, adjoining the dining room, with a sleeping porch above. When such an addition is made, the construction will be more simple, as dining porches usually were merely screened in, being placed in a position where there is more privacy.

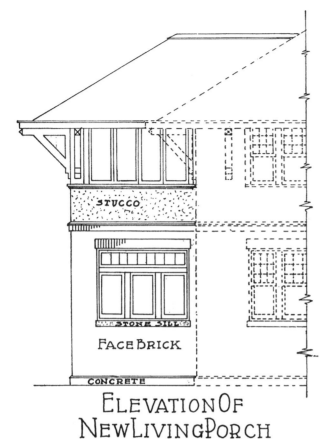

ELEVATION OF NEW LIVING PORCH

Showing How a Sun Parlor and Sleeping Porch Can be Added to Many Homes.

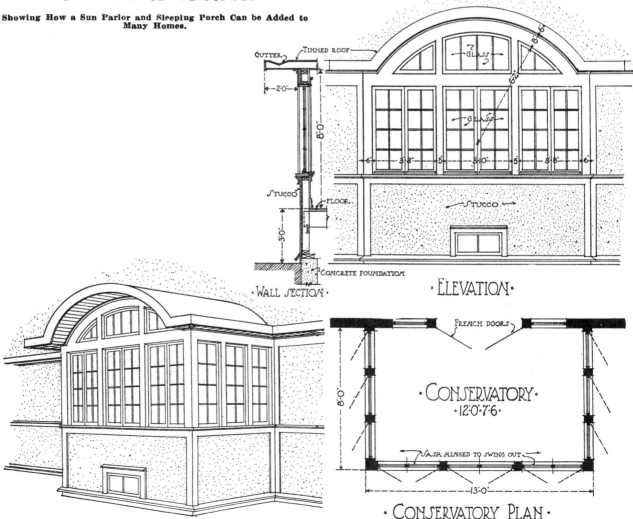

Perspective Sketch, Floor Plan and Details of an Artistic Sun Parlor or Conservatory Addition to be Built onto a Stucco House

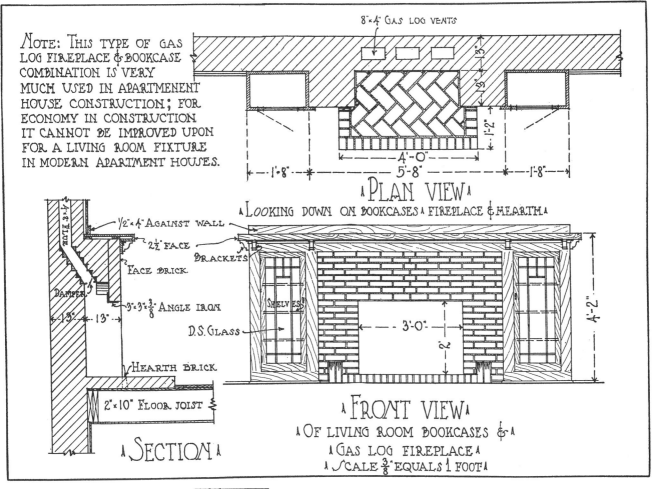

NOTE: THIS TYPE OF GAS LOG FIREPLACE & BOOKCASE COMBINATION IS VERY MUCH USED IN APARTMENT HOUSE CONSTRUCTION; FOR ECONOMY IN CONSTRUCTION IT CANNOT BE IMPROVED UPON FOR A LIVING ROOM FIXTURE IN MODERN APARTMENT HOUSES.

8"x4" GAS LOG VENTS

1'-8"   4'-0"   1'-8"
5'-8"

PLAN VIEW
LOOKING DOWN ON BOOKCASES, FIREPLACE & HEARTH

4"x3" FLUE
½"x4" AGAINST WALL
2½" FACE
BRACKETS
FACE BRICK
DAMPER
3"x3"x⅜" ANGLE IRON
D.S. GLASS
13"   13"
HEARTH BRICK
2"x10" FLOOR JOIST

SHELVES
3'-0"
2'
4'-2"

SECTION

FRONT VIEW
OF LIVING ROOM BOOKCASES &
GAS LOG FIREPLACE
SCALE ⅜" EQUALS 1 FOOT

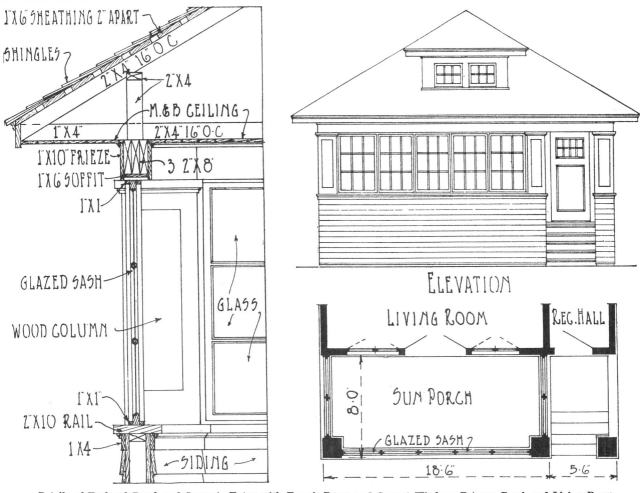

1"x6 SHEATHING 2" APART
SHINGLES
2"x4" 16" O.C.
2"x4
M.&B CEILING
1"X4"   2"x4" 16" O.C.
1"x10" FRIEZE
1"x6 SOFFIT
3 2"x8
1"x1
GLAZED SASH
WOOD COLUMN
GLASS
1"x1
2"x10 RAIL
1"x4
SIDING

ELEVATION

LIVING ROOM   REG. HALL
8'-0
SUN PORCH
GLAZED SASH
18'-6"   5'-6"

Details of Enclosed Porch and Separate Entry with French Doors and Cement Windows Between Porch and Living Room.

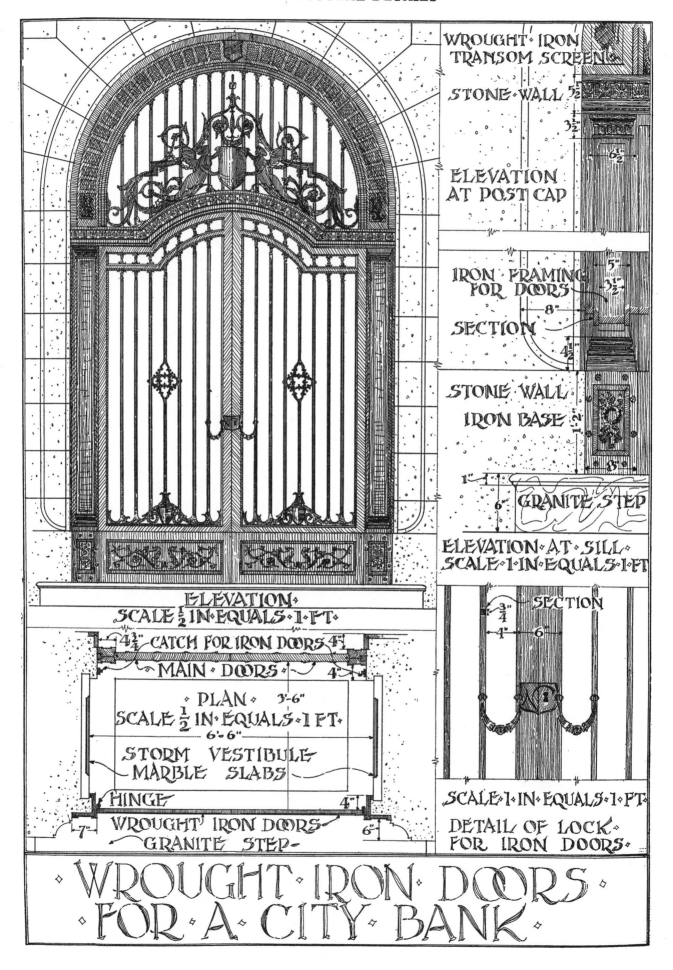

WROUGHT·IRON
TRANSOM·SCREEN

STONE·WALL 5½"

3½"

6½"

ELEVATION
AT·POST·CAP

IRON·FRAMING
FOR·DOORS   5"
             3½"

SECTION   8"

             4½"

STONE·WALL
IRON·BASE   1'-2"

             8"

1"

6" GRANITE·STEP

ELEVATION·AT·SILL
SCALE·1·IN·EQUALS·1·FT

ELEVATION·
SCALE·½·IN·EQUALS·1·FT·

4½" CATCH·FOR·IRON·DOORS 4½"

MAIN·DOORS   4"

·PLAN· 3'-6"
SCALE·½·IN·EQUALS·1·FT·
6'-6"

STORM·VESTIBULE
MARBLE·SLABS

HINGE   4"

WROUGHT·IRON·DOORS
GRANITE·STEP·
7"   6"

SECTION
¾"
4"   6"

SCALE·1·IN·EQUALS·1·FT

DETAIL·OF·LOCK·
FOR·IRON·DOORS·

WROUGHT·IRON·DOORS·
FOR·A·CITY·BANK·

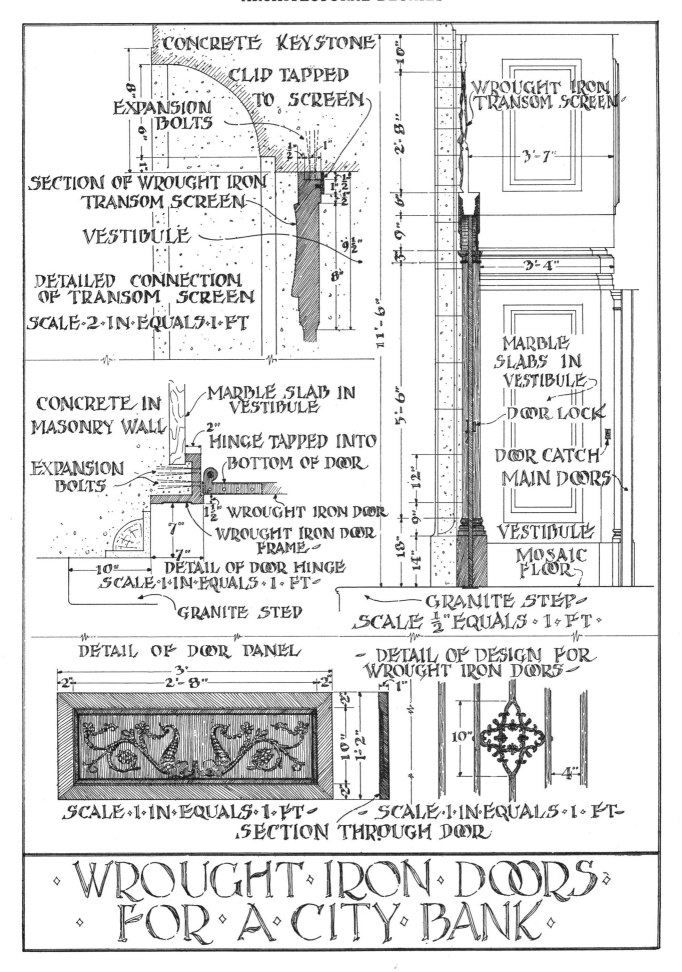

CONCRETE KEYSTONE

CLIP TAPPED TO SCREEN

EXPANSION BOLTS

8"
6"
1"

WROUGHT IRON TRANSOM SCREEN

3'-7"

10"

2'-8"

6"

SECTION OF WROUGHT IRON TRANSOM SCREEN

VESTIBULE

DETAILED CONNECTION OF TRANSOM SCREEN

SCALE·2·IN·EQUALS·1·FT

9'-0"

9½"

8"

11'-6"

3'-0"

3'-4"

MARBLE SLABS IN VESTIBULE

CONCRETE IN MASONRY WALL

MARBLE SLAB IN VESTIBULE

2"

HINGE TAPPED INTO BOTTOM OF DOOR

EXPANSION BOLTS

1½" WROUGHT IRON DOOR

WROUGHT IRON DOOR FRAME

7"
7"

DETAIL OF DOOR HINGE
SCALE·1·IN·EQUALS·1·FT

10"

GRANITE STEP

5'-6"

18"

9"
12"
14"

DOOR LOCK

DOOR CATCH MAIN DOORS

VESTIBULE

MOSAIC FLOOR

GRANITE STEP
SCALE ½" EQUALS·1·FT

DETAIL OF DOOR PANEL

3'
2'-8"
2"   2"

2"
10"
1'-2"
2"

DETAIL OF DESIGN FOR WROUGHT IRON DOORS

1"

10"

4"

SCALE·1·IN·EQUALS·1·FT
SECTION THROUGH DOOR

SCALE·1·IN·EQUALS·1·FT

WROUGHT·IRON·DOORS·
·FOR·A·CITY·BANK·

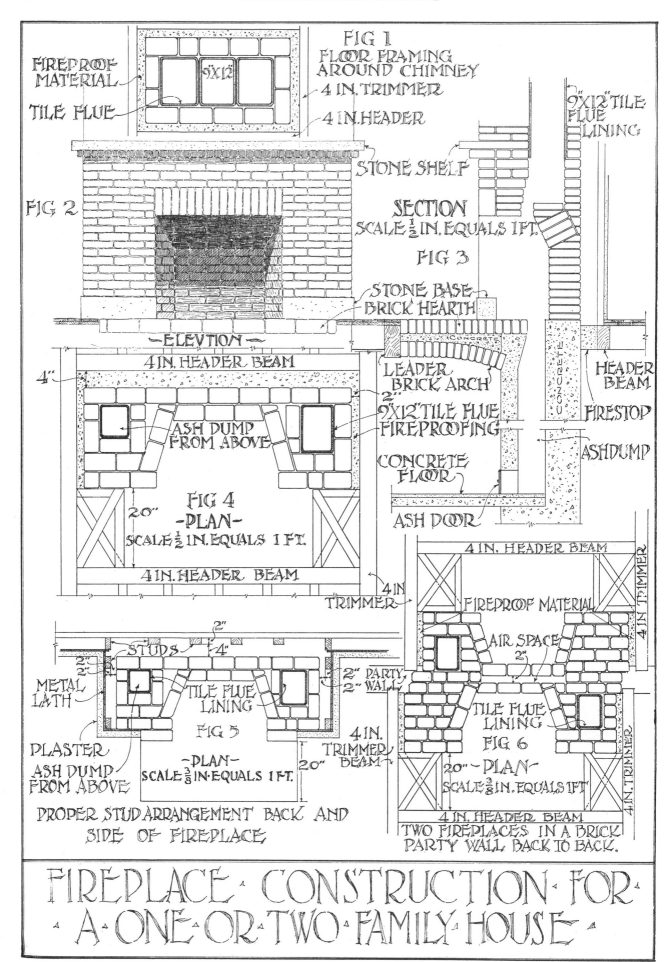

FIREPROOF MATERIAL

TILE FLUE

FIG 1
FLOOR FRAMING
AROUND CHIMNEY
4 IN. TRIMMER
4 IN. HEADER

9"X12"

9"X12" TILE FLUE LINING

FIG 2

STONE SHELF

SECTION
SCALE ½ IN. EQUALS 1FT.

FIG 3

STONE BASE
BRICK HEARTH

~ELEVTION~

4 IN. HEADER BEAM

4"

ASH DUMP FROM ABOVE

LEADER BRICK ARCH
2"
9"X12" TILE FLUE
FIREPROOFING

CONCRETE FLOOR

ASH DOOR

HEADER BEAM

FIRESTOP

ASHDUMP

20"

FIG 4
-PLAN-
SCALE ½ IN. EQUALS 1 FT.

4 IN. HEADER BEAM

4 IN TRIMMER

4 IN. HEADER BEAM

4 IN TRIMMER

FIREPROOF MATERIAL

AIR SPACE
2"

2"
STUDS   4"

2"
2"

METAL LATH

TILE FLUE LINING

FIG 5

2" PARTY WALL

TILE FLUE LINING
FIG 6

PLASTER
ASH DUMP FROM ABOVE

-PLAN-
SCALE ⅜ IN. EQUALS 1 FT.

4 IN. TRIMMER BEAM

20"

20" -PLAN-
SCALE ⅜ IN. EQUALS 1 FT

4 IN. TRIMMER

PROPER STUD ARRANGEMENT BACK AND
SIDE OF FIREPLACE

4 IN. HEADER BEAM
TWO FIREPLACES IN A BRICK
PARTY WALL BACK TO BACK.

FIREPLACE · CONSTRUCTION · FOR · A · ONE · OR · TWO · FAMILY · HOUSE ·

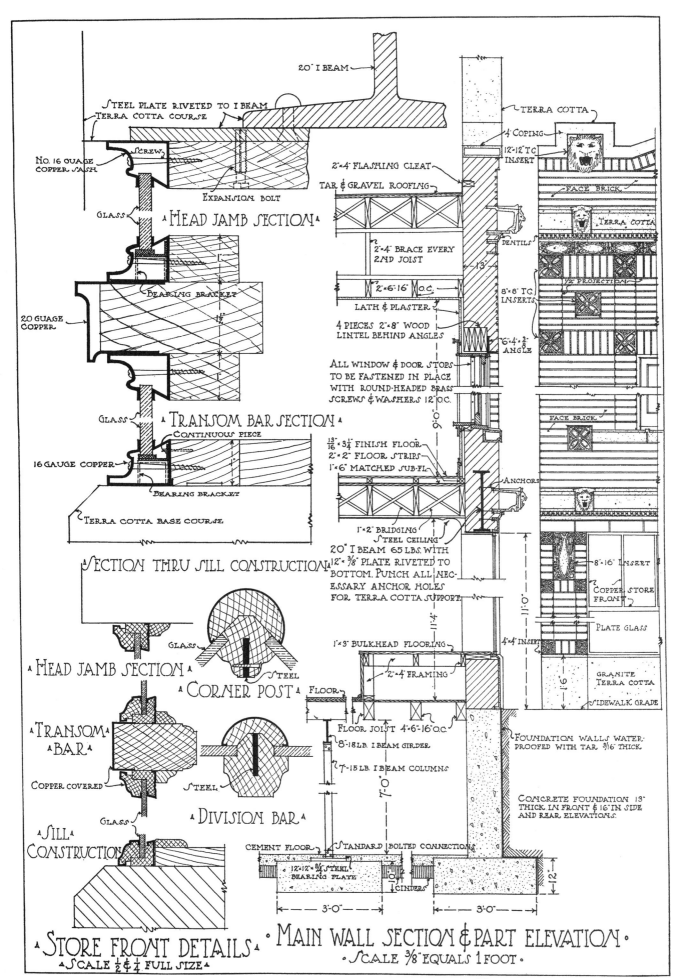

Show Window and Front Wall Construction of Store Building.

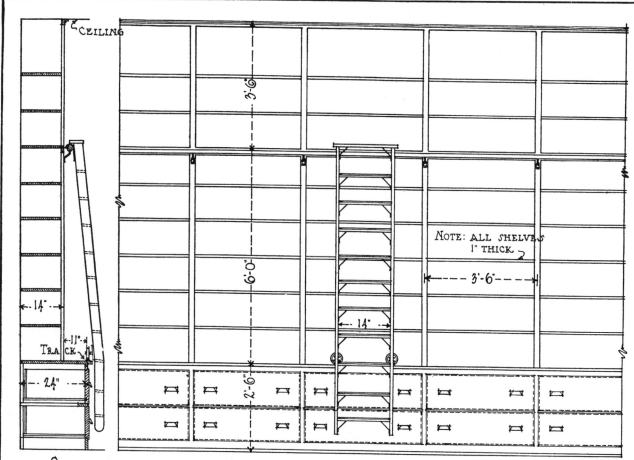

· SECTION · AND · ELEVATION · OF · SHOE · STORE · SHELVING ·
· SCALE · ⅜ · INCH · EQUALS · ONE · FOOT ·

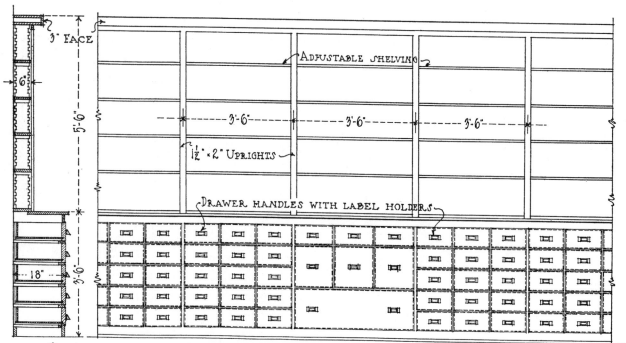

· SECTION · AND · ELEVATION · OF · DRUG · STORE · FIXTURES ·
· SCALE · ⅜ · INCH · EQUALS · ONE · FOOT ·

Details of Shelves and Fixtures Suitable for Shoe Stores and Drug Stores. The Ladder Construction for Handling the Shoe Store Shelving Is a Feature. The Drug Store Design Is a Standard Design Such as Might Be Found in a Well Arranged Drug Store.

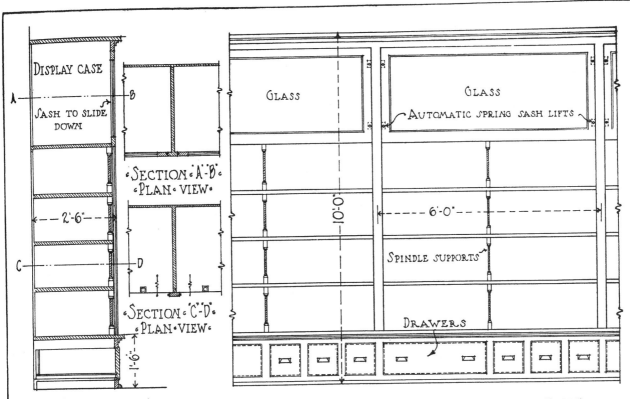

DISPLAY CASE

A

B

SASH TO SLIDE DOWN

·SECTION·A·B· ·PLAN·VIEW·

2'-6"

C

D

·SECTION·C·D· ·PLAN·VIEW·

1'-6"

GLASS

GLASS

AUTOMATIC SPRING SASH LIFTS

10'-0"

6'-0"

SPINDLE SUPPORTS

DRAWERS

·SECTION & ELEVATION·OF·DRY·GOODS·STORE·FIXTURES·
·SCALE ⅜ INCH EQUALS ONE FOOT·

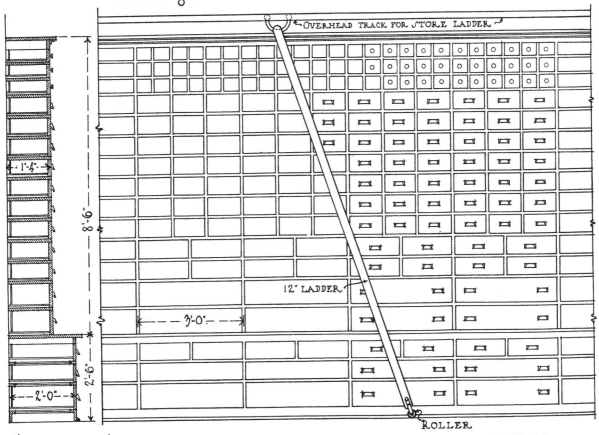

OVERHEAD TRACK FOR STORE LADDER

1'-4"

8'-6"

12" LADDER

3'-0"

2'-6"

2'-0"

ROLLER

·SECTION & ELEVATION·OF·HARDWARE·STORE·FIXTURES·
·SCALE ⅜ INCH EQUALS ONE FOOT·

Shelves and Fixture Arrangements for a Modern Dry Goods Store and a Hardware Store. The Small Labeled Drawers Are the Most Useful for a Hardware Store. The Broad Shelves for the Dry Goods Do Not Need to Be Marked as the Material Can Be Easily Seen.

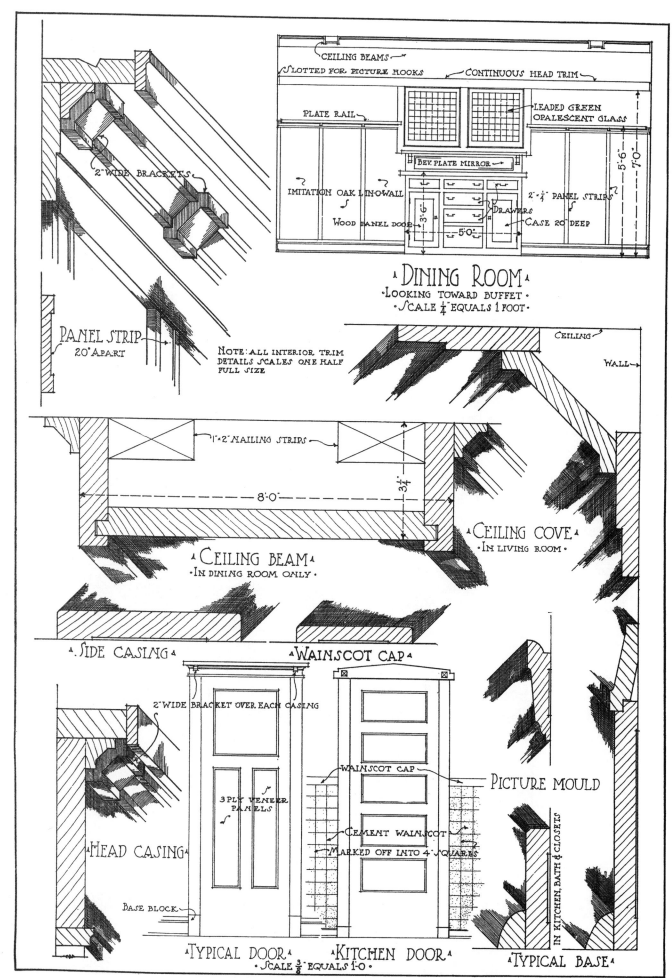

2" WIDE BRACKETS

PANEL STRIP
20" APART

NOTE: ALL INTERIOR TRIM
DETAILS SCALES ONE HALF
FULL SIZE

CEILING BEAMS
SLOTTED FOR PICTURE HOOKS

CONTINUOUS HEAD TRIM

PLATE RAIL

LEADED GREEN
OPALESCENT GLASS

BEV. PLATE MIRROR

IMITATION OAK LIN-O-WALL

2"·¼" PANEL STRIPS

WOOD PANEL DOOR

DRAWERS
CASE 20" DEEP

3'-6"

5'-0"

5'-6"

7'-0"

·DINING ROOM·
·LOOKING TOWARD BUFFET·
·SCALE ¼" EQUALS 1 FOOT·

CEILING

WALL

1"×2" NAILING STRIPS

8'-0"

3¼"

·CEILING COVE·
·IN LIVING ROOM·

·CEILING BEAM·
·IN DINING ROOM ONLY·

·SIDE CASING·

·WAINSCOT CAP·

2" WIDE BRACKET OVER EACH CASING

3 PLY VENEER
PANELS

HEAD CASING

BASE BLOCK

WAINSCOT CAP

CEMENT WAINSCOT
MARKED OFF INTO 4" SQUARES

PICTURE MOULD

IN KITCHEN, BATH & CLOSETS

·TYPICAL DOOR·   ·KITCHEN DOOR·
·SCALE ⅜" EQUALS 1'-0"·

·TYPICAL BASE·

Details of Interior Finish in Second and Third Floor Apartments.

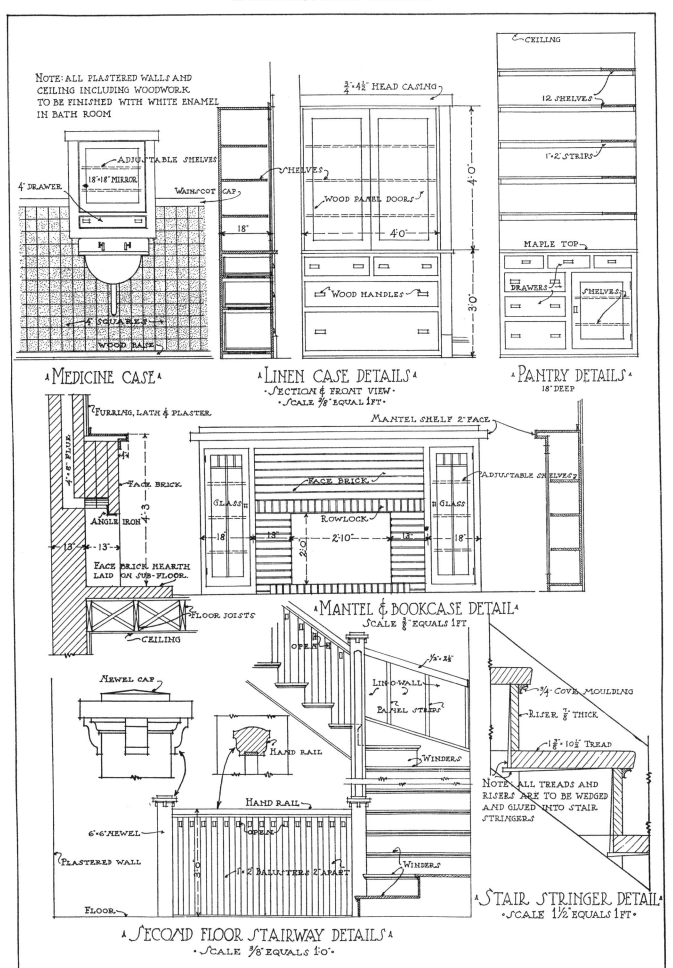

NOTE: ALL PLASTERED WALLS AND CEILING INCLUDING WOODWORK TO BE FINISHED WITH WHITE ENAMEL IN BATH ROOM

ADJUSTABLE SHELVES
18"×18" MIRROR
4" DRAWER
WAINSCOT CAP
SHELVES
18"
4" SQUARES
WOOD BASE

· MEDICINE CASE ·

¾"×4½" HEAD CASING
WOOD PANEL DOORS
4'·0"
4'·0"
3'·0"
WOOD HANDLES

· LINEN CASE DETAILS ·
· SECTION & FRONT VIEW ·
· SCALE ⅜" EQUAL 1 FT ·

CEILING
12 SHELVES
1"·2" STRIPS
MAPLE TOP
DRAWERS
SHELVES

· PANTRY DETAILS ·
18" DEEP

FURRING, LATH & PLASTER
4"·8" FLUE
4"
FACE BRICK
4'·3"
ANGLE IRON
13"   13"
FACE BRICK HEARTH LAID ON SUB-FLOOR.
FLOOR JOISTS
CEILING

MANTEL SHELF 2" FACE
FACE BRICK
GLASS   GLASS
ROWLOCK
18"   13"   2'·10"   13"   18"
2'·0"
ADJUSTABLE SHELVES

· MANTEL & BOOKCASE DETAIL ·
SCALE ⅜" EQUALS 1 FT

OPEN
LIN-O-WALL
PANEL STRIPS
½"·2½"
WINDERS

NEWEL CAP
HAND RAIL
HAND RAIL
6"×6" NEWEL
OPEN
PLASTERED WALL
3'·0"
1"·2" BALUSTERS 2" APART
WINDERS
FLOOR

· SECOND FLOOR STAIRWAY DETAILS ·
· SCALE ⅜" EQUALS 1'·0" ·

¾" COVE MOULDING
RISER ⅞" THICK
1⅜"·10½" TREAD
NOTE: ALL TREADS AND RISERS ARE TO BE WEDGED AND GLUED INTO STAIR STRINGERS

· STAIR STRINGER DETAIL ·
· SCALE 1½" EQUALS 1 FT ·

Details of Special Interior Trim in Hall and in Living Quarters.

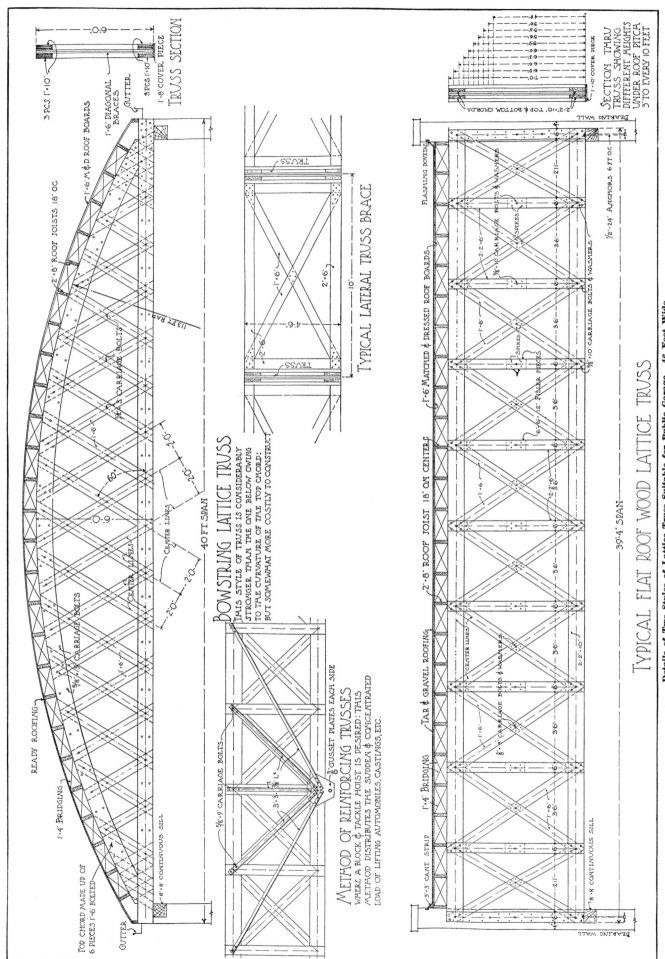

Details of Two Styles of Lattice Truss Suitable for Public Garage, 46 Feet Wide.

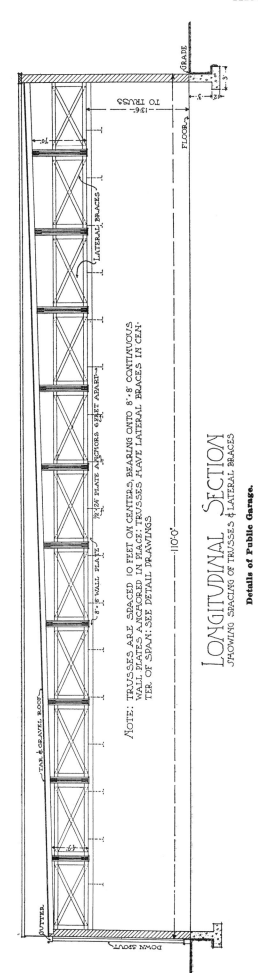

LONGITUDINAL SECTION
SHOWING SPACING OF TRUSSES & LATERAL BRACES

Details of Public Garage.

NOTE: TRUSSES ARE SPACED 10 FEET ON CENTERS, BEARING ONTO 8"·8" CONTINUOUS WALL PLATES ANCHORED IN PLACE: TRUSSES HAVE LATERAL BRACES IN CENTER OF SPAN: SEE DETAIL DRAWINGS

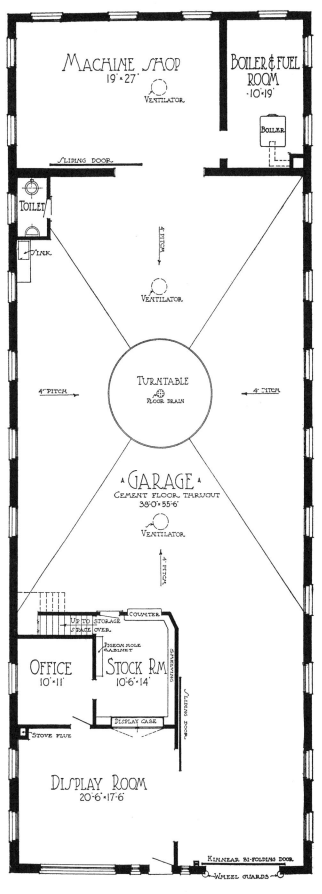

MACHINE SHOP
19'·27'

BOILER & FUEL ROOM
·10'·19'

GARAGE
CEMENT FLOOR THRUOUT
38'·0"×55'·6'

TURNTABLE

OFFICE
10'·11'

STOCK RM.
10'·6"×14'

DISPLAY ROOM
20'·6"·17'·6'

Floor Plan of Garage Showing the Arrangement of the Various Parts. The Front of the Building Contains a Display Room for Accessories and Show Cars. Back of This is the Stock Room and Office Which Can be Easily Made Very Attractive From the Front. The Turntable in the Center Simplifies the Handling of Cars. There is a Commodious Shop at the Rear.

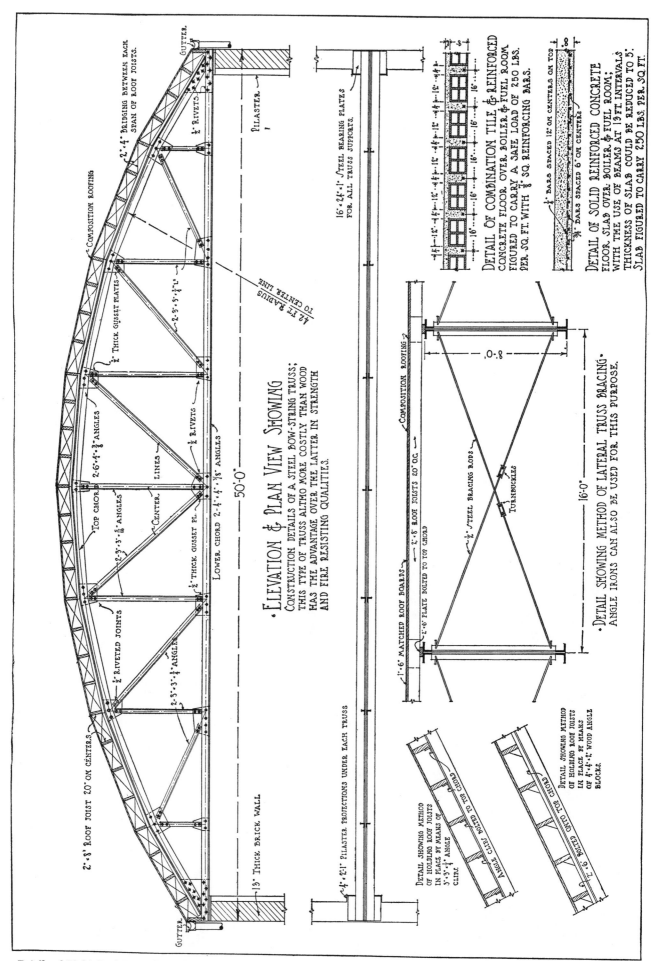

Elevation & Plan View Showing

Construction details of a steel bow-string truss; this type of truss altho more costly than wood has the advantage over the latter in strength and fire resisting qualities.

Detail of Combination Tile & Reinforced Concrete Floor over Boiler & Fuel Room figured to carry a safe load of 250 lbs. per. sq. ft. with ⅜" sq. reinforcing bars.

Detail of Solid Reinforced Concrete Floor. Slab over Boiler & Fuel Room; with the use of beams at 13 ft. intervals thickness of slab could be reduced to 5". Slab figured to carry 250 lbs. per. sq. ft.

Detail Showing Method of Lateral Truss Bracing. Angle irons can also be used for this purpose.

Detail Showing Method of Holding Roof Joists in place by means of 3"·3"·¼" Angle Clips.

Detail Showing Method of Holding Roof Joists in place by means of 4"·4"·4" Wood Angle Blocks.

Details of Light Steel Truss for 50-Foot Span Curving Roof Garage, Also of Concrete Floor Over Heating Room in Public Garage.

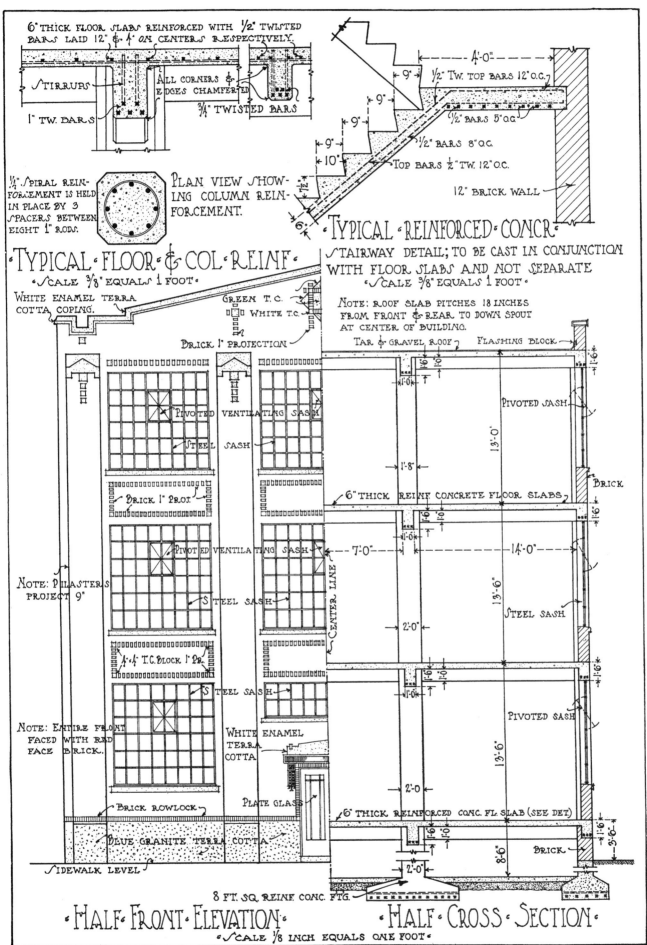

6" THICK FLOOR SLABS REINFORCED WITH 1/2" TWISTED BARS LAID 12" & 4" ON CENTERS RESPECTIVELY.

STIRRUPS

1" TW. BARS

ALL CORNERS & EDGES CHAMFERED

3/4" TWISTED BARS

1/4" SPIRAL REINFORCEMENT IS HELD IN PLACE BY 3 SPACERS BETWEEN EIGHT 1" RODS.

PLAN VIEW SHOWING COLUMN REINFORCEMENT.

·TYPICAL·FLOOR·&·COL·REINF·
·SCALE 3/8" EQUALS 1 FOOT·

4'-0"
9"
1/2" TW. TOP BARS 12" O.C.
9"
1/2" BARS 5" O.C.
9"
1/2" BARS 8" O.C.
9"
10"
TOP BARS 1/2" TW. 12" O.C.
7 1/2"
12" BRICK WALL
6"

·TYPICAL·REINFORCED·CONCR·
STAIRWAY DETAIL; TO BE CAST IN CONJUNCTION WITH FLOOR SLABS AND NOT SEPARATE
·SCALE 3/8" EQUALS 1 FOOT·

NOTE: ROOF SLAB PITCHES 18 INCHES FROM FRONT & REAR TO DOWN SPOUT AT CENTER OF BUILDING.

WHITE ENAMEL TERRA COTTA COPING.

GREEN T.C.
WHITE T.C.
BRICK 1" PROJECTION

TAR & GRAVEL ROOF   FLASHING BLOCK

PIVOTED SASH

PIVOTED VENTILATING SASH

STEEL SASH

13'-0"

BRICK 1" PROJ.

6" THICK REINF. CONCRETE FLOOR SLABS

1'-8"

PIVOTED VENTILATING SASH

STEEL SASH

CENTER LINE

7'-0"   14'-0"

13'-6"

STEEL SASH

2'-0"

NOTE: PILASTERS PROJECT 9"

4"x4" T.C. BLOCK 1" PR.

STEEL SASH.

PIVOTED SASH

13'-6"

NOTE: ENTIRE FRONT FACED WITH RED FACE BRICK.

WHITE ENAMEL TERRA COTTA

PLATE GLASS

2'-0"

BRICK ROWLOCK

6" THICK REINFORCED CONC. FL. SLAB (SEE DET)

BRICK

BLUE GRANITE TERRA COTTA

8'-6"

SIDEWALK LEVEL

2'-0"

8 FT. SQ. REINF CONC. FTG.

3'-6"

·HALF·FRONT·ELEVATION·   ·HALF·CROSS·SECTION·
·SCALE 1/8 INCH EQUALS ONE FOOT·

Details of Reinforced Concrete Factory Building.   Reinforcing of Floors, Girders, and Columns Are Shown and Also Arrangement of Exterior Finish.

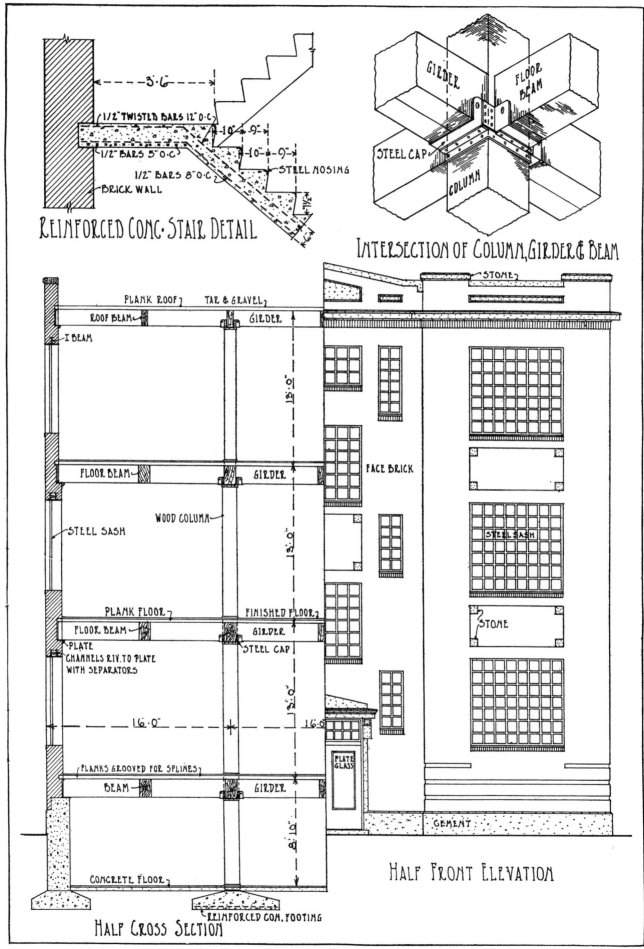

REINFORCED CONC. STAIR DETAIL

INTERSECTION OF COLUMN, GIRDER & BEAM

HALF CROSS SECTION

HALF FRONT ELEVATION

Working Details Standard Mill Construction Factory Building.

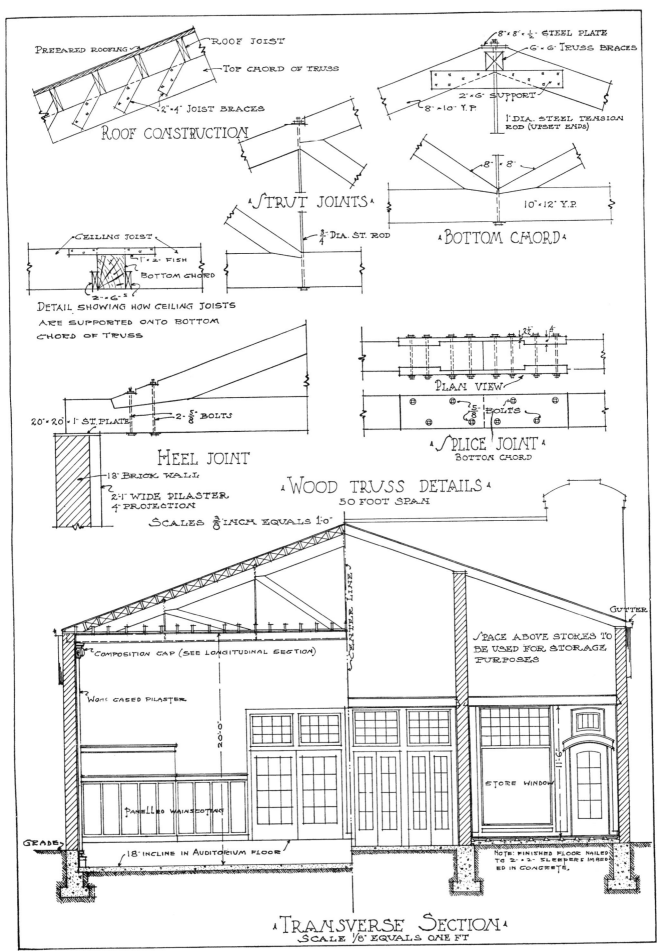

ROOF CONSTRUCTION

PREPARED ROOFING — ROOF JOIST — TOP CHORD OF TRUSS — 2"×4" JOIST BRACES

8"×8"×½" STEEL PLATE — 6"×6" TRUSS BRACES — 2"×6" SUPPORT — 8"×10" Y.P. — 1" DIA. STEEL TENSION ROD (UPSET ENDS)

STRUT JOINTS

¾" DIA. ST. ROD

BOTTOM CHORD
8"×8" — 10"×12" Y.P.

CEILING JOIST — 1"×2" FISH — BOTTOM CHORD — 2"×6"-S

DETAIL SHOWING HOW CEILING JOISTS ARE SUPPORTED ONTO BOTTOM CHORD OF TRUSS

PLAN VIEW — 2½" — 4"

SPLICE JOINT
BOTTOM CHORD
⅝" BOLTS

HEEL JOINT
20"×20"×1" ST. PLATE — 2-⅝" BOLTS
13" BRICK WALL
2'-1" WIDE PILASTER 4" PROJECTION
SCALES ⅜ INCH EQUALS 1'-0"

WOOD TRUSS DETAILS
50 FOOT SPAN

CENTER LINE

COMPOSITION CAP (SEE LONGITUDINAL SECTION)

WOOD CASED PILASTER

SPACE ABOVE STORES TO BE USED FOR STORAGE PURPOSES

GUTTER

20'-0"

11'-6"

STORE WINDOW

PANELLED WAINSCOTING

GRADE

18" INCLINE IN AUDITORIUM FLOOR

NOTE: FINISHED FLOOR NAILED TO 2"×2" SLEEPERS IMBEDDED IN CONCRETE.

TRANSVERSE SECTION
SCALE ⅛" EQUALS ONE FT

Details of Construction of Modern Photo Play House.

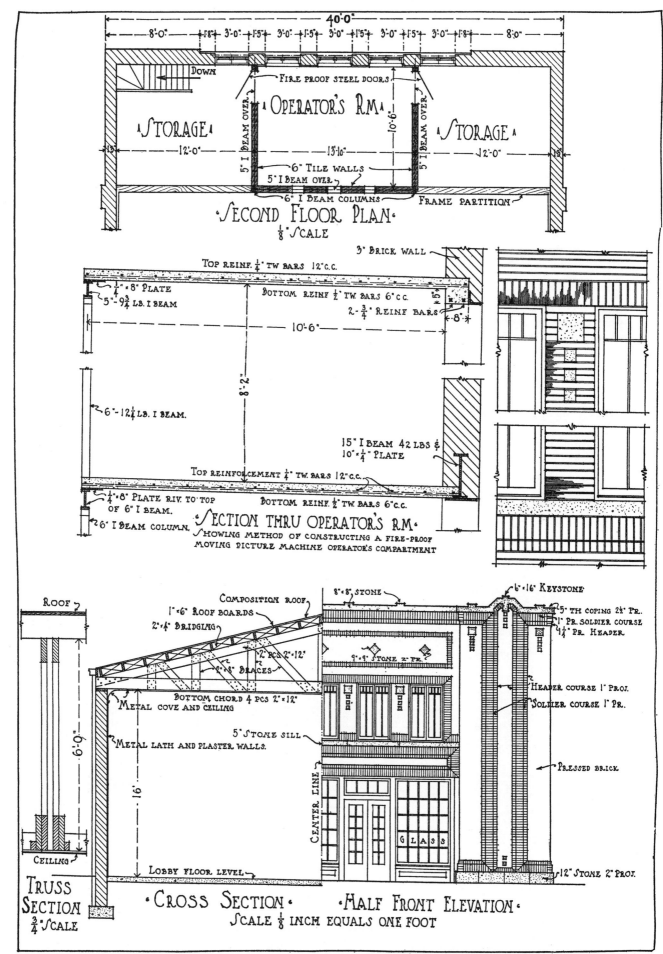

SECOND FLOOR PLAN
⅛" SCALE

SECTION THRU OPERATOR'S RM
SHOWING METHOD OF CONSTRUCTING A FIRE-PROOF
MOVING PICTURE MACHINE OPERATOR'S COMPARTMENT

TRUSS SECTION
¾" SCALE

CROSS SECTION

HALF FRONT ELEVATION
SCALE ⅛ INCH EQUALS ONE FOOT

Details of Construction of One-Story Theater. An Up-to-Date Business Attracting Front is Provided and the Operator's Room is of Fireproof Construction.

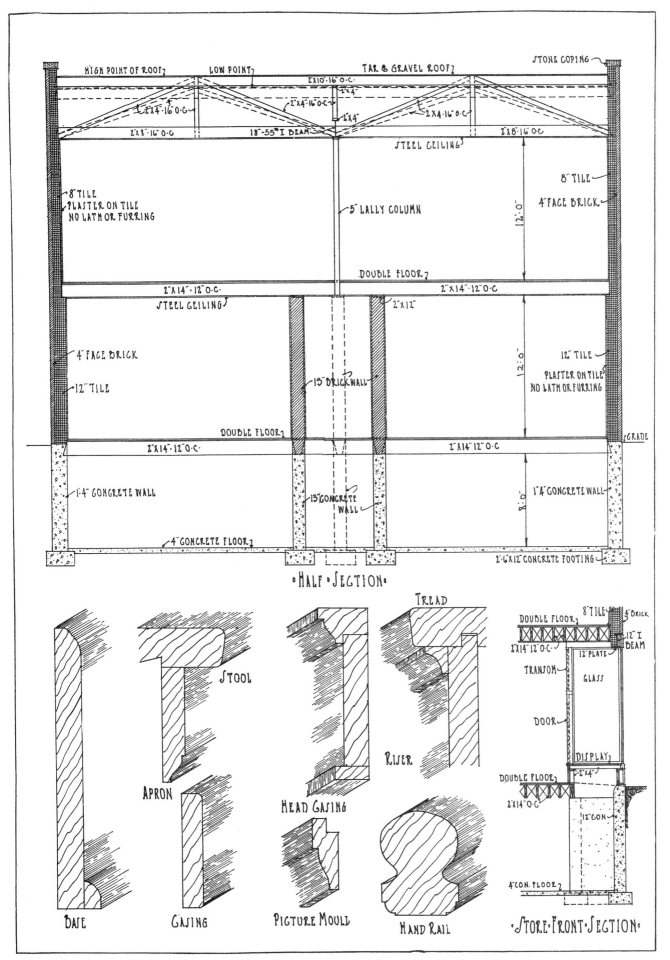

HIGH POINT OF ROOF LOW POINT TAR & GRAVEL ROOF STONE COPING
2"X10"-16" O.C.
2"X4"
2"X14"-16"O.C. 2"X4"-16"O.C. 2"X4" 2"X4"-16"O.C.
2"X8"-16" O.C. 18"-55# I BEAM 2"X8"-16" O.C.
STEEL CEILING
8" TILE 8" TILE
PLASTER ON TILE 4" FACE BRICK
NO LATH OR FURRING
5" LALLY COLUMN 12'-0"
DOUBLE FLOOR
2"X14"-12" O.C. 2"X14"-12" O.C.
STEEL CEILING 2"X12"
4" FACE BRICK 12"-0"
12" TILE 12" TILE
15" BRICK WALL PLASTER ON TILE
NO LATH OR FURRING
DOUBLE FLOOR
2"X14"-12" O.C. 2"X14"-12" O.C. GRADE
1'-4" CONCRETE WALL 1'4" CONCRETE WALL
13" CONCRETE 8'-0"
WALL
4" CONCRETE FLOOR 2'-6"X12" CONCRETE FOOTING

·HALF·SECTION·

TREAD
STOOL
RISER
APRON
HEAD CASING
BASE CASING PICTURE MOULD HAND RAIL

DOUBLE FLOOR 8" TILE 4"BRICK
2"X14"-12"O.C. 12" I BEAM
TRANSOM 12" PLATE
GLASS
DOOR
DISPLAY
DOUBLE FLOOR 2"X4"
2"X14"-O.C.
12" CON.
4"CON. FLOOR
·STORE·FRONT·SECTION·

Details of Construction and Finish of Stores with Lodge Hall Above.

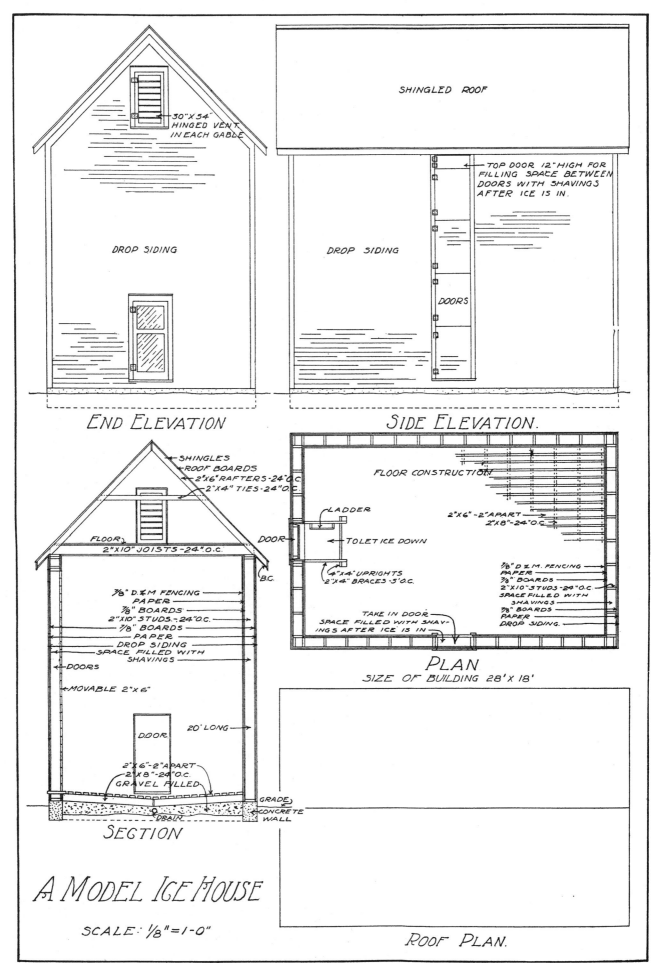

END ELEVATION

SIDE ELEVATION.

SHINGLED ROOF

DROP SIDING

30"X 54"
HINGED VENT
IN EACH GABLE

DROP SIDING

TOP DOOR 12" HIGH FOR
FILLING SPACE BETWEEN
DOORS WITH SHAVINGS
AFTER ICE IS IN.

DOORS

SHINGLES
ROOF BOARDS
2"X6" RAFTERS-24"O.C.
2"X4" TIES-24"O.C.

FLOOR
2"X10" JOISTS-24".O.C.

B.C.

7/8" D.&M. FENCING
PAPER
7/8" BOARDS
2"X10" STUDS.-24"O.C.
7/8" BOARDS
PAPER
DROP SIDING
SPACE FILLED WITH
SHAVINGS
DOORS

MOVABLE 2"X6"

20' LONG

DOOR

2"X6"-2" APART
2"X8"-24"O.C.
GRAVEL FILLED

GRADE
CONCRETE
WALL
DRAIN

SECTION

FLOOR CONSTRUCTION

LADDER

TO LET ICE DOWN

2"X6"-2"APART
2"X8"-24"O.C.

DOOR

4"X4"UPRIGHTS
2"X4" BRACES-5'O.C.

7/8" D.&M. FENCING
PAPER
7/8" BOARDS
2"X10"STUDS-24"O.C.
SPACE FILLED WITH
SHAVINGS
7/8" BOARDS
PAPER
DROP SIDING.

TAKE IN DOOR
SPACE FILLED WITH SHAV-
INGS AFTER ICE IS IN

PLAN
SIZE OF BUILDING 28' X 18'

A MODEL ICE HOUSE

SCALE: 1/8"=1-0"

ROOF PLAN.

Design and Arrangement for Model Ice House.

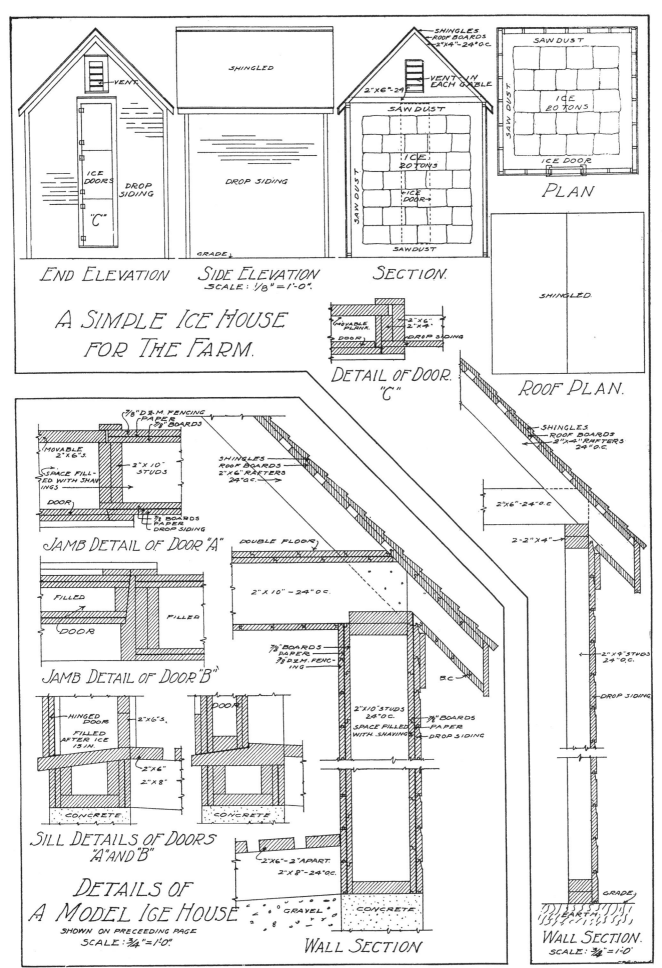

END ELEVATION

SIDE ELEVATION
SCALE: 1/8" = 1'-0".

SECTION.

A SIMPLE ICE HOUSE FOR THE FARM.

DETAIL OF DOOR. "C"

PLAN

ROOF PLAN.

JAMB DETAIL OF DOOR "A"

JAMB DETAIL OF DOOR "B"

SILL DETAILS OF DOORS "A" AND "B"

DETAILS OF A MODEL ICE HOUSE
SHOWN ON PRECEEDING PAGE
SCALE: 3/4" = 1'-0".

WALL SECTION

WALL SECTION.
SCALE: 3/4" = 1'-0"

Design and Details of Simple Farm Ice House.

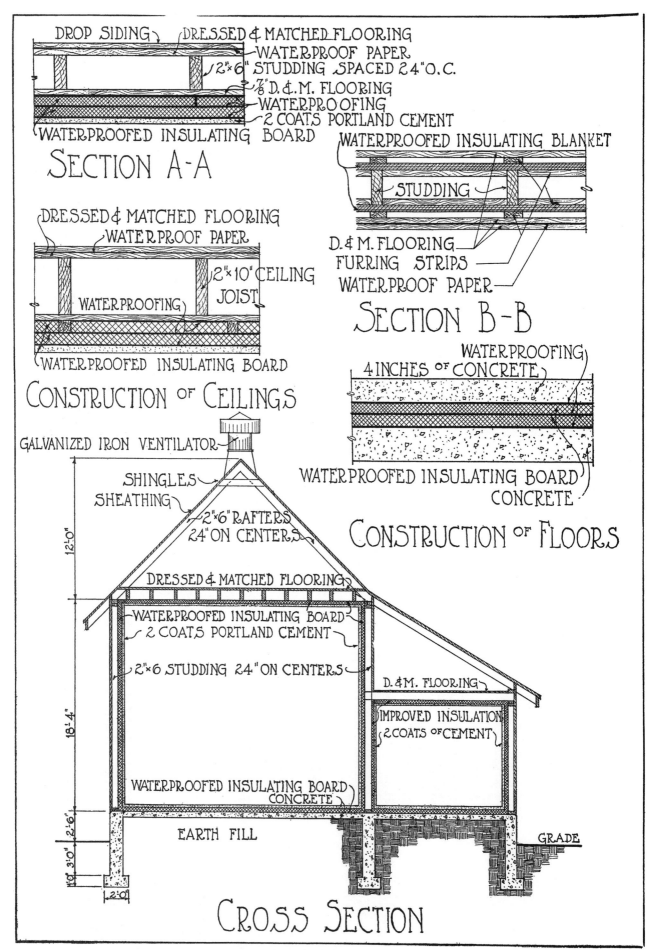

DROP SIDING — DRESSED & MATCHED FLOORING
WATERPROOF PAPER
2"×6" STUDDING SPACED 24" O.C.
⅞" D. & M. FLOORING
WATERPROOFING
2 COATS PORTLAND CEMENT
WATERPROOFED INSULATING BOARD

SECTION A-A

DRESSED & MATCHED FLOORING
WATERPROOF PAPER
2"×10" CEILING JOIST
WATERPROOFING
WATERPROOFED INSULATING BOARD

CONSTRUCTION OF CEILINGS

WATERPROOFED INSULATING BLANKET
STUDDING

D. & M. FLOORING
FURRING STRIPS
WATERPROOF PAPER

SECTION B-B

WATERPROOFING
4 INCHES OF CONCRETE

WATERPROOFED INSULATING BOARD
CONCRETE

CONSTRUCTION OF FLOORS

GALVANIZED IRON VENTILATOR
SHINGLES
SHEATHING
2"×6" RAFTERS 24" ON CENTERS
DRESSED & MATCHED FLOORING
WATERPROOFED INSULATING BOARD
2 COATS PORTLAND CEMENT
2"×6 STUDDING 24" ON CENTERS
D. & M. FLOORING
IMPROVED INSULATION
2 COATS OF CEMENT
WATERPROOFED INSULATING BOARD
CONCRETE
EARTH FILL
GRADE

12'-0"
18'-4"
2'-6"
3'-0"
2'-0"

CROSS SECTION

Details of Construction of Community Cold Storage Plant and Ice House, Showing Special Insulation.

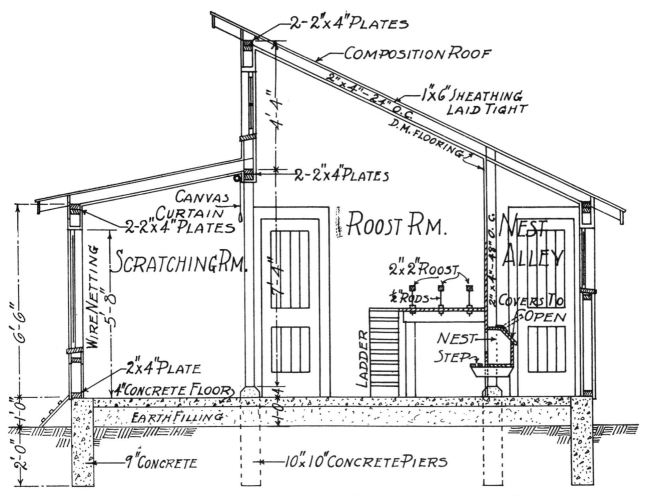

CROSS SECTION OF POULTRY HOUSE

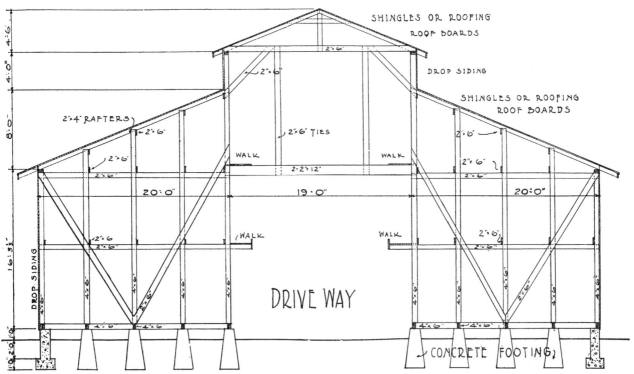

Cross-Section of Lumber Yard Shed, Showing Approved Method of Construction.

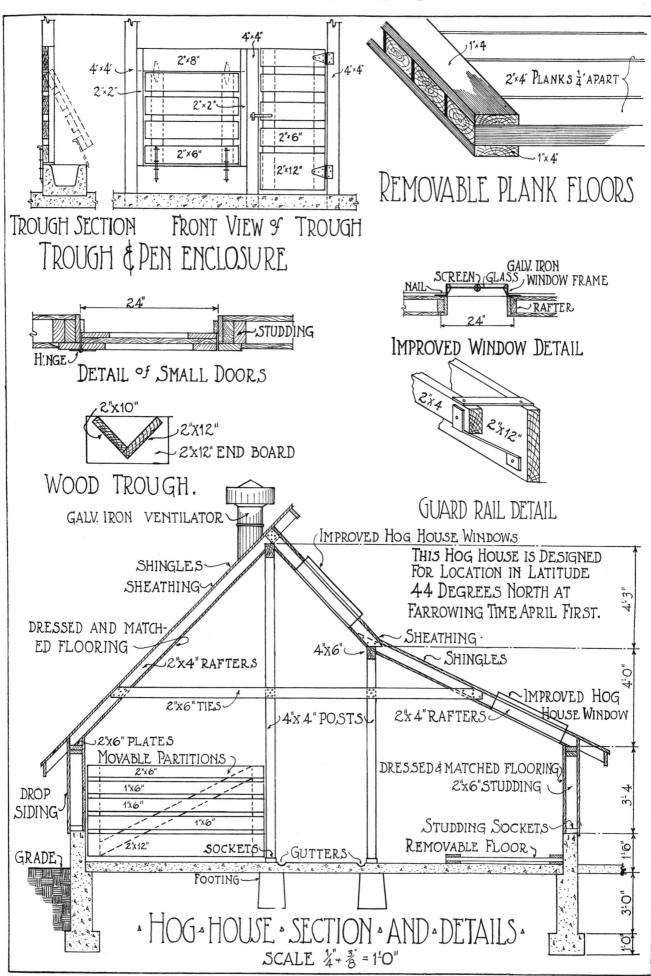

REMOVABLE PLANK FLOORS

TROUGH SECTION   FRONT VIEW OF TROUGH

TROUGH & PEN ENCLOSURE

DETAIL OF SMALL DOORS

IMPROVED WINDOW DETAIL

WOOD TROUGH.

GUARD RAIL DETAIL

THIS HOG HOUSE IS DESIGNED FOR LOCATION IN LATITUDE 44 DEGREES NORTH AT FARROWING TIME APRIL FIRST.

HOG·HOUSE·SECTION·AND·DETAILS

SCALE ¼" + ⅜" = 1'0"

Details of Winter Hog House of Modified Saw-Tooth Roof Type. Face This Building Toward the South, and It Will be Warm and Well Lighted All Winter.

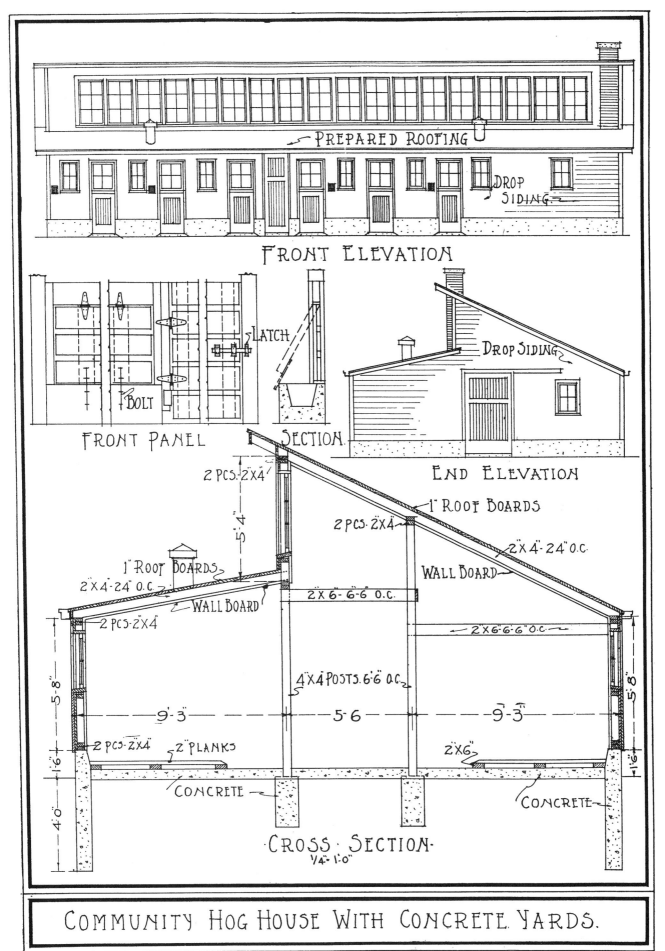

PREPARED ROOFING

DROP SIDING

FRONT ELEVATION

LATCH

BOLT

FRONT PANEL

SECTION

DROP SIDING

END ELEVATION

2 PCS. 2 X 4

5'-4"

1" ROOF BOARDS

2 PCS. 2 X 4

2" X 4" - 24" O.C.

WALL BOARD

1" ROOF BOARDS

2" X 4" - 24" O.C.

WALL BOARD

2 X 6 - 6'-6 O.C.

2" X 6 - 6'-6" O.C.

2 PCS. 2 X 4

4" X 4" POSTS. 6'-6 O.C.

5'-8"

5'-8"

9'-3"

5'-6"

9'-3"

1'-6"

1'-6"

2 PCS. 2 X 4

2" PLANKS

2" X 6"

4'-0"

CONCRETE

CONCRETE

CROSS SECTION
1/4 = 1'-0"

COMMUNITY HOG HOUSE WITH CONCRETE YARDS.

Working Drawings of Community Hog House Design. Elevations Drawn to Scale ⅛ Inch Equals One Foot. Cross Section Detail, ¼ Inch Equals One Foot.

Bank Building and Lodge Hall

SINCE the building which is to contain a banking business and lodge hall is sure to become the center of business and social activities among the men in the community in which it is erected such a building should be somewhat out of the class of commonplace structures. Good substantial construction to which is added the necessary artistic treatment required to place it in somewhat of a class by itself are the most important of the several factors to be considered in the design of such a building. The finish of the exterior may be made very impressive by the use of ornamental face brick with terra cotta trim. The use of these materials has come to be standard in city construction and there is nothing which impresses the stranger with the progressiveness of a town more than to see the business section being built up with structures in which these modern materials are used.

The building illustrated here occupies a corner lot and is 30 by 50 feet. The entire first floor is designed as a bank and the second floor is taken up by the lodge hall. The ornamental front is placed on the 30-foot side of the building. The portions of the front wall above the first floor windows and between the sets of second floor windows are finished with face brick while the entrance, columns and entablature are built of terra cotta. The small-paned windows add a great deal to the distinctive appearance of the building. There is a sufficiently elaborate treatment given all of the details to mark this building as one of importance among the various structures along the street upon which it would be placed.

The heavy brass trimmed door of the bank opens into a small vestibule in which there are entrance and exit doors connecting with the main corridor. At the right upon enter-

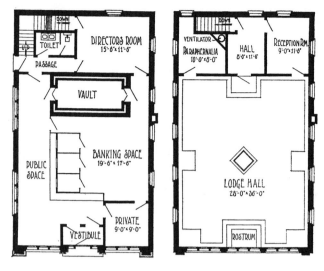

First Floor Plan.   Second Floor Plan.

Arrangement of Bank Building.

ing is a private office having doors both into the public square and into the banking space. Three cages are placed facing the side wall of the building and bounding the main corridor near the front of the bank. These cages are built up of wood panels from the floor to the counter, which extends from the private office along the side of the first cage and along the front of the three cages down the corridor. Above the counter there is a bronze grillwork on the outside of the cages and steel lattice partitions are used between cages.

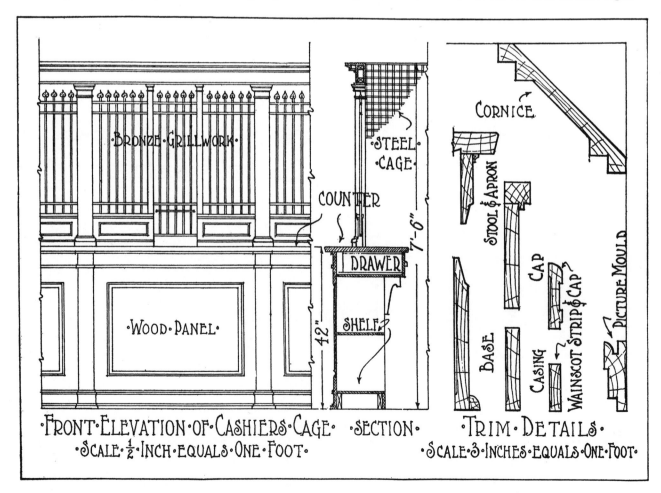

Front Elevation of Cashier's Cage and Trim Details in Bank Building.

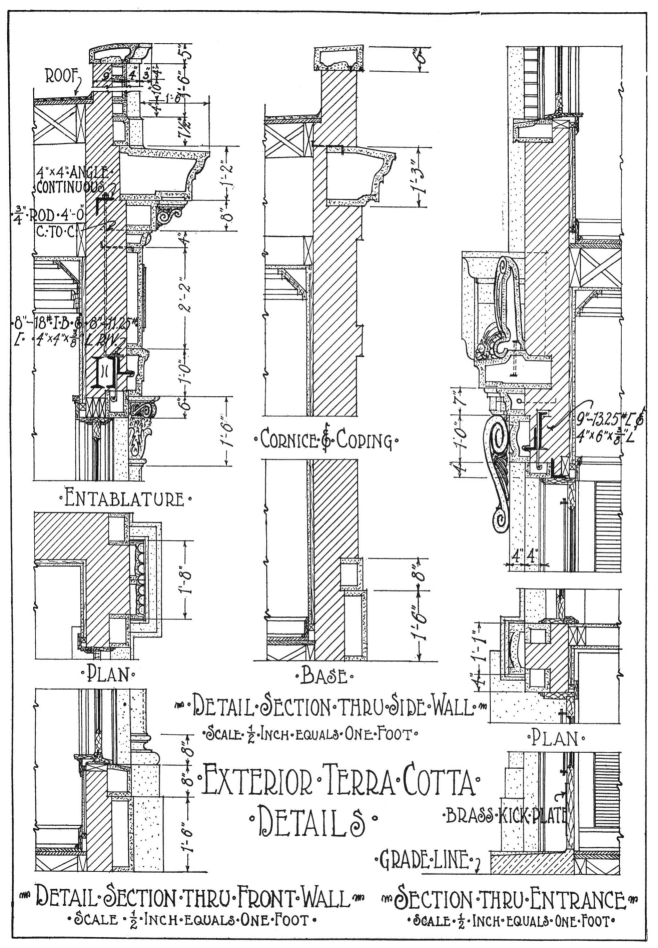

ROOF

4"×4" ANGLE
CONTINUOUS

3/4" ROD 4'-0"
C. TO C.

8"-18# I.B.6. 8"-11.25#
L. 4"×4"×3/8" L RIV.

· ENTABLATURE ·

· PLAN ·

· CORNICE & COPING ·

· BASE ·

∿ DETAIL · SECTION · THRU · SIDE · WALL ∿
· SCALE · ½ · INCH · EQUALS · ONE · FOOT ·

EXTERIOR · TERRA · COTTA
· DETAILS ·

· PLAN ·

9"-13.25# L
4"×6"×3/8" L

· BRASS · KICK · PLATE ·

· GRADE · LINE ·

∿ DETAIL · SECTION · THRU · FRONT · WALL ∿
· SCALE · ½ · INCH · EQUALS · ONE · FOOT ·

∿ SECTION · THRU · ENTRANCE ∿
· SCALE · ½ · INCH · EQUALS · ONE · FOOT ·

Details of Terra Cotta Ornamentation on Exterior of Bank Building.

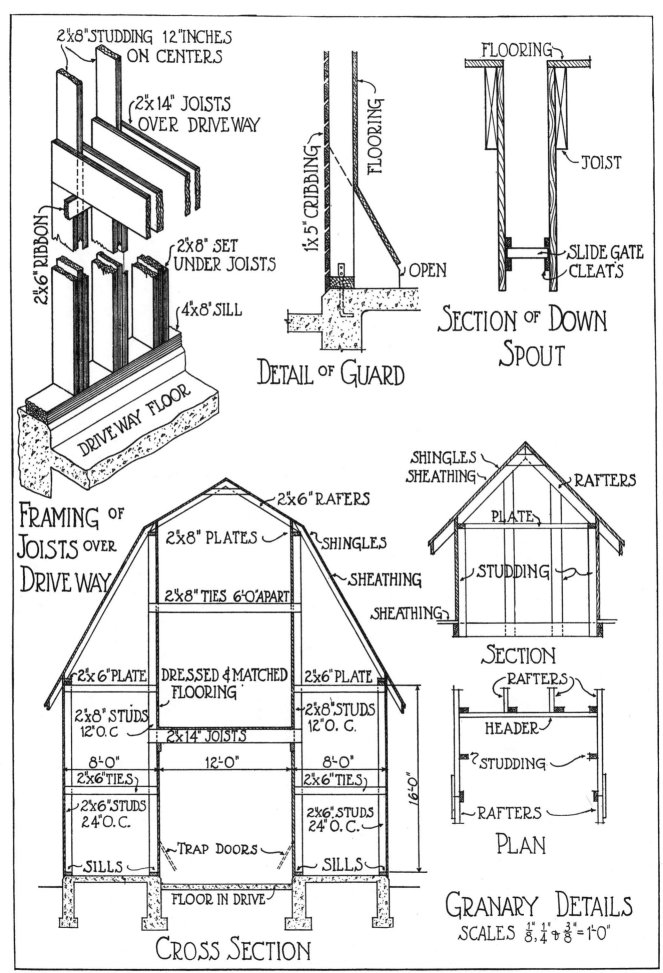

2"x8" STUDDING 12"INCHES ON CENTERS

2"x14" JOISTS OVER DRIVEWAY

2"x6" RIBBON

2"x8" SET UNDER JOISTS

4"x8" SILL

DRIVE WAY FLOOR

FRAMING OF JOISTS OVER DRIVE WAY

1"x5" CRIBBING

FLOORING

OPEN

DETAIL OF GUARD

FLOORING

FLOORING

JOIST

SLIDE GATE CLEATS

SECTION OF DOWN SPOUT

SHINGLES
SHEATHING

RAFTERS

PLATE

STUDDING

SHEATHING

SECTION

RAFTERS

HEADER

STUDDING

RAFTERS

PLAN

2"x6" RAFERS

2"x8" PLATES

SHINGLES

SHEATHING

2"x8" TIES 6'-0" APART

2"x6" PLATE

DRESSED & MATCHED FLOORING

2"x6" PLATE

2"x8" STUDS 12"O.C

2"x8" STUDS 12"O.C.

2"x14" JOISTS

8'-0"   12'-0"   8'-0"

2"x6" TIES

2"x6" TIES

16'-0"

2"x6" STUDS 24"O.C.

2"x6" STUDS 24"O.C.

TRAP DOORS

SILLS

SILLS

FLOOR IN DRIVE

CROSS SECTION

GRANARY DETAILS
SCALES $\frac{1}{8}$, $\frac{1}{4}$ & $\frac{3}{8}$" = 1'-0"

Construction Details of Two-Story Gambrel Roof Corn Crib and Granary.

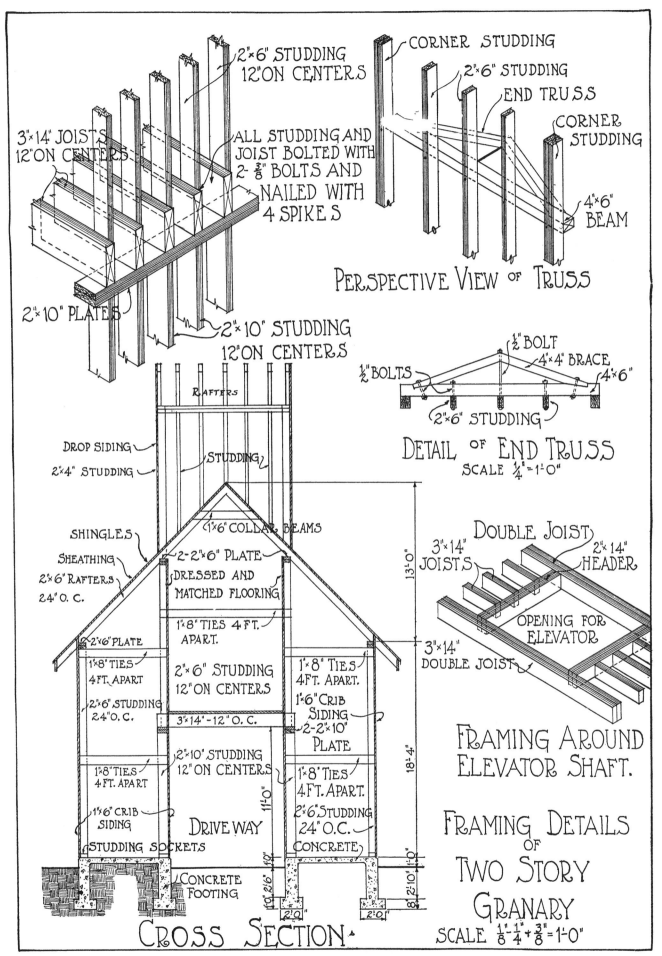

2"×6" STUDDING 12" ON CENTERS

CORNER STUDDING

2"×6" STUDDING

END TRUSS

CORNER STUDDING

3"×14" JOISTS 12" ON CENTERS

ALL STUDDING AND JOIST BOLTED WITH 2-⅜" BOLTS AND NAILED WITH 4 SPIKES

4"×6" BEAM

2"×10" PLATES

2"×10" STUDDING 12" ON CENTERS

PERSPECTIVE VIEW OF TRUSS

½" BOLT
4"×4" BRACE
4"×6"
½" BOLTS
2"×6" STUDDING

DETAIL OF END TRUSS
SCALE ¼" = 1'-0"

RAFTERS

DROP SIDING
2"×4" STUDDING

STUDDING

SHINGLES
SHEATHING
2"×6" RAFTERS
24" O.C.

1"×6" COLLAR BEAMS
2-2"×6" PLATE
DRESSED AND MATCHED FLOORING

1"×8" TIES 4 FT. APART.

2"×6" PLATE

1"×8" TIES 4 FT. APART

2"×6" STUDDING 24" O.C.

2"×6" STUDDING 12" ON CENTERS

1"×8" TIES 4 FT. APART.

1"×6" CRIB SIDING
2-2"×10" PLATE

3"×14"-12" O.C.

2"×10" STUDDING 12" ON CENTERS

1"×8" TIES 4 FT. APART

1"×8" TIES 4 FT. APART.

1"×6" CRIB SIDING

DRIVEWAY

STUDDING SOCKETS

2"×6" STUDDING 24" O.C.

CONCRETE

CONCRETE FOOTING

13'-0"

18'-4"

11'-0"

8' 2'10" 1'-0"

1'-0" 2'6" 4'0"

2'-0"

2'-0"

CROSS SECTION

DOUBLE JOIST
3"×14" JOISTS
2"×14" HEADER

OPENING FOR ELEVATOR

3"×14" DOUBLE JOIST

FRAMING AROUND ELEVATOR SHAFT.

FRAMING DETAILS OF TWO STORY GRANARY
SCALE ⅛" - ¼" + ⅜" = 1'-0"

Details of Construction of Two-Story Gable Roof Combined Corn Crib and Granary.

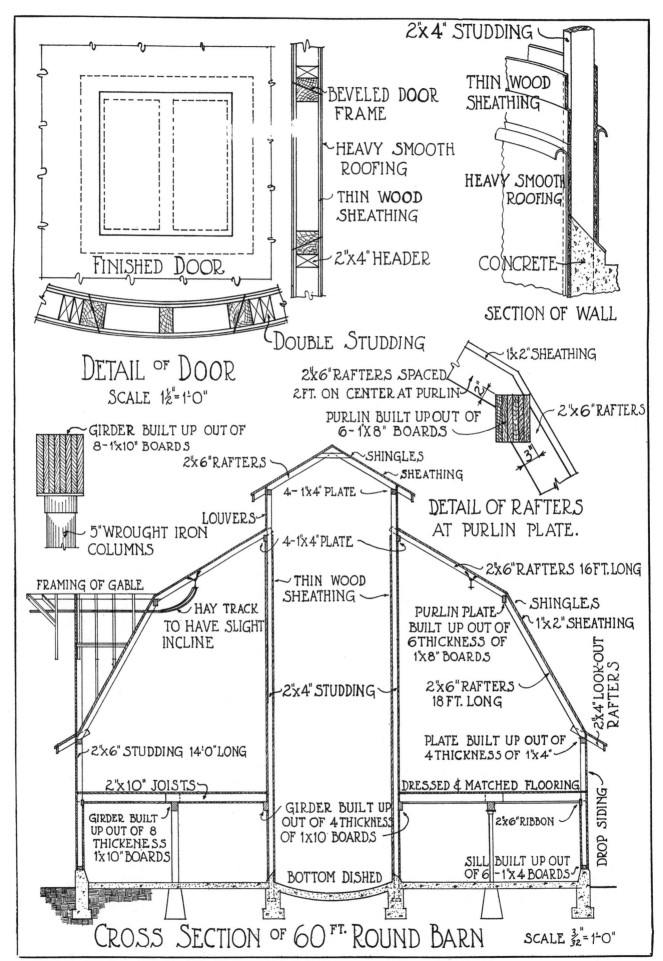

FINISHED DOOR

BEVELED DOOR FRAME

HEAVY SMOOTH ROOFING

THIN WOOD SHEATHING

2"x4" HEADER

2"x4" STUDDING

THIN WOOD SHEATHING

HEAVY SMOOTH ROOFING

CONCRETE

SECTION OF WALL

DETAIL OF DOOR
SCALE 1½"=1'0"

DOUBLE STUDDING

2"x6" RAFTERS SPACED 2 FT. ON CENTER AT PURLIN

PURLIN BUILT UP OUT OF 6-1"x8" BOARDS

1"x2" SHEATHING

2"x6" RAFTERS

GIRDER BUILT UP OUT OF 8-1"x10" BOARDS

2"x6" RAFTERS

4- 1"x4" PLATE

SHINGLES

SHEATHING

DETAIL OF RAFTERS AT PURLIN PLATE.

LOUVERS

4- 1"x4" PLATE

5" WROUGHT IRON COLUMNS

FRAMING OF GABLE

HAY TRACK TO HAVE SLIGHT INCLINE

THIN WOOD SHEATHING

2"x6" RAFTERS 16 FT. LONG

SHINGLES
1"x2" SHEATHING

PURLIN PLATE BUILT UP OUT OF 6 THICKNESS OF 1"x8" BOARDS

2"x4" STUDDING

2"x6" RAFTERS 18 FT. LONG

2"x4" LOOK-OUT RAFTERS

PLATE BUILT UP OUT OF 4 THICKNESS OF 1"x4"

2"x6" STUDDING 14'0" LONG

2"x10" JOISTS

DRESSED & MATCHED FLOORING

GIRDER BUILT UP OUT OF 8 THICKENESS 1"x10" BOARDS

GIRDER BUILT UP OUT OF 4 THICKNESS OF 1"x10" BOARDS

2"x6" RIBBON

DROP SIDING

SILL BUILT UP OUT OF 6 -1"x4" BOARDS

BOTTOM DISHED

CROSS SECTION OF 60 FT. ROUND BARN

SCALE 3/32"=1'0"

Details of Construction of 60-Foot Diameter Barn with Central Silo.

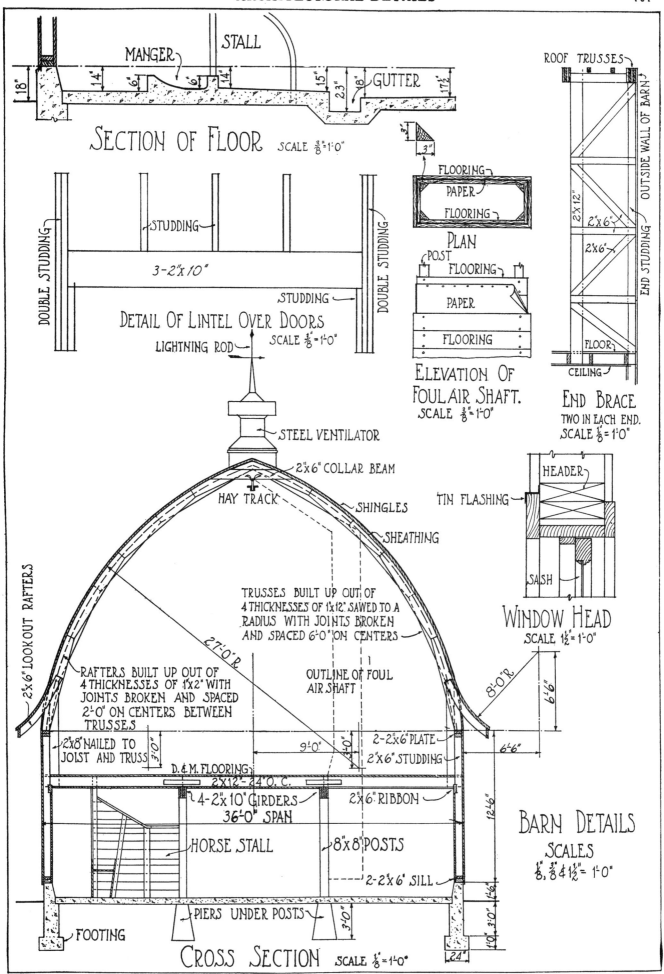

SECTION OF FLOOR SCALE ⅜"=1'0"

MANGER STALL GUTTER

DOUBLE STUDDING STUDDING 3-2"x10" STUDDING DOUBLE STUDDING

DETAIL OF LINTEL OVER DOORS SCALE ⅜"=1'0"

FLOORING PAPER FLOORING
PLAN

POST FLOORING PAPER FLOORING
ELEVATION OF FOUL AIR SHAFT. SCALE ⅜"=1'0"

ROOF TRUSSES OUTSIDE WALL OF BARN
2"x12" 2"x6" 2"x6" END STUDDING FLOOR CEILING
END BRACE TWO IN EACH END. SCALE ⅛"=1'0"

HEADER TIN FLASHING SASH
WINDOW HEAD SCALE 1½"=1'0"

LIGHTNING ROD
STEEL VENTILATOR
2"x6" COLLAR BEAM
HAY TRACK
SHINGLES
SHEATHING

2"x6" LOOKOUT RAFTERS

TRUSSES BUILT UP OUT OF 4 THICKNESSES OF 1"x12" SAWED TO A RADIUS WITH JOINTS BROKEN AND SPACED 6'-0" ON CENTERS

27'-0" R

OUTLINE OF FOUL AIR SHAFT

8'-0" R
6'-6"

RAFTERS BUILT UP OUT OF 4 THICKNESSES OF 1"x2" WITH JOINTS BROKEN AND SPACED 2'-0" ON CENTERS BETWEEN TRUSSES

2"x8" NAILED TO JOIST AND TRUSS
3'-0"
D. & M. FLOORING
2"x12"-24"O.C.
9'-0"
3'-0"
2-2"x6" PLATE
2"x6" STUDDING
6'-6"

4-2"x10" GIRDERS 36'-0" SPAN
HORSE STALL
2"x6" RIBBON
8"x8" POSTS
2-2"x6" SILL
12'-6"

BARN DETAILS
SCALES
⅛", ⅜" & 1½" = 1'-0"

PIERS UNDER POSTS
3'-0"
1'-0" 3'-0"
24"
FOOTING

CROSS SECTION SCALE ⅛"=1'0"

Details of Gothic or Curving Roof Barn.

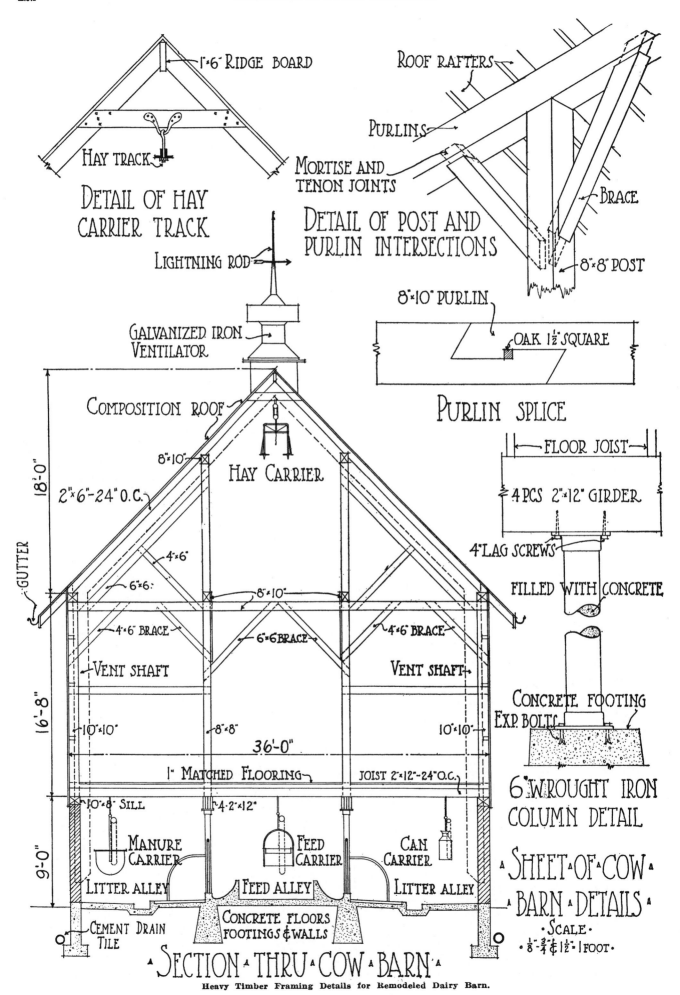

1"×6" RIDGE BOARD

HAY TRACK

DETAIL OF HAY CARRIER TRACK

ROOF RAFTERS

PURLINS

MORTISE AND TENON JOINTS

DETAIL OF POST AND PURLIN INTERSECTIONS

BRACE

8"×8" POST

8"×10" PURLIN

OAK 1½" SQUARE

PURLIN SPLICE

LIGHTNING ROD

GALVANIZED IRON VENTILATOR

COMPOSITION ROOF

HAY CARRIER

8"×10"

2"×6"-24" O.C.

GUTTER

18'-0"

4"×6"

6"×6"

8"×10"

4"×6" BRACE

6"×6" BRACE

4"×6" BRACE

VENT SHAFT

VENT SHAFT

16'-8"

10"×10"

8"×8"

10"×10"

36'-0"

1" MATCHED FLOORING

JOIST 2"×12"-24" O.C.

10"×8" SILL

4-2"×12"

9'-0"

MANURE CARRIER

FEED CARRIER

CAN CARRIER

LITTER ALLEY

FEED ALLEY

LITTER ALLEY

CEMENT DRAIN TILE

CONCRETE FLOORS FOOTINGS & WALLS

SECTION THRU COW BARN

Heavy Timber Framing Details for Remodeled Dairy Barn.

FLOOR JOIST

4 PCS 2"×12" GIRDER

4" LAG SCREWS

FILLED WITH CONCRETE

CONCRETE FOOTING

EXP. BOLTS

6" WROUGHT IRON COLUMN DETAIL

SHEET OF COW BARN DETAILS

SCALE
⅛" - ¾" & 1½" - 1 FOOT

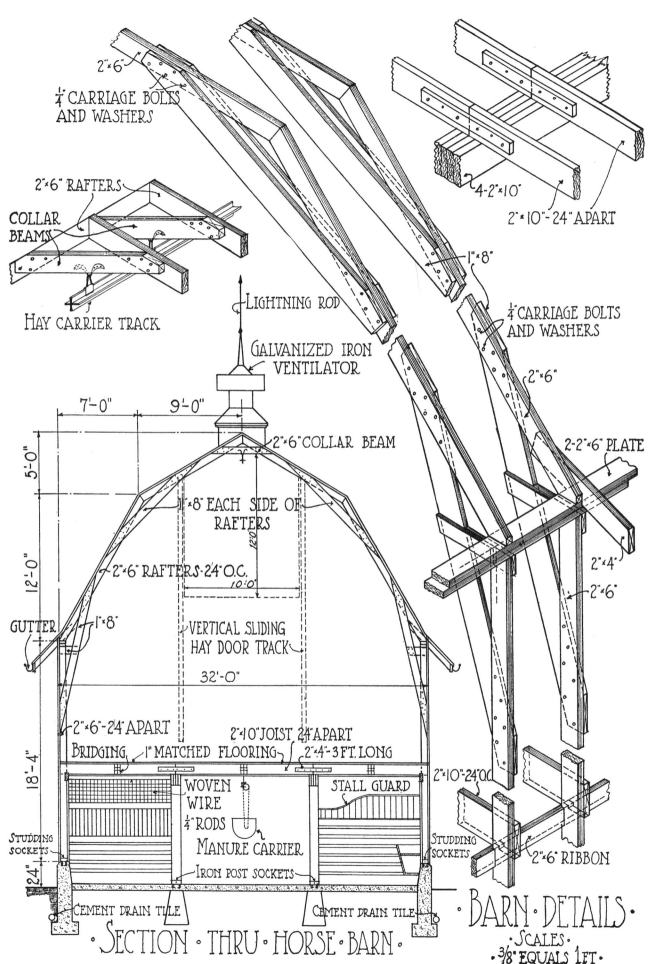

2"×6"

¼" CARRIAGE BOLTS AND WASHERS

2"×6" RAFTERS

COLLAR BEAMS

HAY CARRIER TRACK

4-2"×10"

2"×10"-24" APART

1"×8"

¼" CARRIAGE BOLTS AND WASHERS

2"×6"

2-2"×6" PLATE

2"×4"

2"×6"

LIGHTNING ROD

GALVANIZED IRON VENTILATOR

7'-0"   9'-0"

5'-0"

2"×6" COLLAR BEAM

1"×8" EACH SIDE OF RAFTERS

120"

2"×6" RAFTERS-24" O.C.

10'-0"

12'-0"

VERTICAL SLIDING HAY DOOR TRACK

32'-0"

GUTTER   1"×8"

2"×6"-24" APART

BRIDGING   1" MATCHED FLOORING

2"×10" JOIST 24" APART

2"×4"-3 FT. LONG

2"×10"-24" O.C.

18'-4"

WOVEN WIRE ¼" RODS

STALL GUARD

MANURE CARRIER

STUDDING SOCKETS

IRON POST SOCKETS

STUDDING SOCKETS

2"×6" RIBBON

24"

CEMENT DRAIN TILE

CEMENT DRAIN TILE

·SECTION·THRU·HORSE·BARN·

·BARN·DETAILS·
·SCALES·
·⅜" EQUALS 1 FT·

Details of Horse Barn. Roof Is Self-Supporting Plank Frame Construction of the Type Where Every Rafter Forms a Truss. Rafters Spaced on 24-Inch Centers.

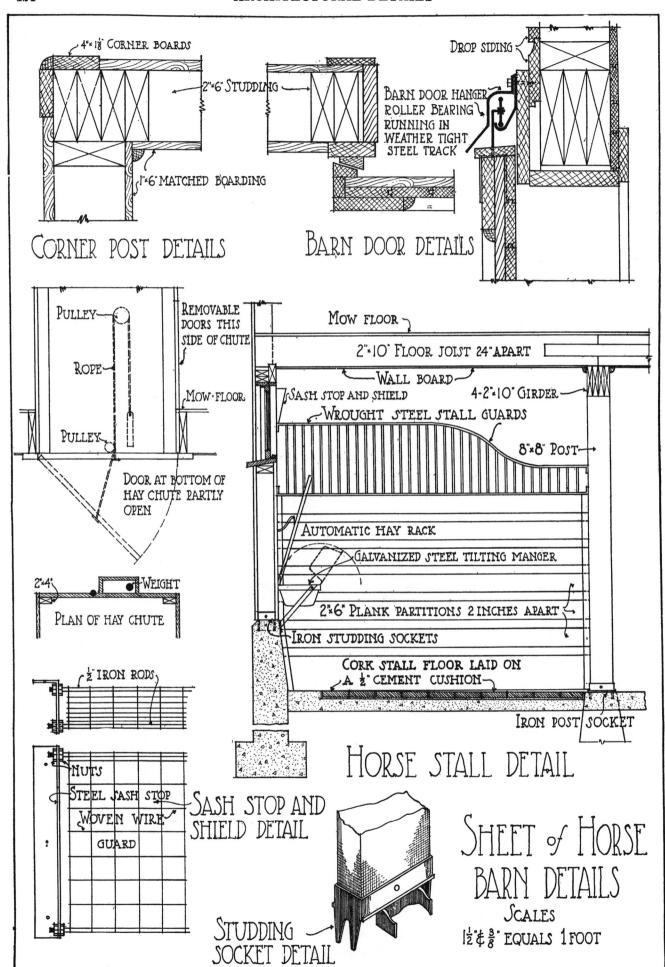

4"×1⅞" CORNER BOARDS

2"×6" STUDDING

1"×6" MATCHED BOARDING

CORNER POST DETAILS

DROP SIDING

BARN DOOR HANGER ROLLER BEARING RUNNING IN WEATHER TIGHT STEEL TRACK

BARN DOOR DETAILS

PULLEY

ROPE

PULLEY

REMOVABLE DOORS THIS SIDE OF CHUTE

MOW FLOOR

DOOR AT BOTTOM OF HAY CHUTE PARTLY OPEN

MOW FLOOR

2"×10" FLOOR JOIST 24" APART

WALL BOARD

4-2"×10" GIRDER

SASH STOP AND SHIELD

WROUGHT STEEL STALL GUARDS

8"×8" POST

AUTOMATIC HAY RACK

GALVANIZED STEEL TILTING MANGER

2"×6" PLANK PARTITIONS 2 INCHES APART

2"×4"   WEIGHT

PLAN OF HAY CHUTE

IRON STUDDING SOCKETS

CORK STALL FLOOR LAID ON A ½" CEMENT CUSHION

IRON POST SOCKET

HORSE STALL DETAIL

½" IRON RODS

NUTS

STEEL SASH STOP

WOVEN WIRE

GUARD

SASH STOP AND SHIELD DETAIL

STUDDING SOCKET DETAIL

SHEET of HORSE BARN DETAILS

SCALES
1½" & ⅜" EQUALS 1 FOOT

Working Details of Construction and Special Equipment for Horse Barn.

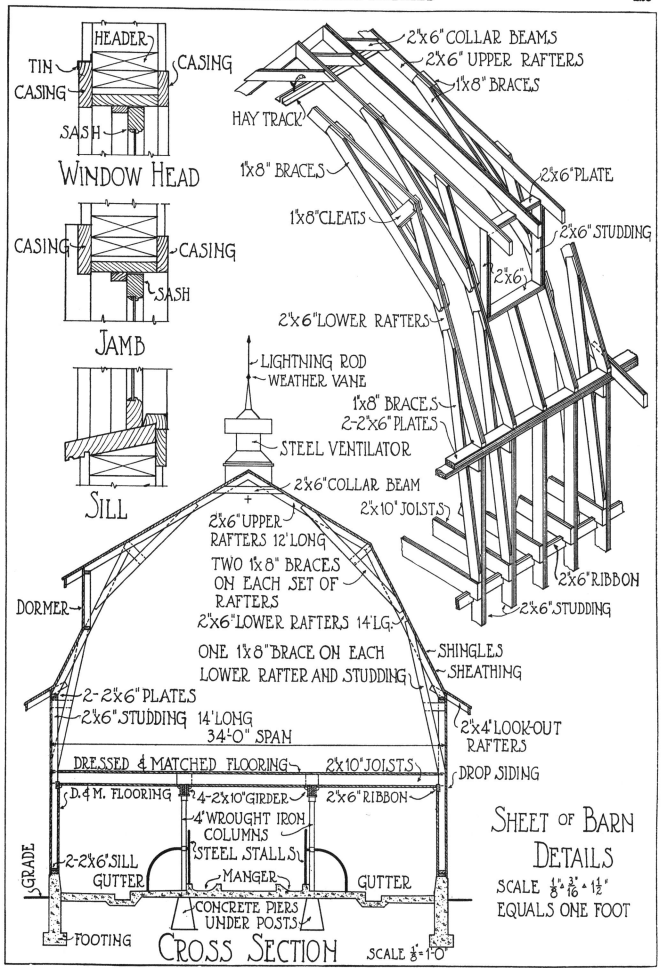

WINDOW HEAD

HEADER

TIN
CASING
CASING
SASH

JAMB

CASING
CASING
SASH

SILL

2"x6" COLLAR BEAMS
2"x6" UPPER RAFTERS
1"x8" BRACES
HAY TRACK
1"x8" BRACES
2"x6" PLATE
1"x8" CLEATS
2"x6" STUDDING
2"x6"
2"x6" LOWER RAFTERS
1"x8" BRACES
2-2"x6" PLATES
2"x10" JOISTS
2"x6" RIBBON
2"x6" STUDDING

LIGHTNING ROD
WEATHER VANE
STEEL VENTILATOR
2"x6" COLLAR BEAM
2"x6" UPPER
RAFTERS 12' LONG
TWO 1"x8" BRACES
ON EACH SET OF
RAFTERS
2"x6" LOWER RAFTERS 14' LG.
ONE 1"x8" BRACE ON EACH
LOWER RAFTER AND STUDDING

DORMER
SHINGLES
SHEATHING
2-2"x6" PLATES
2"x6" STUDDING 14' LONG
34'-0" SPAN
2"x4" LOOK-OUT
RAFTERS
DRESSED & MATCHED FLOORING
2"x10" JOISTS
DROP SIDING
D. & M. FLOORING
4-2"x10" GIRDER
2"x6" RIBBON
4" WROUGHT IRON
COLUMNS
STEEL STALLS
GRADE
2-2"x6" SILL
GUTTER
MANGER
GUTTER
CONCRETE PIERS
UNDER POSTS
FOOTING

SHEET of BARN
DETAILS
SCALE $\frac{1}{8}" \triangle \frac{3}{16}" \triangle 1\frac{1}{2}"$
EQUALS ONE FOOT

CROSS SECTION   SCALE $\frac{1}{8}" = 1'-0"$

Details of Construction Drawn to Exact Scale of Gambrel Roof Barn with Dormers.

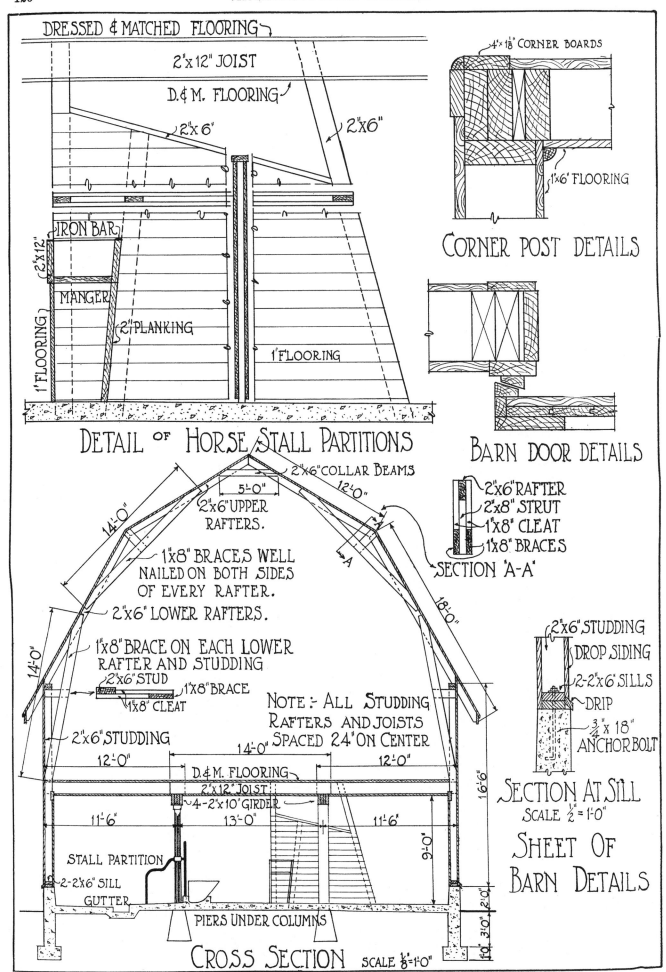

DRESSED & MATCHED FLOORING

2"x 12" JOIST

D. & M. FLOORING

2"x 6"

2"x 6"

IRON BAR

2"x 12"

MANGER

2" PLANKING

1' FLOORING

1' FLOORING

DETAIL OF HORSE STALL PARTITIONS

2"x 6" COLLAR BEAMS

5'-0"

12'-0"

2"x 6" UPPER RAFTERS.

14'-0"

1"x 8" BRACES WELL NAILED ON BOTH SIDES OF EVERY RAFTER.

2"x 6" LOWER RAFTERS.

1"x 8" BRACE ON EACH LOWER RAFTER AND STUDDING

14'-0"

2"x 6" STUD

1"x 8" BRACE

1"x 8" CLEAT

18'-0"

NOTE :- ALL STUDDING RAFTERS AND JOISTS SPACED 24" ON CENTER

2"x 6" STUDDING

12'-0"

14'-0"

12'-0"

D. & M. FLOORING

2"x 12" JOIST

4-2"x 10" GIRDER

16'-6"

11'-6"

13'-0"

11'-6"

9'-0"

STALL PARTITION

2-2"x 6" SILL

GUTTER

PIERS UNDER COLUMNS

2'-0"

3'-0"

1'-0"

CROSS SECTION SCALE ⅛"= 1'-0"

4"x 1⅛" CORNER BOARDS

1"x 6" FLOORING

CORNER POST DETAILS

BARN DOOR DETAILS

2"x 6" RAFTER
2"x 8" STRUT
1"x 8" CLEAT
1"x 8" BRACES

SECTION 'A-A'

A

A

2"x 6" STUDDING

DROP SIDING

2-2"x 6" SILLS

DRIP

¾"x 18" ANCHOR BOLT

SECTION AT SILL SCALE ½"= 1'-0"

SHEET OF BARN DETAILS

Construction Details of Small Farm Barn with Self-Supporting Gambrel Roof.

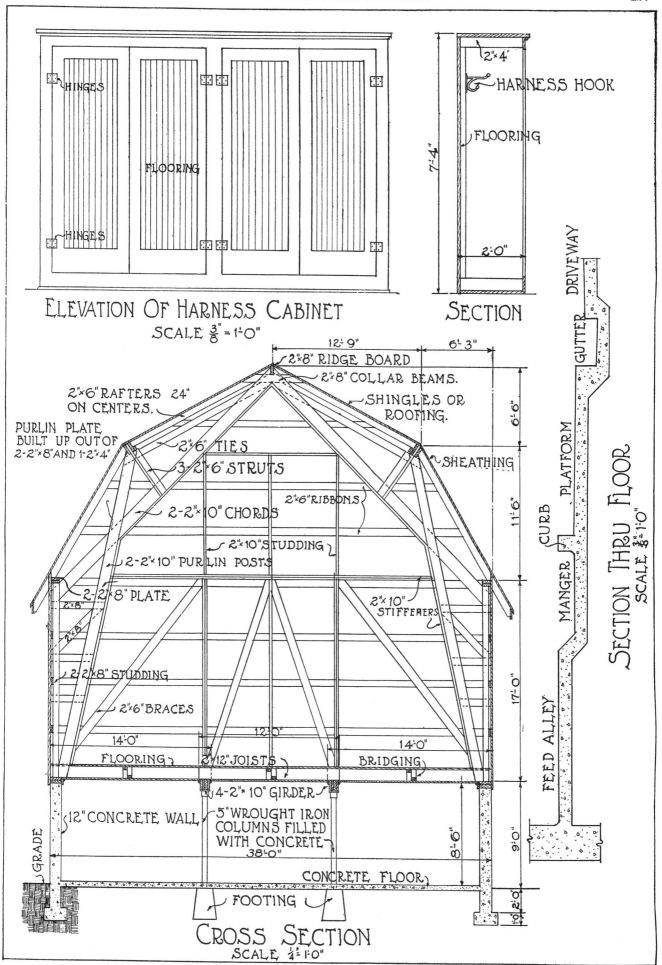

ELEVATION OF HARNESS CABINET
SCALE $\frac{3}{8}$" = 1'-0"

HINGES

FLOORING

HINGES

SECTION

2"×4"

HARNESS HOOK

FLOORING

7'-4"

2'-0"

DRIVEWAY

GUTTER

PLATFORM

CURB

MANGER

FEED ALLEY

SECTION THRU FLOOR
SCALE $\frac{3}{8}$" = 1'-0"

12'-9"   6'-3"

2"×8" RIDGE BOARD
2"×8" COLLAR BEAMS.
SHINGLES OR ROOFING.

2"×6" RAFTERS 24" ON CENTERS.

PURLIN PLATE BUILT UP OUT OF 2-2"×8" AND 1-2"×4"

2"×6" TIES

3-2"×6" STRUTS

SHEATHING

2"×6" RIBBONS

2-2"×10" CHORDS

2"×10" STUDDING

2-2"×10" PURLIN POSTS

2-2"×8" PLATE

2"×8"

2"×8"

2"×10" STIFFENERS

2-2"×8" STUDDING

2"×6" BRACES

6'-6"

11'-6"

17'-0"

14'-0"   12'-0"   14'-0"

FLOORING   2"×12" JOISTS   BRIDGING

4-2"×10" GIRDER

12" CONCRETE WALL   5" WROUGHT IRON COLUMNS FILLED WITH CONCRETE 38'-0"

8'-6"   9'-0"

GRADE

CONCRETE FLOOR

FOOTING

2'-0"

CROSS SECTION
SCALE $\frac{1}{4}$" = 1'-0"

Cross-Section Thru Self-Supporting Gambrel Roof of Barn, Showing Also End Framing. Roof Trusses Are Spaced About 12 Feet Apart.

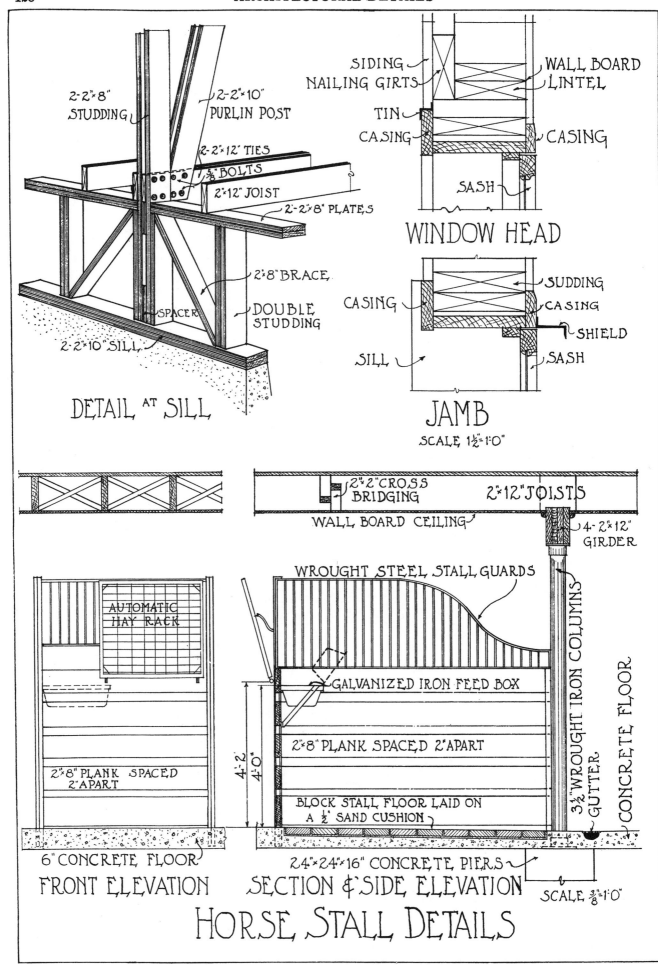

2-2"×8" STUDDING

2-2"×10" PURLIN POST

2-2"×12" TIES

⅜" BOLTS

2"×12" JOIST

2-2"×8" PLATES

2"×8" BRACE

SPACER

DOUBLE STUDDING

2-2"×10" SILL

DETAIL AT SILL

SIDING

NAILING GIRTS

TIN

CASING

WALL BOARD

LINTEL

CASING

SASH

WINDOW HEAD

CASING

SILL

SUDDING

CASING

SHIELD

SASH

JAMB

SCALE 1½"=1'0"

2"×2" CROSS BRIDGING

2"×12" JOISTS

WALL BOARD CEILING

4-2"×12" GIRDER

WROUGHT STEEL STALL GUARDS

3½" WROUGHT IRON COLUMNS

CONCRETE FLOOR

AUTOMATIC HAY RACK

GALVANIZED IRON FEED BOX

2"×8" PLANK SPACED 2" APART

BLOCK STALL FLOOR LAID ON A ½" SAND CUSHION

GUTTER

2"×8" PLANK SPACED 2" APART

4'-2"

4'-0"

6" CONCRETE FLOOR

FRONT ELEVATION

24"×24"×16" CONCRETE PIERS

SECTION & SIDE ELEVATION

SCALE ⅜"=1'0"

HORSE STALL DETAILS

Details of Horse Stable Part of Combination Barn. Note Improved Stall Flooring of Creosoted Blocks Laid on the Concrete. Plank Frame Construction at Sill Also Clearly Shown.

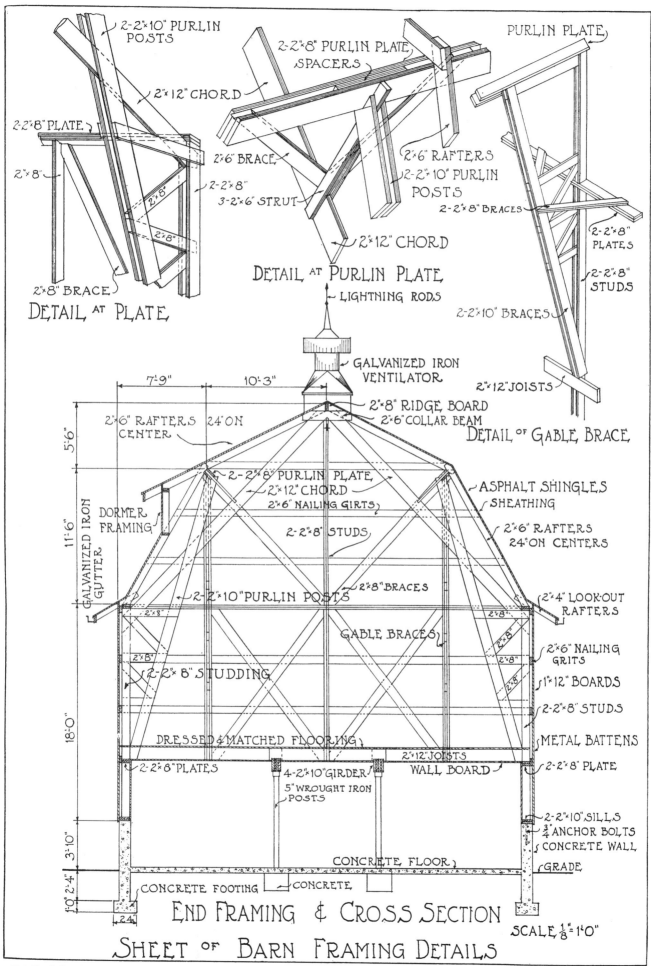

DETAIL AT PLATE

2-2"×10" PURLIN POSTS
2"×12" CHORD
2-2"×8" PLATE
2"×8"
2"×8"
2"×8"
2"×8"
2"×8" BRACE

DETAIL AT PURLIN PLATE
2-2"×8" PURLIN PLATE SPACERS
2"×6" BRACE
2-2"×8"
3-2"×6" STRUT
2"×6" RAFTERS
2-2"×10" PURLIN POSTS
2"×12" CHORD

PURLIN PLATE
2-2"×8" BRACES
2-2"×8" PLATES
2-2"×8" STUDS
2-2"×10" BRACES
2"×12" JOISTS

DETAIL OF GABLE BRACE

LIGHTNING RODS
GALVANIZED IRON VENTILATOR
2"×8" RIDGE BOARD
2"×6" COLLAR BEAM

7'-9"
10'-3"
5'-6"
11'-6"
18'-0"
3'-10"
1'-0" 2'-4"

2"×6" RAFTERS 24" ON CENTER
DORMER FRAMING
GALVANIZED IRON GUTTER
2"×8"
2"×8"
2-2"×10" PURLIN POSTS
2"×8"
2-2"×8" STUDDING

2-2"×8" PURLIN PLATE
2"×12" CHORD
2"×6" NAILING GIRTS
2-2"×8" STUDS
2"×8" BRACES
GABLE BRACES

ASPHALT SHINGLES
SHEATHING
2"×6" RAFTERS 24" ON CENTERS
2"×4" LOOK-OUT RAFTERS
2"×8"
2"×8"
2"×8"
2"×6" NAILING GRITS
1"×12" BOARDS
2-2"×8" STUDS
METAL BATTENS

DRESSED & MATCHED FLOORING
2-2"×8" PLATES
4-2"×10" GIRDER
5" WROUGHT IRON POSTS
2"×12" JOISTS
WALL BOARD
2-2"×8" PLATE

2-2"×10" SILLS
3/4" ANCHOR BOLTS
CONCRETE WALL
GRADE

CONCRETE FLOOR
CONCRETE FOOTING
CONCRETE
24"

END FRAMING & CROSS SECTION
SCALE 1/8" = 1'-0"

SHEET OF BARN FRAMING DETAILS

Detail of Gambrel Roof Horse Barn, Showing End Framing, and Also Intermediate Plank Frame Truss. Sketches Above Show Clearly the Principal Connections in This Type of Truss.

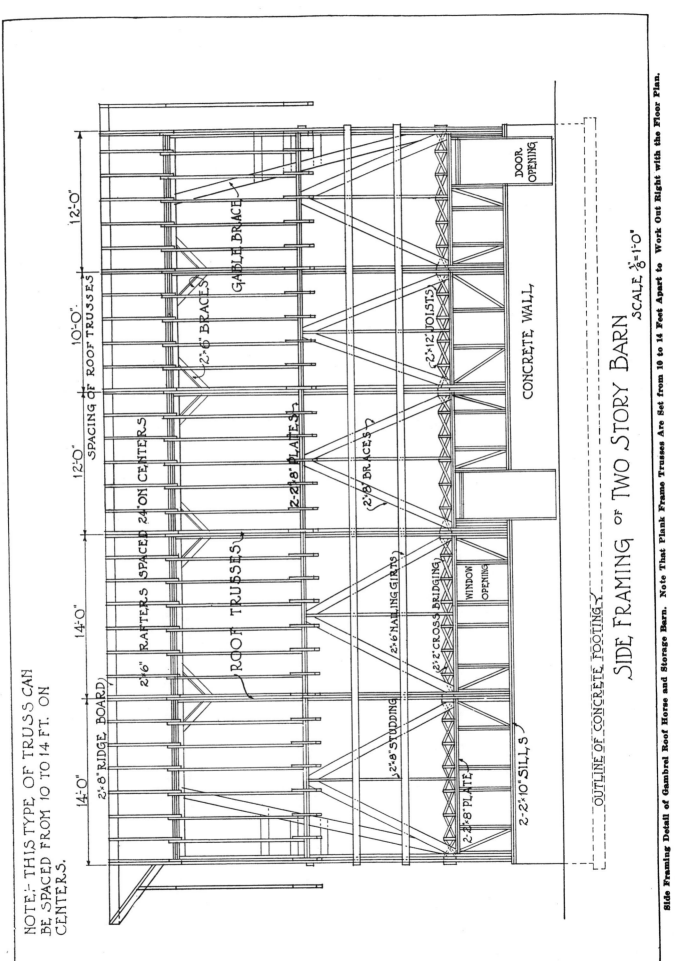

Side Framing Detail of Gambrel Roof Horse and Storage Barn. Note That Plank Frame Trusses Are Set from 10 to 14 Feet Apart to Work Out Right with the Floor Plan.

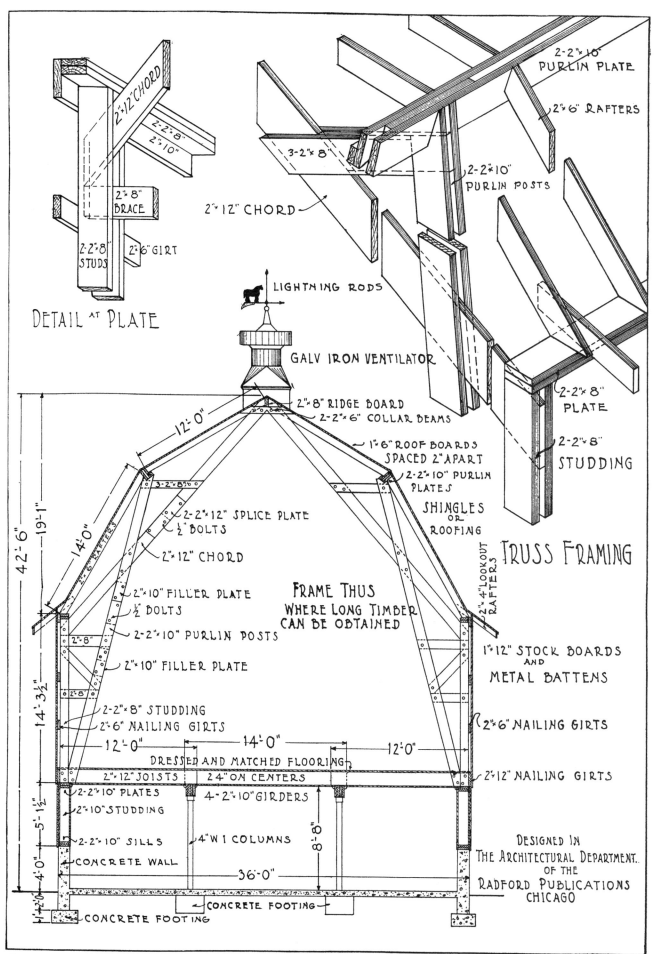

2-2"x 10"
PURLIN PLATE

2"x6" RAFTERS

2"x12" CHORD

2-2"x10"
PURLIN POSTS

3-2"x8"

2"x12" CHORD

2"x8"
BRACE

2-2"x8"
STUDS   2"x6" GIRT

DETAIL AT PLATE

2-2"x8"
PLATE

2-2"x8"
STUDDING

LIGHTNING RODS

GALV IRON VENTILATOR

2"x8" RIDGE BOARD
2-2"x6" COLLAR BEAMS

1"x6" ROOF BOARDS
SPACED 2" APART

2-2"x10" PURLIN
PLATES

SHINGLES
OR
ROOFING

TRUSS FRAMING

12'-0"

2-2"x12" SPLICE PLATE
½" BOLTS

2"x12" CHORD

FRAME THUS
WHERE LONG TIMBER
CAN BE OBTAINED

2"x4" LOOKOUT
RAFTERS

3-2"x8"

2"x6" RAFTERS

2"x10" FILLER PLATE
½ BOLTS

2-2"x10" PURLIN POSTS

2"x10" FILLER PLATE

2"x8"

2"x8"

2-2"x8" STUDDING
2"x6" NAILING GIRTS

1"x12" STOCK BOARDS
AND
METAL BATTENS

2"x6" NAILING GIRTS

42'-6"

19'-1"

14'-0"

14'-3½"

5'-1½"

4'-0"

12'-0"   14'-0"   12'-0"

DRESSED AND MATCHED FLOORING

2"x12" JOISTS   24" ON CENTERS

2-2"x10" PLATES   4-2"x10" GIRDERS

2"x10" STUDDING

2-2"x10" SILLS   4"W I COLUMNS   8'-8"

CONCRETE WALL

2"x12" NAILING GIRTS

DESIGNED IN
THE ARCHITECTURAL DEPARTMENT
OF THE
RADFORD PUBLICATIONS
CHICAGO

36'-0"

CONCRETE FOOTING

CONCRETE FOOTING

Cross-Section Thru Gambrel Roof Barn. This Is an Example of Radford's Standardized Plank Frame Construction, Making Use of 2-Inch Plank Carried Regularly in Stock at All Lumber Yards.

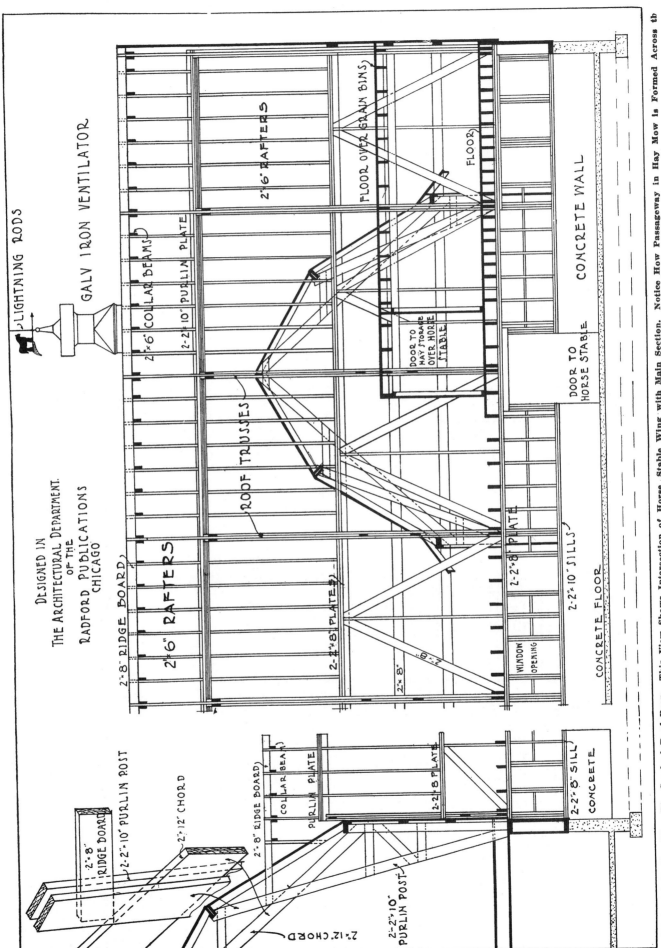

Longitudinal Section Thru Big Gambrel Roof Barn. This View Shows Intersection of Horse Stable Wing with Main Section. Notice How Passageway in Hay Mow is Formed Across the Center of the Barn to Make All Parts of the Mow Accessible, Even When the Center is Filled.

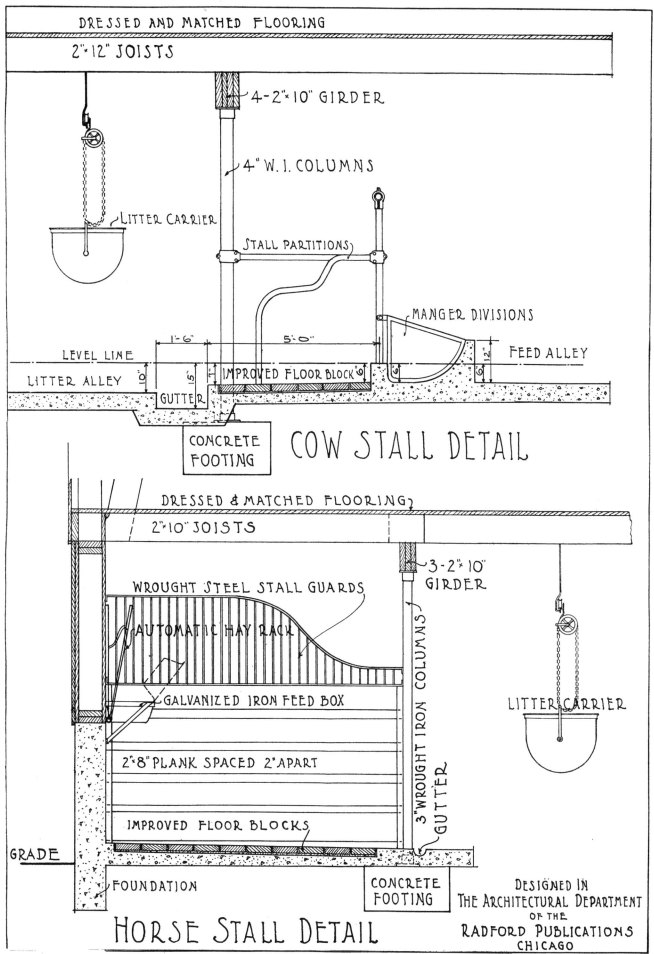

DRESSED AND MATCHED FLOORING

2"×12" JOISTS

4-2"×10" GIRDER

4" W.I. COLUMNS

LITTER CARRIER

STALL PARTITIONS

MANGER DIVISIONS

1'-6"   5'-0"   FEED ALLEY

LEVEL LINE

LITTER ALLEY   10"   15"   IMPROVED FLOOR BLOCK 6"   6"   6"   12"

GUTTER

CONCRETE FOOTING   COW STALL DETAIL

DRESSED & MATCHED FLOORING

2"×10" JOISTS

3-2"×10" GIRDER

WROUGHT STEEL STALL GUARDS

AUTOMATIC HAY RACK

GALVANIZED IRON FEED BOX

LITTER CARRIER

2"×8" PLANK SPACED 2" APART

3" WROUGHT IRON COLUMNS

GUTTER

IMPROVED FLOOR BLOCKS

GRADE

FOUNDATION

CONCRETE FOOTING

HORSE STALL DETAIL

DESIGNED IN
THE ARCHITECTURAL DEPARTMENT
OF THE
RADFORD PUBLICATIONS
CHICAGO

Details of Sanitary Cow Stalls and Horse Stalls in Big Barn.

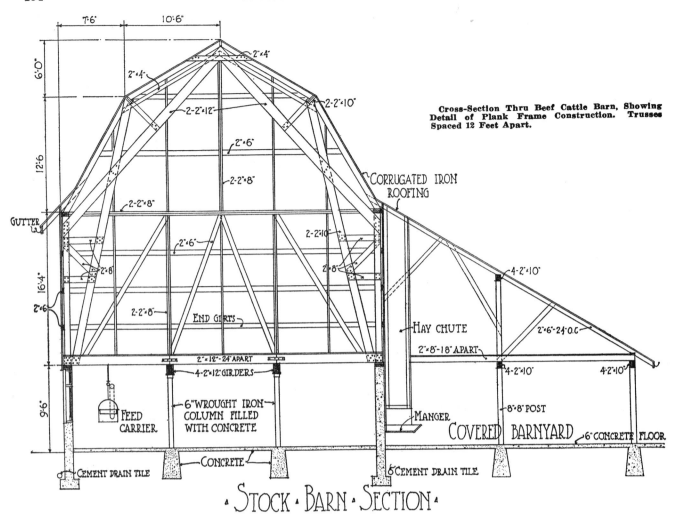

Cross-Section Thru Beef Cattle Barn, Showing Detail of Plank Frame Construction. Trusses Spaced 12 Feet Apart.

· STOCK · BARN · SECTION ·

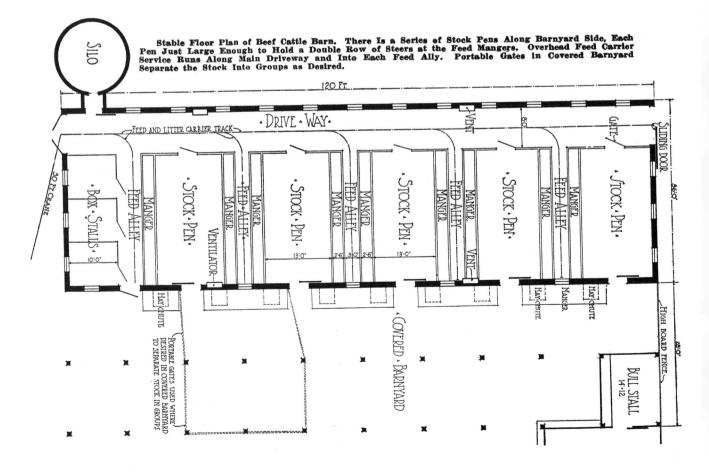

Stable Floor Plan of Beef Cattle Barn. There Is a Series of Stock Pens Along Barnyard Side, Each Pen Just Large Enough to Hold a Double Row of Steers at the Feed Mangers. Overhead Feed Carrier Service Runs Along Main Driveway and Into Each Feed Ally. Portable Gates in Covered Barnyard Separate the Stock Into Groups as Desired.

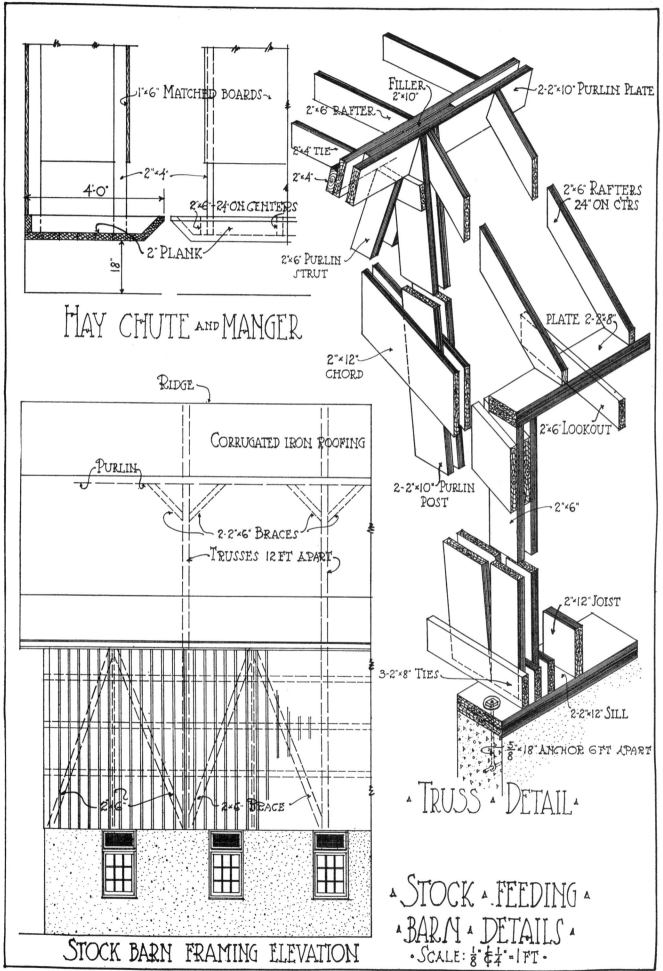

1"×6" MATCHED BOARDS

FILLER 2"×10"

2"-2"×10" PURLIN PLATE

2"×6" RAFTER

2"×4" TIE

2"×4"

2"×6" RAFTERS 24" ON CTRS

4'-0"

2"×4"

2"×6"-24" ON CENTERS

2" PLANK

2"×6" PURLIN STRUT

18"

PLATE 2-2"×8"

2"×12" CHORD

HAY CHUTE AND MANGER

2"×6" LOOKOUT

2-2"×10" PURLIN POST

RIDGE

CORRUGATED IRON ROOFING

2"×6"

PURLIN

2-2"×6" BRACES

TRUSSES 12 FT APART

2"×12" JOIST

3-2"×8" TIES

2-2"×12" SILL

$\frac{5}{8}$"×18" ANCHOR 6 FT APART

2"×6"

2"×6" BRACE

TRUSS DETAIL

STOCK FEEDING BARN DETAILS

SCALE: $\frac{1}{8}$" & $\frac{1}{4}$"=1 FT

STOCK BARN FRAMING ELEVATION

Details of Plank Frame Construction for Beef Cattle Barn. These Trusses Are Built Up of 2-Inch Planks and Are Spaced 12 Feet Apart.

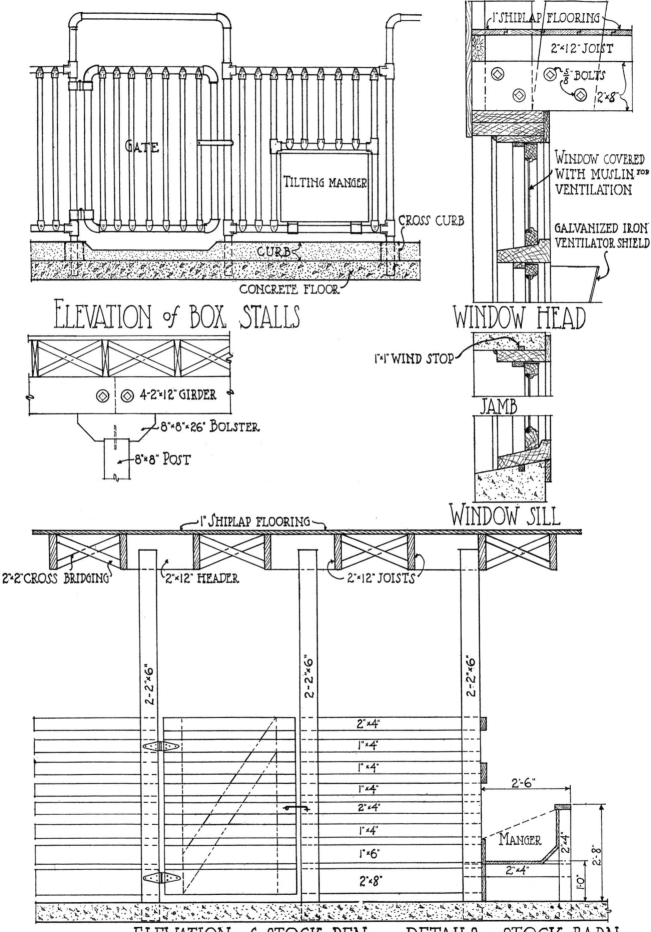

ELEVATION of BOX STALLS

GATE

TILTING MANGER

CROSS CURB

CURB

CONCRETE FLOOR

4-2"×12" GIRDER

8"×8"×26" BOLSTER

8"×8" POST

WINDOW HEAD

1" SHIPLAP FLOORING

2"×12" JOIST

⅝ BOLTS

2"×8"

WINDOW COVERED WITH MUSLIN FOR VENTILATION

GALVANIZED IRON VENTILATOR SHIELD

1"×1" WIND STOP

JAMB

WINDOW SILL

1" SHIPLAP FLOORING

2"×2" CROSS BRIDGING

2"×12" HEADER

2"×12" JOISTS

2-2"×6"

2-2"×6"

2-2"×6"

2"×4"

1"×4"

1"×4"

1"×4"

2"×4"

1"×4"

1"×6"

2"×8"

2'-6"

MANGER

2"×4"

2"×4"

2'-8"

1'-0"

ELEVATION of STOCK PEN AND DETAILS IN STOCK BARN

SCALES ⅜" & ¾" = 1'-0"

Details of Stock Pens, Etc., for Beef Cattle Barn.

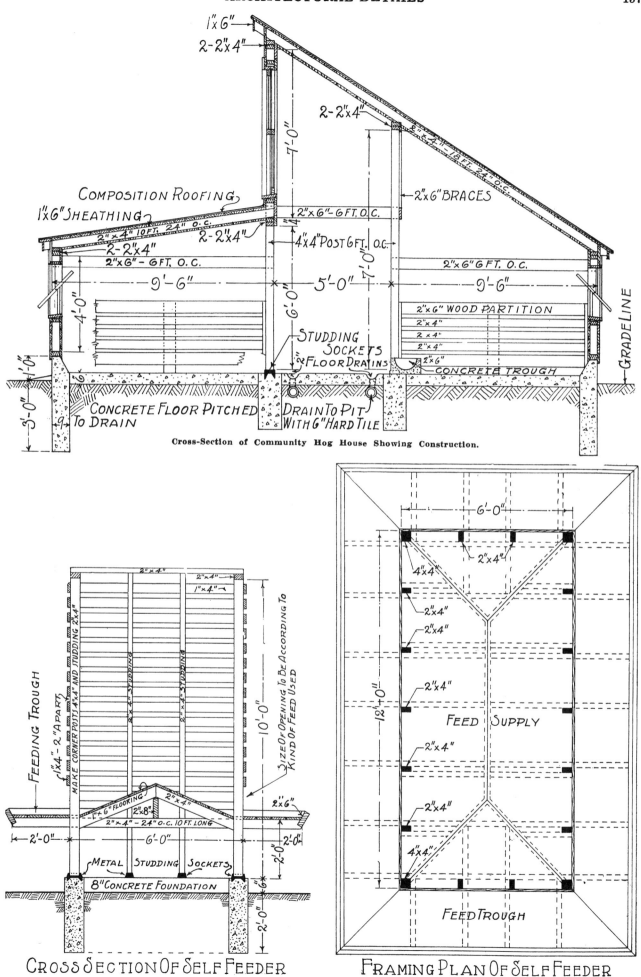

Cross-Section of Community Hog House Showing Construction.

CROSS SECTION OF SELF FEEDER

FRAMING PLAN OF SELF FEEDER

Details of Large Self-Feeder for Cattle.

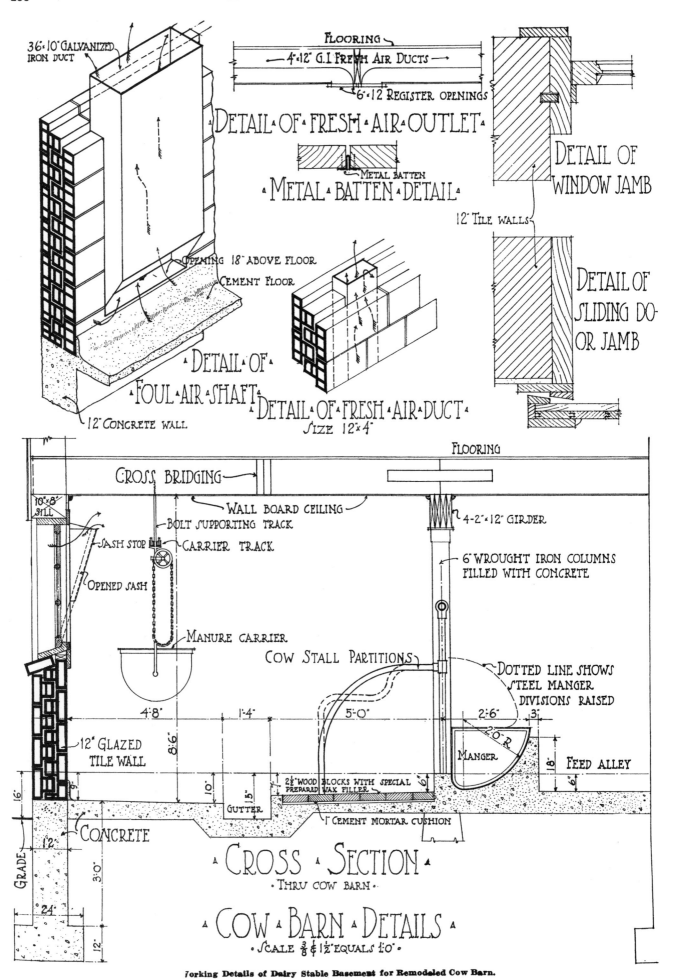

36"x10" GALVANIZED IRON DUCT

FLOORING
4"x12" G.I. FRESH AIR DUCTS
6"x12 REGISTER OPENINGS

·DETAIL·OF·FRESH·AIR·OUTLET·

METAL BATTEN
·METAL·BATTEN·DETAIL·

DETAIL OF WINDOW JAMB

12" TILE WALLS

DETAIL OF SLIDING DOOR JAMB

OPENING 18" ABOVE FLOOR

CEMENT FLOOR

·DETAIL·OF· FOUL·AIR·SHAFT·

·DETAIL·OF·FRESH·AIR·DUCT· SIZE 12"x4"

12" CONCRETE WALL

FLOORING

CROSS BRIDGING

WALL BOARD CEILING

4-2"x12" GIRDER

10"x8" SILL

BOLT SUPPORTING TRACK
SASH STOP   CARRIER TRACK

6" WROUGHT IRON COLUMNS FILLED WITH CONCRETE

OPENED SASH

MANURE CARRIER

COW STALL PARTITIONS

DOTTED LINE SHOWS STEEL MANGER DIVISIONS RAISED

4'8"   1'4"   5'0"   2'6"   3'

8'6"

12" GLAZED TILE WALL

2'0" R

MANGER

FEED ALLEY

18"

9"

10"   1'5"

2½" WOOD BLOCKS WITH SPECIAL PREPARED WAX FILLER   6"

6"

GUTTER

1" CEMENT MORTAR CUSHION

16"

GRADE

CONCRETE

12"

3'0"

·CROSS·SECTION·
·THRU·COW·BARN·

24"

12"

·COW·BARN·DETAILS·
·SCALE ⅜ & 1½ EQUALS 1'0"·

Working Details of Dairy Stable Basement for Remodeled Cow Barn.

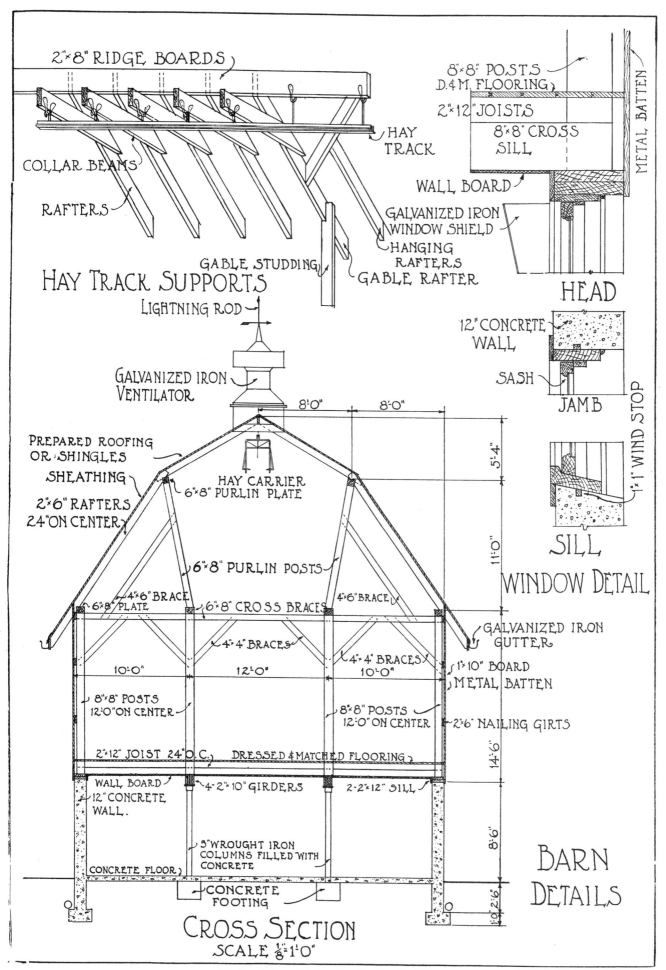

2"×8" RIDGE BOARDS

8"×8" POSTS
D.&M. FLOORING
2"×12" JOISTS
8"×8" CROSS SILL

METAL BATTEN

HAY TRACK

COLLAR BEAMS

RAFTERS

WALL BOARD

GALVANIZED IRON WINDOW SHIELD

HAY TRACK SUPPORTS

GABLE STUDDING

HANGING RAFTERS

GABLE RAFTER

HEAD

LIGHTNING ROD

12" CONCRETE WALL

SASH

JAMB

GALVANIZED IRON VENTILATOR

8'0"   8'0"

1"×1" WIND STOP

PREPARED ROOFING OR SHINGLES

SHEATHING

2"×6" RAFTERS 24" ON CENTER

HAY CARRIER
6"×8" PURLIN PLATE

5'-4"

SILL

WINDOW DETAIL

6"×8" PURLIN POSTS

11'-0"

4"×6" BRACE
6"×8" PLATE
6"×8" CROSS BRACES
4"×6" BRACE

GALVANIZED IRON GUTTER

4"×4" BRACES

10'-0"   12'-0"   4"×4" BRACES   10'-0"

1"×10" BOARD
METAL BATTEN

8"×8" POSTS
12'-0" ON CENTER

8"×8" POSTS
12'-0" ON CENTER

2"×6" NAILING GIRTS

2"×12" JOIST 24" O.C.   DRESSED & MATCHED FLOORING

14'-6"

WALL BOARD
12" CONCRETE WALL.

4-2"×10" GIRDERS

2-2"×12" SILL

5" WROUGHT IRON COLUMNS FILLED WITH CONCRETE

8'-6"

BARN DETAILS

CONCRETE FLOOR

CONCRETE FOOTING

2'-6"

CROSS SECTION
SCALE ⅛" = 1'0"

Details of Heavy Timber Framing for Stock Barn.

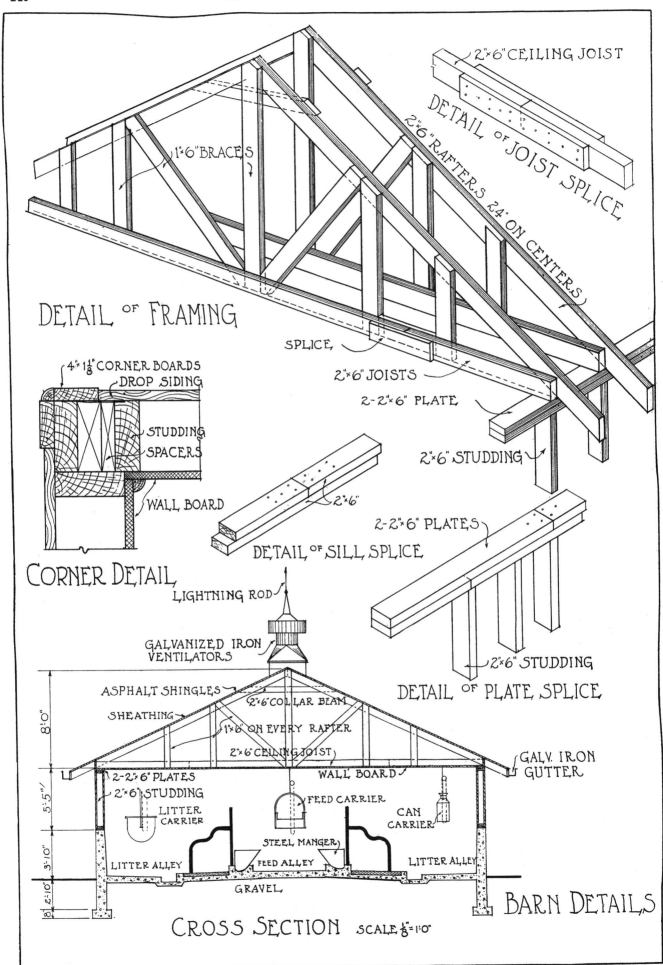

2"x6" CEILING JOIST

DETAIL OF JOIST SPLICE

DETAIL OF FRAMING

1"x6" BRACES

2"x6" RAFTERS 24" ON CENTERS

SPLICE

2"x6" JOISTS

2-2"x6" PLATE

2"x6" STUDDING

4"x1⅛" CORNER BOARDS
DROP SIDING

STUDDING

SPACERS

WALL BOARD

CORNER DETAIL

2"x6"

DETAIL OF SILL SPLICE

2-2"x6" PLATES

2"x6" STUDDING

DETAIL OF PLATE SPLICE

LIGHTNING ROD

GALVANIZED IRON VENTILATORS

ASPHALT SHINGLES

SHEATHING

2"x6" COLLAR BEAM

1"x6" ON EVERY RAFTER

2"x6" CEILING JOIST

GALV. IRON GUTTER

8'-0"

2-2"x6" PLATES

WALL BOARD

2"x6" STUDDING

FEED CARRIER

LITTER CARRIER

CAN CARRIER

5'-5"

STEEL MANGER

3'-10"

LITTER ALLEY

FEED ALLEY

LITTER ALLEY

2'-10"

GRAVEL

BARN DETAILS

8"

CROSS SECTION   SCALE ⅛"=1'0"

Details of Gable Roof Dairy Stable. Span of Roof 32 Feet. Concrete Foundation Walls Extend Up 3 Feet 10 Inches. Above This the Inside Is Lined with Wall Board, for Both Side Walls and Ceiling.

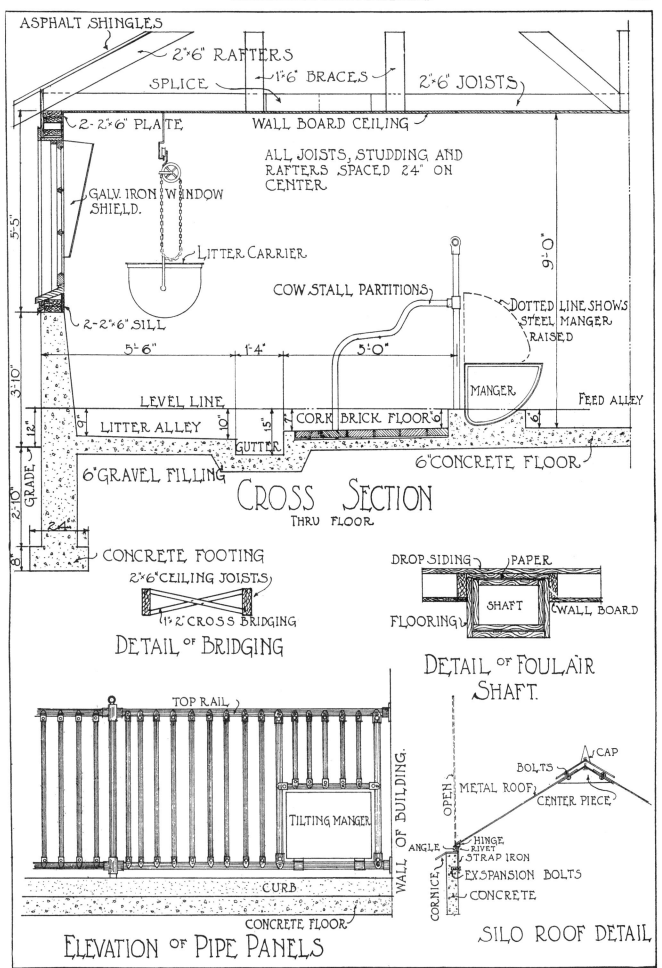

ASPHALT SHINGLES
2"×6" RAFTERS
SPLICE
1"×6" BRACES
2"×6" JOISTS
2-2"×6" PLATE
WALL BOARD CEILING
ALL JOISTS, STUDDING AND RAFTERS SPACED 24" ON CENTER
GALV. IRON WINDOW SHIELD.
LITTER CARRIER
COW STALL PARTITIONS
9'-0"
DOTTED LINE SHOWS STEEL MANGER RAISED
5'-5"
2-2"×6" SILL
5'-6"
1'-4"
5'-0"
MANGER
FEED ALLEY
3'-10"
LEVEL LINE
LITTER ALLEY
9"
10"
15"
7"
CORK BRICK FLOOR
6"
6"
GUTTER
12"
GRADE
6" CONCRETE FLOOR
2'-10"
6' GRAVEL FILLING

CROSS SECTION
THRU FLOOR

24"
8"
CONCRETE FOOTING
2"×6" CEILING JOISTS
1"×2" CROSS BRIDGING

DETAIL OF BRIDGING

DROP SIDING
PAPER
SHAFT
FLOORING
WALL BOARD

DETAIL OF FOUL AIR SHAFT.

TOP RAIL
WALL OF BUILDING.
CAP
BOLTS
OPEN
METAL ROOF
CENTER PIECE
TILTING MANGER
ANGLE
HINGE
RIVET
STRAP IRON
CORNICE
EXPANSION BOLTS
CONCRETE
CURB
CONCRETE FLOOR

ELEVATION OF PIPE PANELS

SILO ROOF DETAIL

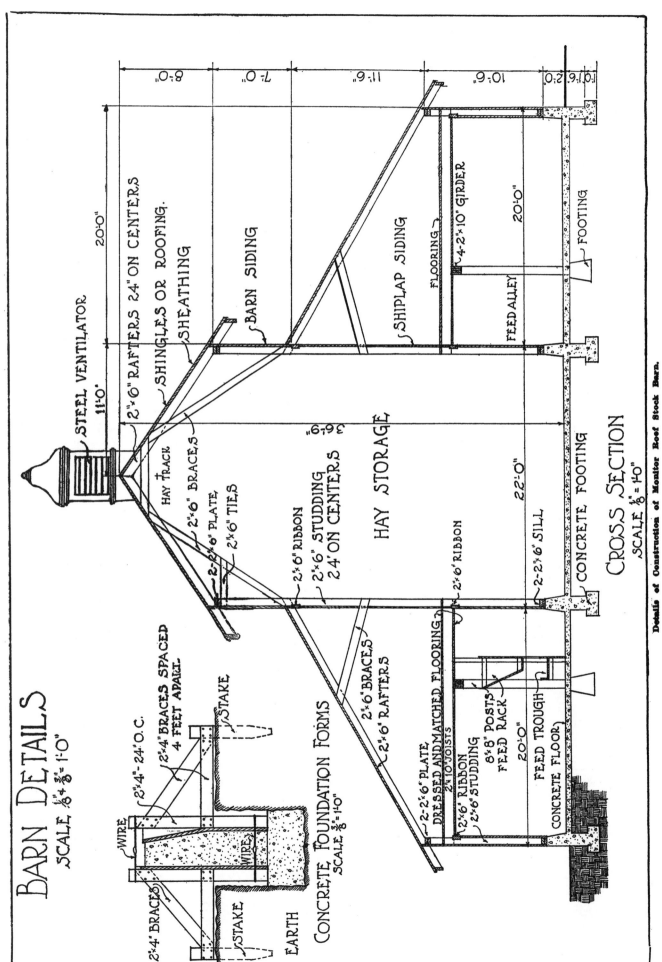

BARN DETAILS
SCALE ⅛" & ⅜" = 1'-0"

STEEL VENTILATOR

2"×6" RAFTERS 24" ON CENTERS
SHINGLES OR ROOFING.
SHEATHING

BARN SIDING

SHIPLAP SIDING

FLOORING

4-2"×10" GIRDER

FEED ALLEY

FOOTING

HAY STORAGE

2"×6" STUDDING 24" ON CENTERS

2"×6" RIBBON

2"×6" TIES

2"×6" PLATE

2-2"×6" PLATE

2"×6" BRACES

HAY TRACK

2"×4" BRACES SPACED 4 FEET APART.

2"×4"-24" O.C.

WIRE

STAKE

2"×4" BRACES

STAKE

EARTH

CONCRETE FOUNDATION FORMS
SCALE ⅜" = 1'-0"

2-2"×6" PLATE
DRESSED AND MATCHED FLOORING
2"×10" JOISTS
2"×6" RIBBON
2"×6" STUDDING

8"×8" POSTS
FEED RACK

FEED TROUGH

CONCRETE FLOOR

20'-0"

2"×6" RIBBON

2-2"×6" SILL

CONCRETE FOOTING

22'-0"

2"×6" BRACES
2"×6" RAFTERS

CROSS SECTION
SCALE ⅛" = 1'-0"

Details of Construction of Monitor Roof Stock Barn.

8'-0" 7'-0" 11'-6" 10'-6" 10'-6' 2'-0"

20'-0"

11'-0"

36'-9"

20'-0"

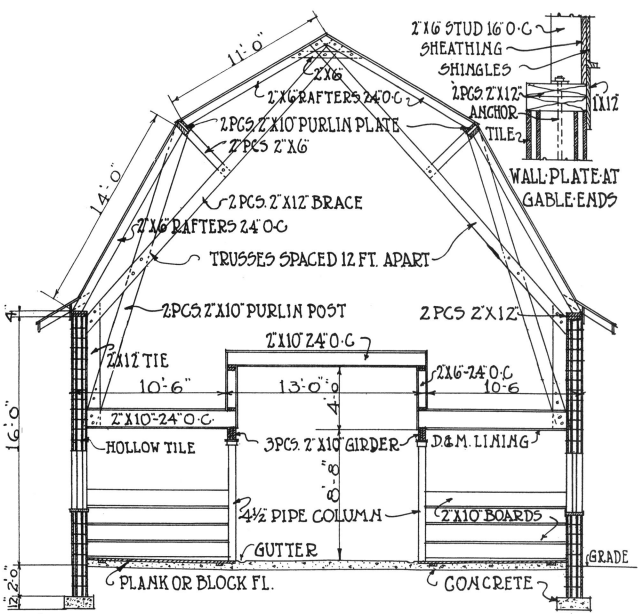

11'-0"

14'-0"

2"X6"

2"X6" RAFTERS 24" O.C.

2 PCS. 2"X10" PURLIN PLATE

2 PCS 2"X6"

2 PCS. 2"X12" BRACE

2"X6" RAFTERS 24" O.C.

TRUSSES SPACED 12 FT. APART

2 PCS. 2"X10" PURLIN POST

2 PCS 2"X12"

2"X10" 24" O.C.

2"X12" TIE

10'-6"

13'-0"-0

2"X6"-24" O.C.
10'-6

2"X10"-24" O.C.

16'-0"

HOLLOW TILE

3 PCS. 2"X10" GIRDER

D. & M. LINING

4'

8'-8"

4½" PIPE COLUMN

2"X10" BOARDS

GUTTER

GRADE

2'-0"

PLANK OR BLOCK FL.

CONCRETE

2'X6" STUD 16" O.C.
SHEATHING
SHINGLES
2 PCS. 2"X12"
ANCHOR
TILE
1"X12"

WALL·PLATE·AT
GABLE·ENDS

Section Thru Hollow Tile Horse and Cow Barn, Showing Framing for Self-Supporting Roof. The Tile Walls Extend Clear Up to the Eaves. The Purlin Braces Come Down to the Floor Joists and Are Tied to the Ends of the Truss Chord Above at the Plate Line by Means of Two Pieces of 2 by 12 for Each Truss. This Takes the Outward Thrust Away from the Top of the Tile Wall.

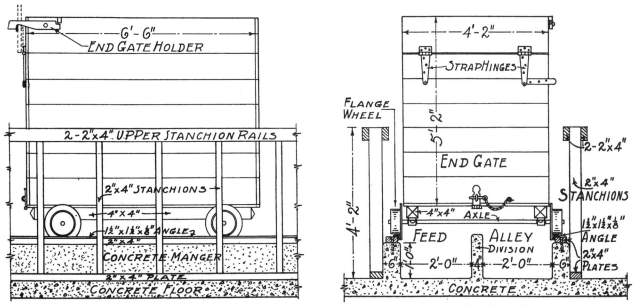

6'-6"

END GATE HOLDER

2-2"x4" UPPER STANCHION RAILS

2"x4" STANCHIONS

4" x 4"

1½"x1½"x⅛" ANGLE

2"x4"

CONCRETE MANGER

2"x4" PLATE

CONCRETE FLOOR

4'-2"

STRAP HINGES

FLANGE
WHEEL

5'-2"

END GATE

2-2"x4"

2"x4"
STANCHIONS

AXLE

4"x4"

FEED

ALLEY
DIVISION

1½"x1½"x⅛"
ANGLE

2"x4"
PLATES

4'-2"

10"

6"

2'-0"

2'-0"

6"

CONCRETE

Working Drawings of Handy Cart for Feeding Silage. The Cart Runs on a Light Angle-Iron Track the Length of the Feed Alley. It Is Filled Directly from the Silo, and When the End Gate Is Opened the Silage Is Raked Out and Distributed with a Minimum of Time and Labor.

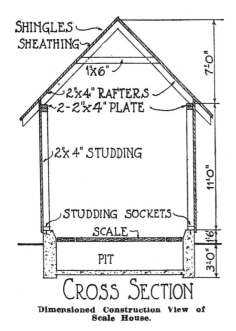

CROSS SECTION

**Dimensioned Construction View of
Scale House.**

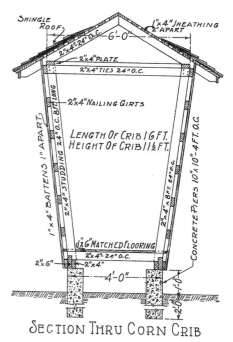

SECTION THRU CORN CRIB

**Small Single Corn Crib of the Good Old-Fashioned Type Resting
on Concrete Posts 12 Inches Above Ground to Keep Out the Rats
and Mice. The Building Is 4 Feet Wide at the Base, Sloping Outward to a 6-Foot Width at the Plates. The Height Is 11½ Feet and
the Length 16 Feet; 1 by 4-Inch Battens Placed 1 Inch Apart Form
the Sloping Side Walls and Assure Plenty of Ventilation. For
Convenience in Filling, There Are Two Small Doors High Up in the
Side. A Good, Tight, Well Framed Roof Is Provided, Making This
a Very Secure Corn Crib.**

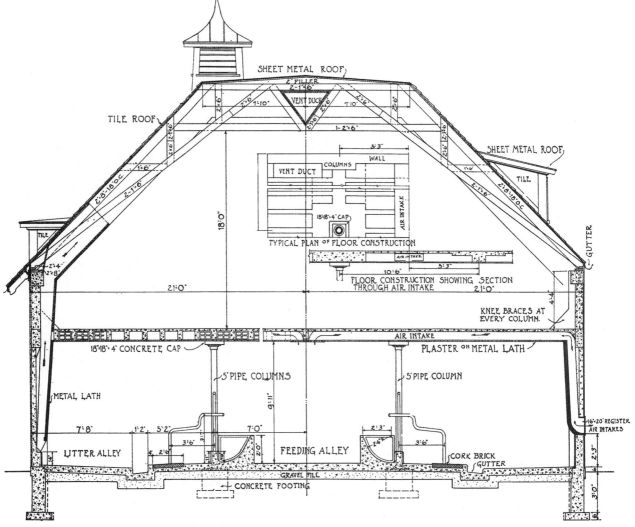

**Cross-Section of Fireproof Dairy Stable of Reinforced Concrete, Showing Some of the Construction Features. The Air Intake Is Built
Thru the Ceiling Over the Stable, Which Is of Concrete and Tile. The Truss Framing for the Roof Is Unusual.**

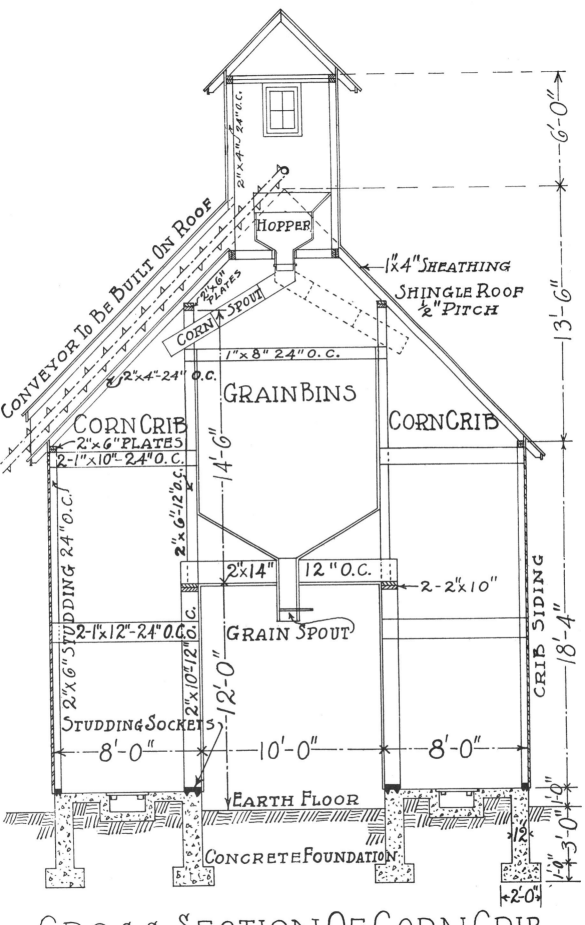

CROSS SECTION OF CORN CRIB

Details of Construction of High Corn Crib and Granary. Note How the Distributing Hopper Is Arranged in the Cupola.

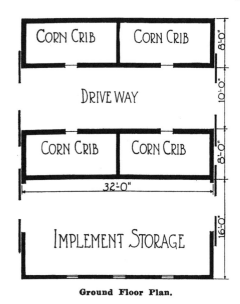

Upper Floor Plan.

Ground Floor Plan.

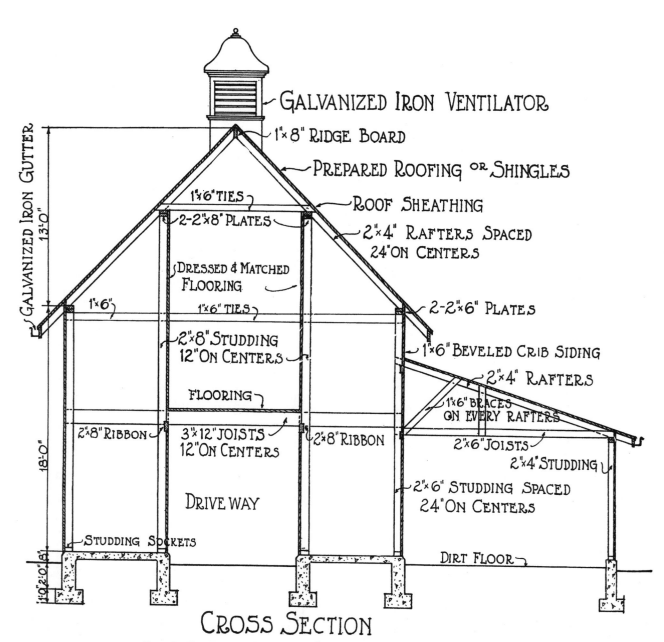

CROSS SECTION

Cross-Section Thru Combined Corn Crib, Grain House and Implement Storage Shed.

Roof Truss for 36-Foot Barn

Question—Would plank frame construction be heavy enough for a barn 36 feet wide, or would it be advisable to use another form of truss? What size plank should be used in a barn 36 feet wide, using 18-foot studding, 2 by 6's? There will be 2 by 6 rafters, two 2 by 6's for plates, 4 by 6's for sills, 2 by 10's for joists, and two 2 by 12's for girders, with 4 by 6 supports placed 9 feet apart. The joists would be 16 feet long between wall and girder.

Would you advise tying with a 2 by 6 at a point just below the plate to the floor joists, say at an angle of 45 deg.? The braces on the rafters are to be 1 by 8's.

Answer—If you will cover the joints of the intersecting rafters with 1 by 8-inch cleats on each side, it will strengthen this point very much (see detail at section A-A). The 1 by 8-inch braces on each side of the rafters are heavy enough for a barn of ordinary construction, if it is not exposed too much to high wind.

For a barn with 18-foot studding use 2 by 6-inch timbers instead of 1 by 8-inch for the lower brace.

If the barn is exposed to high winds, we would advise tying with a 2 by 6-inch at the point just below the floor joists, spaced 8 feet on centers.

In regard to the floor joists, 2 by 10-inch are not heavy enough for a span of 16 feet with the amount of hay storage that you have to carry. We would recommend using 2 by 12-inch joists and spacing the posts 11 feet 6 inches from the outside wall. This would make the span more evenly spaced.

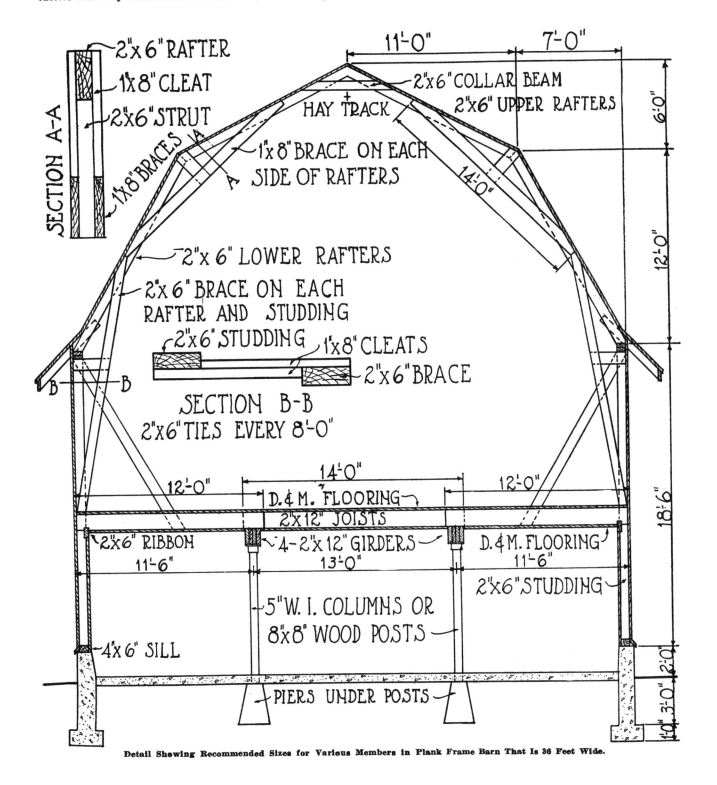

Detail Showing Recommended Sizes for Various Members in Plank Frame Barn That Is 36 Feet Wide.

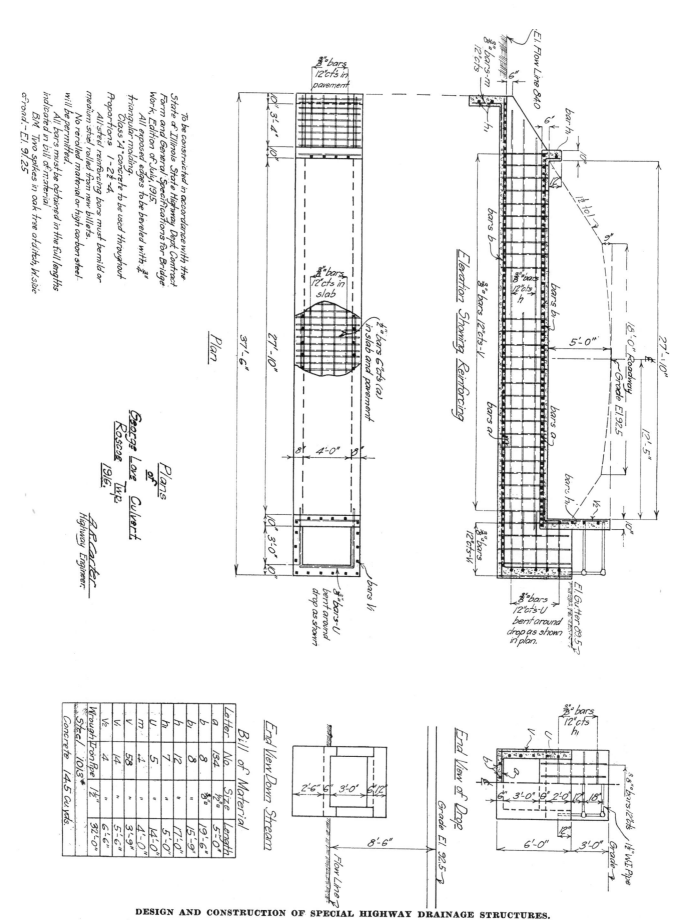

To be constructed in accordance with the
State of Illinois State Highway Dept Contract
Form and General Specifications for Bridge
Work, Edition of July, 1915.

All exposed edges to be beveled with a $\frac{3}{4}$"
triangular molding.

Class "A" concrete to be used throughout.

Proportions 1–2$\frac{1}{2}$–4.

All steel reinforcing bars must be mild or
medium steel rolled from new billets.

No rerolled material or high carbon steel
will be permitted.

All bars must be obtained in the full lengths
indicated in bill of material.

BM Two spikes in oak tree at ditch, W.side
of road.– El. 91.25

Plan

Plans
of
George Lake Culvert
Roscoe Twp.
1916.

A.R.Carter
Highway Engineer.

Elevation Showing Reinforcing

End View Down Stream

End View of Drop

Bill of Material

Letter	No.	Size	Length
a	134	$\frac{1}{2}$"⌀	5'-0"
b	8	$\frac{3}{8}$"	19'-6"
b₁	8	"	15'-9"
h	12	"	17'-0"
U	5	"	5'-0"
m	4	"	14'-0"
h₁	7	"	4'-0"
V	58	"	3'-9"
V₁	14	"	5'-6"
V₂	4	"	6'-6"
Wrought Iron Pipe	12	4"	32'-0"
Steel 1013#			
Concrete 14.5 Cu.yds.			

DESIGN AND CONSTRUCTION OF SPECIAL HIGHWAY DRAINAGE STRUCTURES.

Detail Illustrating a Type of Box Culvert Used to Drop Elevation of Water Flow Line Without Scouring of Soil.

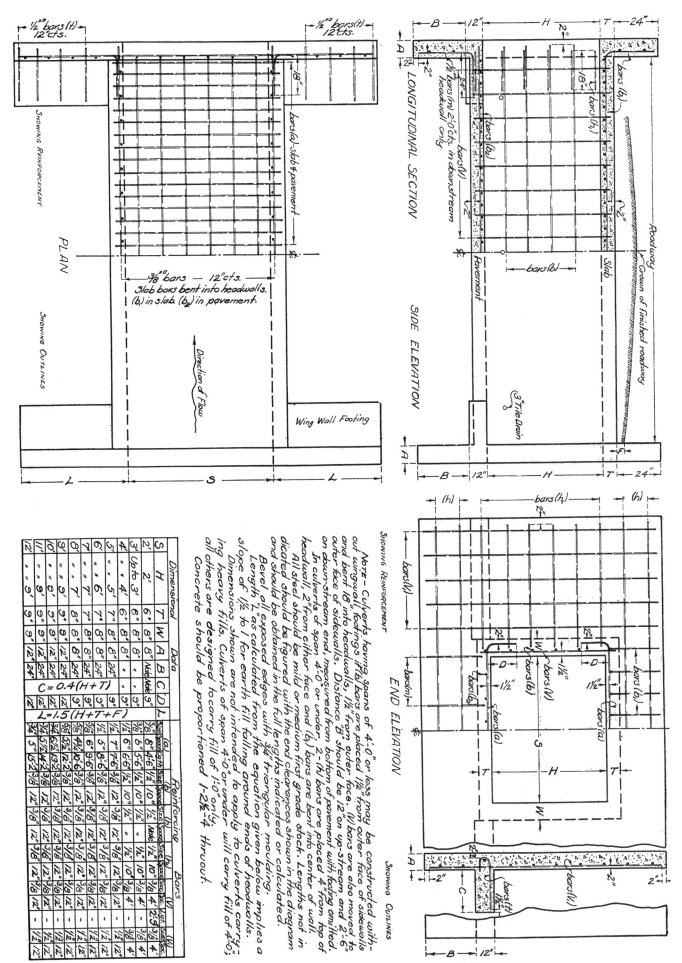

DESIGN AND CONSTRUCTION OF SPECIAL HIGHWAY DRAINAGE STRUCTURES.
Plan for Reinforced Concrete Box Culverts of Span 12 Feet or Less and Height 9 Feet or Less.

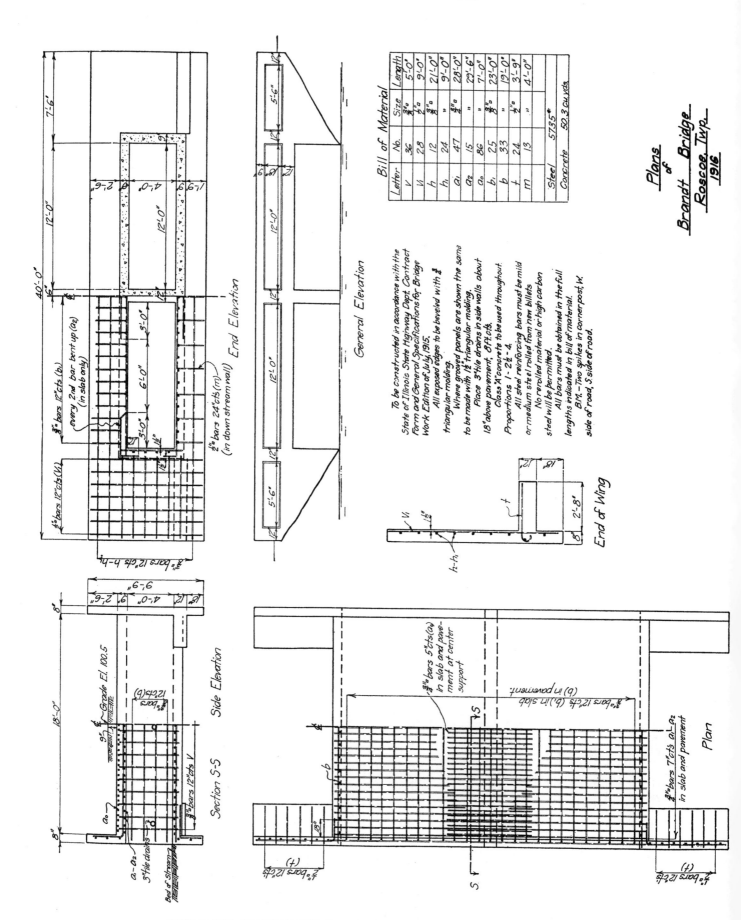

DESIGN AND CONSTRUCTION OF SPECIAL HIGHWAY DRAINAGE STRUCTURES.

Double Box Culvert Designed to Reduce the Cost of a Long Span Necessary Because of Limited Vertical Clearance.

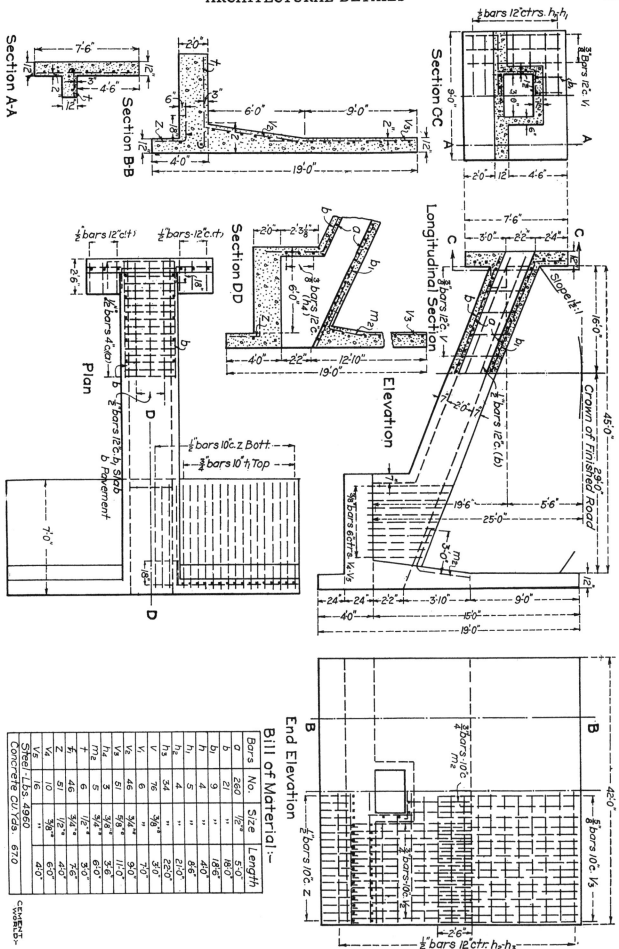

Bars	No.	Size	Length
a	260	½"ø	5'-0"
b	21	"	18'-0"
b₁	9	"	18'-6"
b₂	4	"	4'-0"
h	4	"	8'-6"
h₁	5	"	21'-0"
h₂	4	"	21'-0"
h₃	34	"	22'-0"
v	76	⅜"	3'-0"
v₁	6	"	7'-0"
v₂	46	¾"	9'-0"
v₃	51	⅝"	11'-0"
m₂	5	⅜"	3'-6"
t	6	½"	3'-0"
t₁	46	¾"	7'-6"
z	51	½"	4'-0"
v₄	10	⅜"	6'-0"
v₅	16	"	4'-0"
Steel - Lbs. 4960			
Concrete Cu.Yds. 67.0			

Bill of Material:—

DESIGN AND CONSTRUCTION OF SPECIAL HIGHWAY DRAINAGE STRUCTURES.
Reinforced Concrete Culvert to Bring Water Down to a Lower Level. Conditions Requiring This Type of Culvert Are Common in McDonough County, Illinois, Where This Design Was Developed in State Aid Highway Drainage Work.

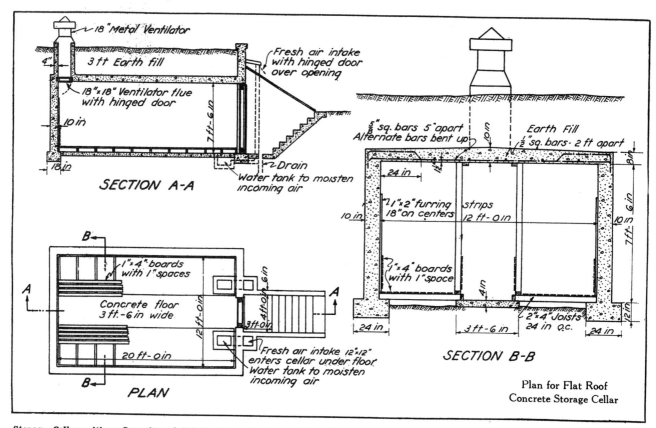

Storage Cellar with a Capacity of 800 Bushels. Greater or Less Capacity Can Be Secured by Adding to or Taking from the Length of the Plan, Each Additional Foot of Length Increasing the Storage Capacity 40 Bushels.

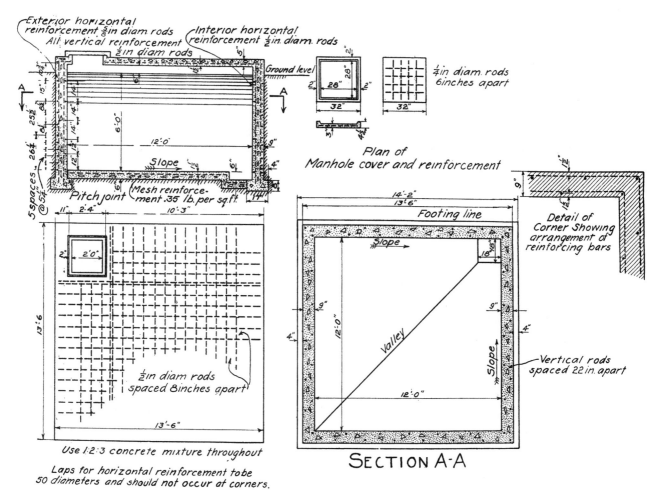

Construction Details of a Reinforced Concrete Tank Designed to Hold 6,000 Gallons of Oil.

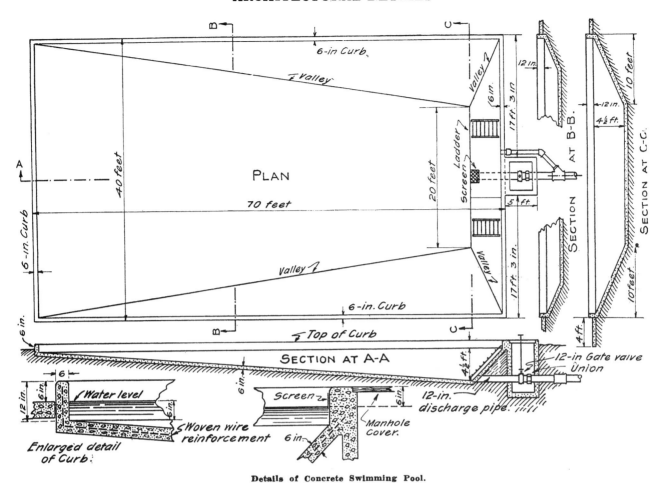

Details of Concrete Swimming Pool.

Plans for a Concrete Dipping Vat for Cattle, as Recommended by the U. S. Department of Agriculture.

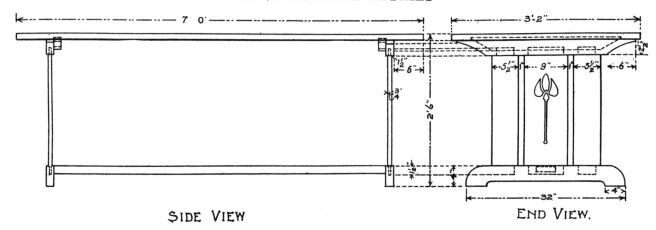

SIDE VIEW   END VIEW.

ARCHITECT'S OR BUILDER'S TABLE.

STOCK BILL FOR OFFICE TABLE

Top, 1 piece, 1⅛ by 38½ by 85 inches, S-2-S.
Top end rails, 2 pieces, 1½ by 3¼ by 38 inches, S-2-S.
Bottom end rails, 2 pieces, 1½ by 4¼ by 32½ inches, S-2-S.

Cleats, 2 pieces, 1½ by 2½ by 32 inches, S-2-S.
Stretcher, 1 piece, 1½ by 7¼ by 70 inches, S-2-S.
Slats, 2 pieces, ¾ by 9¼ by 26 inches, S-2-S.
Slats, 4 pieces, ¾ by 5¾ by 26 inches, S-2-S.

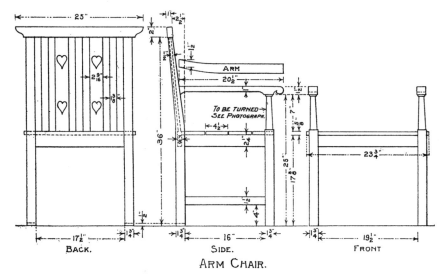

BACK.   SIDE.   FRONT.

ARM CHAIR.

STOCK BILL FOR CHAIR

Front posts, 2 pieces, 1¾ by 1¾ by 26 inches, S-4-S.
Back posts, 1 piece, 1¾ by 5½ by 37 inches, S-2-S.
Seat rails, 2 pieces, ⅞ by 2½ by 18 inches, S-2-S.
Seat rail, 1 piece, ⅞ by 2½ by 21½ inches, S-2-S.
Seat rail, 1 piece, ⅞ by 3⅛ by 19½ inches, S-2-S.
Lower rails, 2 pieces, ⅝ by 1¾ by 18 inches, S-2-S.
Seat, 4 pieces, ⅝ by 4¾ by 24 inches, S-2-S.
Arms, 2 pieces, 1½ by 3 by 21 inches, S-2-S.
Back, 1 piece, 1 by 2¼ by 25½ inches, S-2-S.
Back slats, 2 pieces, ½ by 2¾ by 19 inches, S-2-S.
Back slats, 3 pieces, ½ by 1⅝ by 19 inches, S-2-S.

STOCK BILL FOR DRAFTING TABLE

Top, 1 piece, ⅞ by 24½ by 36½ inches, S-2-S.
Posts, 4 pieces, 1¾ by 1¾ by 40½ inches, S-4-S.
Side paneling—
Rails, 2 pieces, ¾ by 3¼ by 20 inches, S-2-S.
Rails, 2 piece, ¾ by 2¾ by 20 inches, S-2-S.
Munting, 2 pieces, ¾ by 3¾ by 26½ inches, S-2-S.
Panels, 4 pieces, 5/16 by 8½ by 25½ inches, S-2-S.
Back paneling—
Rail, 1 piece, ¾ by 3¼ by 32 inches, S-2-S.
Rail, 1 piece, ¾ by 2¾ by 32 inches, S-2-S.
Munting, 2 pieces, ¾ by 2¾ by 26½ inches, S-2-S.
Panels, 3 pieces, 5/16 by 9 by 25½ inches, S-2-S.
Facing, 1 piece, ¾ by 2⅜ by 32½ inches, S-2-S.
Slide, 2 pieces, ¾ by 1¾ by 22 inches, S-2-S.
Slide, 2 pieces, ¾ by 1¾ by 33 inches, S-2-S.
Slide, 1 piece, ½ by 16 by 28 inches, S-2-S.
Drawer supports, 14 pieces, ⅞ by 2½ by 20 inches, S-2-S.
Drawer supports, 14 pieces, ⅞ by 2½ by 32½ inches, S-2-S.

Drawer guides, 14 pieces, ¾ by ¾ by 20 inches, S-2-S.
Drawer fronts, 6 pieces, ¾ by 4¼ by 30½ inches, S-2-S.
Drawer ends, 12 pieces, ½ by 4¼ by 20 inches, S-2-S.
Drawer backs, 6 pieces, ⅜ by 4 by 30 inches, S-2-S.
Drawer bottoms, 6 pieces, ⅜ by 20 by 30 inches, S-2-S.

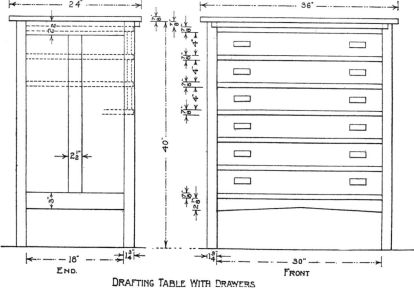

END.   FRONT.

DRAFTING TABLE WITH DRAWERS

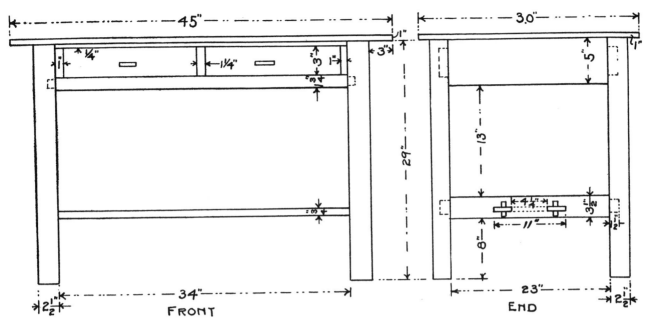

LIBRARY OR STUDY TABLE.

STOCK BILL FOR LIBRARY TABLE

Top, 1 piece, 1 by 30½ by 45½ inches, S-2-S.
Legs, 4 pieces 2½ by 2½ by 29½ inches, S-4-S.
Back rail, 1 piece, ¾ by 5¼ by 37 inches, S-2-S.
End rails, 2 pieces, ¾ by 5¼ by 26 inches, S-2-S.
Front rail, 1 piece, ¾ by 2 by 37 inches, S-2-S.
Shelf, 1 piece, ¾ by 11¼ by 40 inches, S-2-S.
Drawer facings, 2 pieces, ¾ by 3¼ by 16 inches, S-2-S.

Drawer sides, 4 pieces, ⅜ by 3¼ by 26 inches, S-2-S.
Drawer backs, 4 pieces, ⅜ by 3 by 16 inches, S-2-S.
Drawer bottoms, 2 pieces, ⅜ by 26 by 16 inches, S-2-S.
Drawer slides, 3 pieces, ¾ by 2¾ by 26 inches, S-2-S.
Drawer guides, 3 pieces, ¾ by 1½ by 26 inches, S-2-S.
Tie, over drawers, 1 piece, ½ by 2¾ by 36 inches, S-2-S.

The remaining pieces, keys, and short facings about the drawers may be got from scrap stock.

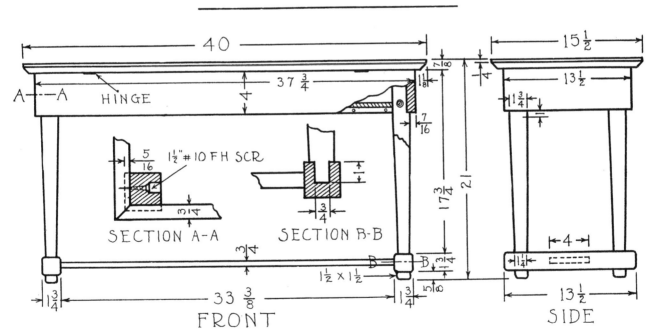

Construction Details of a Strong and Serviceable Piano Bench.

STOCK BILL FOR PIANO BENCH, GIVING FINISHED SIZES

Cover, 1 piece, ⅞ by 15½ by 40.
Posts, 4 pieces, 1¾ by 1¾ by 18¾ (one 1-inch tenon).
Frame, 2 pieces, ¾ by 4 by 37¾.
   2 pieces, ¾ by 4 by 13½.
Lower rail. 2 pieces, 1¾ by 1¾ by 13½.

Stretcher, 1 piece, ¾ by 4 by 35⅛ (two ⅞-inch tenons).
Blocks, 4 pieces, ⅝ by 1½ by 1½.
Bottom, 1 piece, 5/16 by 12 by 36¼ (wallboard).
   2 pieces, ⅜ by ⅜ by 33⅜.
   2 pieces, ⅜ by ⅜ by 9⅛.
Hardware, 1 pair ¾ by 2½ nickel plated butts.
   16 1½-inch No. 10 F. H. screws.

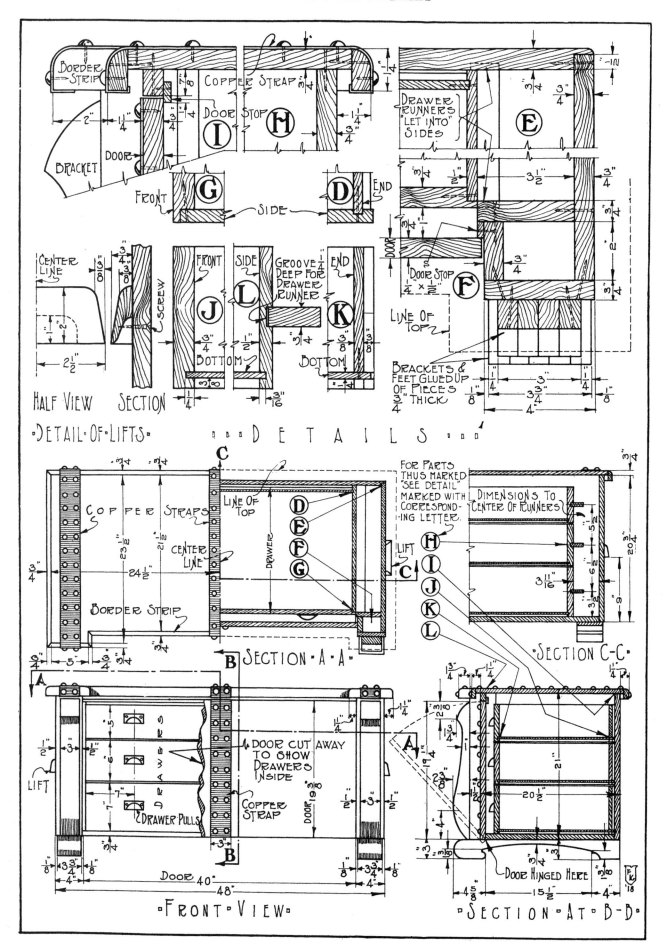

Working Details of a Cedar Chest of Unique and Attractive Design

INDEX TO ARCHITECTURAL DETAILS

For Every Type of Building

A Collection of Authoritative Plates for Contractors, Builders, Lumber Dealers, Millmen, Draftsmen, and Architects